D0261712

A Year in Tibet

ALSO BY SUN SHUYUN

Ten Thousand Miles without a Cloud
The Long March

SUN SHUYUN

A Year in Tibet

Harper
Press

HarperCollins*Publishers*
77–85 Fulham Palace Road, Hammersmith, London w6 8jb

www.harpercollins.co.uk

Published by Harper*Press*,
an Imprint of HarperCollins*Publishers* 2008

1

Copyright © Sun Shuyun 2008

By arrangement with Seven Stones Media

Sun Shuyun asserts the moral right to
be identified as the author of this work

Photographs reproduced by kind permission of Seven Stones Media.

A catalogue record for this book
is available from the British Library

ISBN 978-0-00-726511-4

Set in Minion with Janson and Spectrum display

Printed and bound in Great Britain by Clays Ltd, St Ives plc

All rights reserved. No part of this publication may be
reproduced, stored in a retrieval system, or transmitted,
in any form or by any means, electronic, mechanical,
photocopying, recording or otherwise, without the
prior written permission of the publishers.

Mixed Sources
Product group from well-managed
forests and other controlled sources
www.fsc.org Cert no. SW-COC-1806
© 1996 Forest Stewardship Council

FSC

FSC is a non-profit international organisation established to promote the
responsible management of the world's forests. Products carrying the FSC
label are independently certified to assure consumers that they come
from forests that are managed to meet the social, economic and
ecological needs of present and future generations.

Find out more about HarperCollins and the environment at
www.harpercollins.co.uk/green

To the Rikzin family

Luton Cultural Services Trust	
9 39115489	
Askews	951.506
0 2 MAR 2009	Sun

CONTENTS

PROLOGUE

Tibet has always called to me. In 1986, my last year at Beijing University, I had the chance to volunteer to work in Tibet. For eight years' service I would get Party membership, double pay, housing priority and faster promotion on my return. It seemed like a good deal. I was only twenty-three; I knew it would be tough but I would be set up for life by the time I was thirty. And I had seen a lot of photographs of *Xizang*, the Chinese name for Tibet, which means 'Western Treasure'. It looked beautiful. I was tempted.

This was long before I read *Lost Horizon* by James Hilton, the book that planted the mystic Shangri-la in the minds of foreigners, or the tantalising accounts by early explorers. I wrote to my parents, and received a prompt and stern reply from my father: 'I can't believe anyone in your class has such stupid ideas. Is that the sort of thing you learn in Beijing University? I thought they would have higher ambitions for you. Tibet is not a fit place for us anyway.' He carried on in this vein for a page, warning me of dire consequences if I went. He thought the altitude would finish me off before my eight years were up.

For my parents, Tibet was a barbarous land where men drank blood and lamas made drums from human skin and horns from virgins' thigh bones; where serfs were treated worse than animals; where the moral standards were so low that brothers – and even fathers and sons – shared a wife, and sisters shared a

1

husband. Years of Communist propaganda about Tibet's backwardness had convinced them of all of this. I bowed to their pressure.

We Chinese have always called our country *Zhongguo*, 'centre of the universe'. The land beyond was inhabited by barbarians. In primary school, we learned how China gave the benefits of its superior civilisation to Tibet. In 641 a Chinese princess named Wencheng married Songtsen Gampo, the Tibetan king, and took with her our advanced knowledge of medicine and medical equipment, astrology, plants and seeds, brocade silk, craftsmen, musicians, scholars, Buddhist scriptures, a statue of the Buddha, and Buddhism itself. Today the statue she took to Tibet is still worshipped by the Tibetans in their most holy shrine, the Jokang Temple in Lhasa. In the most exaggerated version of this tale, her beauty and intelligence won the King's heart and he was persuaded to have the Potala Palace built for her. In other words, most good things Tibet has, it owes to her, a mere sixteen-year-old girl.

It is curious though that our annals of history of that period tell us nothing more about her. It is the Tibetan record that gave us perhaps a true reflection of her feelings on hearing the news of the impending marriage; she told the Emperor Taizong she did not want to go:

> How could you send me to the Tibetan land?
> Where there is nothing but snow
> Where it is bitterly cold and rough
> Where dragons and ghosts and devils abound
>
> Where there is no happiness and joy
> Where five cereals do not grow and hunger is prevalent
> Where the inferior carnivorous people live
> Where behaviour is rude and etiquette is lacking ...[1]

The Imperial court started sending officials to Tibet in 1727. They were called Ambans and represented the Emperor's authority in this far-flung corner. But they were mostly posted there as punishment for transgressions of some sort. In the 185 years up till the Last Emperor in 1911, there were a total of 135 of them; they did not stay long. Only a dozen, according to scholars, were competent,[2] while the rest were for the most part passive, contemptuous and corrupt. They disparaged this remote and 'primitive' part of the Empire. One of them described the Tibetans as 'stupid as deer and pigs'. Others wrote in their dispatches that the Tibetans would benefit from the morals of Confucius or from adopting Chinese names, and would be more civilised if they wore trousers under their robes. The Ambans had little time for Tibetan religion either: 'Lamas do not have to recite sutras day and night; they should make money as well in trade, agriculture and industry.'[3] Contempt did not stop many of them from lining their pockets. They had scales of charges for recommending aristocrats to positions in the Tibetan government; for the top job, it was 12,000 ounces of silver.[4] They cared little for what the Tibetans might think of them, or the court they were representing.

Even in the Republican period, the disparagement persisted. Chiang Kaishek's Western-educated envoy to Lhasa wrote: 'When you set foot on the Tibetan land, the question that occupies your mind is: is this Shangri-la, the paradise that is full of rosy and dreamy colours and idyllic smells? ... It is no different from the surrounding areas, only more barren, more poverty stricken, and drowned in a deadly silence.'[5]

I started learning Tibetan at Oxford, with the late Tibetologist Michael Aris, and wrote my master's thesis on Britain's role in Tibet when it withdrew from its empire in India. I made my first trip to Tibet in 1991, to see for myself whether it was hell on earth or Shangri-la. I found a land of emptiness and majesty.

The guidebooks say Tibet is closer to heaven, and that was how I felt: a harmony between nature, man and faith, which had a strong appeal for me. Was I attracted because I grew up in such a crowded country, where nature was being trampled on by the vast population? Was it because I was living in a spiritual void created by disillusionment with communism? Or was I, like the long string of adventurers and explorers before me, looking for a 'land of lost content' that perhaps exists only in the mind? I went back many times, going further and further into the plateau, living with nomads, nuns, and hermits, each trip longer than the previous one. But these were all relatively brief encounters.

Then came my chance – to direct a documentary series about a year in the life of ordinary Tibetans. From July 2006 to June 2007 that is just what I did. I decided to film in Gyantse, 13,000 feet up, Tibet's third largest town, but one with still only 8,000 people. It is also the seat of a county with 60,000 people, big enough for me to find a representative range of characters. It is beautiful and all of a piece, with its ancient fort, well-known monastery, and traditional houses largely intact – a rarity in today's Tibet. Of course, change has come to Gyantse too, along with a growing influx of tourists, migrants, and traders, although they have not, or not yet, altered its character. And Gyantse is a place of history, the scene of Colonel Younghusband's infamous massacres in 1904, when he led an expedition to open up Tibet for the British Empire.

My film crew and I rented a Tibetan house on the edge of town, with an outside toilet and no running water – we had to fetch water in barrels by motor rickshaw, and shower in the public bath. Altogether we were nine, a mixture of Tibetan and Chinese: myself, three cameramen at the start, later reduced to one, two Tibetan researchers, a young Chinese assistant producer, a Chinese production manager, and a Tibetan driver.

We also had a Sichuanese cook and a Tibetan housekeeper who came in daily.

For a year we followed a shaman, a village doctor, a junior Party official, a hotel manager, a rickshaw driver, a builder, and two monks through the ups and downs of their lives. Late summer was tense due to the visit of the controversial Panchen Lama, the Tibetan spiritual leader second only to the Dalai Lama, but the hotel manager had record profits. Autumn brought anxiety to the villagers anticipating the all-important harvest; new technology also cost the shaman his job as warder-off of hailstones. During the long winter we filmed a wedding in which the bride and the grooms had no say, but we also observed a household where three brothers have shared a wife for twenty years. The monastery was burgled and the rickshaw driver had to leave home to find work. The village doctor found herself sick, on top of her struggles to care for the patients in her ill-equipped clinic, and she herself turned to a lama and a pilgrimage in the hope of a cure. In the spring the builder was trying to get a contractor's certificate, for which he had to pass an exam in Chinese, a language he did not speak. The novice monk, our youngest character, was threatened with expulsion for lack of discipline. We were watching a people bound by tradition, but challenged by rapid change.

But this is not the book of the film. Television is good for action, and often with no action, there is no film. At the start of our project, the shaman's mother died. There could not have been a more important occasion to explore Tibetan beliefs. But we could not film the actual death; it would have been too intrusive. The elaborate rituals for her rebirth were not enough; we had to drop the whole event in the final cut. This is where books come into their own; they are also far better at exploring people's innermost feelings and thoughts, their beliefs and their reflections on the past. And this is particularly vital for portraying Tibet, a society so rich and complex, and so different from any other.

In this book, I have followed the dramas of the characters in the film, but I focus mainly on the Rikzin family: the shaman Tseten and his two brothers, Dondan and Loga; their wife, Yangdron; their father, Mila; and their four children. The shaman is at the very heart of Tibetan life. People come to him with headaches, toothaches, broken hearts and sick animals. They consult him about births and deaths, which hospital to go to for operations, who should marry whom, whether or when to start a business, or to pray for a felled tree. Tseten even had a visit from a distraught man wanting to know his dog's next incarnation.

The Rikzin family's stories took me into the most intimate aspects of village life, and beyond – the strength of the Tibetans' beliefs and the importance of their rituals; the joy they take in life; their battle to be educated, and in their own language; the pitiful standards of health care; the success of the few in the midst of poverty and lack of opportunity; the palpable political tensions; the animosity between Tibetans and Chinese.

As a Chinese I felt honoured to be welcomed into this community, and by the Rikzin family. They have enabled me to describe as a witness the everyday lives of rural Tibet. Ninety per cent of Tibetans live in villages and on the pastoral land – yet the vast literature on Tibet rarely refers to them. It is among them that faith is still nurtured, the culture is maintained, and tradition flourishes. This is the real Tibet.

ONE

The Shaman, the Gun and
Mao's Red Book

IT IS EARLY MORNING, and the sky is leaden – not at all like
the crystal blue Tibetan vault on the postcards. Dark clouds
hang over the village of Tangmad and the mountains behind it,
the sky lit now and then by a dramatic flash of lightning. We
are huddled in the Rikzins' kitchen, watching the rain. It is not
heavy, quite gentle in fact, but it is unrelenting. For four days in
a row, the family has got up at two or three in the morning, hoping for it to break. But they – and we – have been disappointed
every time. Loga, the oldest brother, Dondan, the middle one,
Tseten, the youngest, who is also the village shaman, and Yangdron,
the wife they share, are not saying very much. They are drinking
yak-butter tea and eating *tsampa* – roasted barley flour – which
they mix with the tea. Mila, the brothers' father, is praying in his
room.

Yangdron breaks the silence. 'Do you think the rain will stop
this morning? Yesterday, we could not get into the fields. It was
so wet. Last year the harvest was already in by now.'

'It should be all right,' Tseten says breezily, trying to lighten
the atmosphere.

Dondan turns his head to look out of the window. The clouds over the horizon are becoming thicker and thicker. He sighs. 'It could be worse,' he says.

The only truly cheerful one is Loga. He has the mental age of a child. He does not understand; with hot butter tea and *tsampa*, what is there to worry about? It is the start of another day.

I have heard that the village held a festival two weeks ago for the local god Yul Lha. He is one of the most powerful deities. He is supposed to control the mountains, the rivers that flow from them, the land beneath them, the people and animals who live near them – and the weather. It was before we started filming. I ask Tseten to tell me about it.

'We have a shrine to Yul Lha on the edge of the village. Each family brought a bundle of their best crops, barley, mustard seeds, and peas as offerings. I recited mantras to invoke the presence of Yul Lha, asking him to come and enjoy them. You know, he is responsible for just about everything important – the rain and the harvest, sickness and health, the safety of men and animals.'

'Will it be a good harvest this year?' I ask. I noticed that some of the fields we passed on the way to the village looked rather pitiful, like an old man's hair, the stalks short, the ears sagging.

'We could have done with a bit more rain earlier after the planting,' Tseten concedes, 'but we cannot complain.'

I have found mentions of some offerings made in the past in a book I have been reading: widows' or prostitutes' menstrual blood in a bowl made from the skull of an illegitimate child, hearts and livers, flowers, incense, and a sampling of the finest food available. In the 1950s, an assembly of monks required 'one wet intestine, two skulls, and a whole human skin' for a ritual to pray for the Dalai Lama's longevity.[6] The best barley and peas seem a bit ordinary by comparison.

Tseten laughs. 'Yul Lha is not so hard to please. If you are respectful and sincere, he will help you.'

Tseten refers to Yul Lha with reverence, but also with familiarity, as though he is a real presence. Of course it is his job as a shaman, but it still comes as a surprise to me. I know the Cultural Revolution destroyed much of the fabric and culture of Tibetan life, and took from the Tibetans what they had for centuries valued most – their monasteries, their monks, their religious rituals. But I did not realise how many of the old traditions had returned in the years since, how much people's lives were once again dominated by the old beliefs.

I made a mistake when I first came to Tangmad village looking for the Rikzin family in July. I met a little girl with clear, radiant eyes, and a beautiful smile, and she was holding her mother's hand. When I complimented the mother on her daughter's beauty, she did not look at all pleased. She took the girl off in a hurry. My Tibetan researcher, Penpa, told me the woman would probably head for the monastery to pray to her daughter's deity in order to appease any anger or jealousy I might have invoked. I had put the girl at risk.

After three months in Tibet, I have learned that gods are everywhere. One day, I had arranged to follow Tseten on one of his rounds to see what it was like. He was an hour late to meet us. When he appeared, he apologised – he had been praying to the tree god for his neighbours before they cut down a tree to make a beam for their new house. Trees, flowers, crops, animals, humans, houses, wells, springs, rivers, mountains, earth, heaven – all have gods assigned to them. Humans, too, have gods keeping an eye on them: the one over your shoulder is the fighting god, the one under your right armpit is the masculine god and the one under your left the feminine god; the house god is present on the four corners of your roof, and the storage god in the cupboards; there is a god in the well, in the stable, and in the kitchen – if you make the stove dirty, you might offend the stove god, and she will make the whole family sick.

In fact, the story of how Buddhism came to Tibet is embedded in the mythology of these demons and gods. In the eighth century, King Trisong Detsen invited an Indian master to come to teach and to build the first Tibetan monastery. Legend has it that devils did their best to halt the construction. The master's life was also threatened by followers of Bön, the widespread indigenous religion. So another great Indian master, Padmasambhava – or Padam, as he is known – was called upon to travel to Tibet. Again, the same devils put obstacles in his path. The God of Gnyan Chen Tanggola, one of Tibet's holiest and highest mountains, was his most notable assailant. Padam's response was to sit in deep meditation on this mountain top, and, soon enough, the snow started to melt, creating a torrent, bringing earth and rocks down with it. The mountain god surrendered, convinced of Padam's superior powers, and offered his loyalty. Padam made him a protective deity in the Tibetan Buddhist pantheon, together with all his 360 subsidiary gods and goddesses, and numerous other devils and spirits.

These gods and goddesses are duty-bound to protect and to bring prosperity to the monasteries and monks, and the faithful. But they have been allowed to keep their bad habits – they are carnivorous, thirsty for blood, and often consumed by ego, anger, jealousy, and greed. They are quite unBuddhist; they have nothing to do with delivering enlightenment – that is left to the numerous Buddhas and Bodhisattvas.

Traditionally, it is the shaman who intercedes with the deities and spirits, to honour them, to placate them, and to plead with them for help. When we were choosing characters to feature in our documentary film, every Tibetologist we consulted recommended that we include a shaman. After hunting for several weeks in the villages, Penpa, the researcher, came back one day in early August looking very pleased with himself, 'You owe me a big present. I think I've found just the family you want.'

I drove with him the next day to Karmad – one of the eighteen districts (*xiang*) of Gyantse County. We turned off onto a stony track after twenty minutes on the main road to Shigatse, the second biggest city in Tibet. It was lined with willow trees, and through them I could see the vast expanse of yellowing barley fields under brilliant sunshine, stretching to the dark mountains on either side. The track went on straight for miles to the end of the valley, into the huge space of sky and clouds. Where were we going to end up? We crossed the Nyangchu River and passed several villages, all looking very inviting. I asked Penpa repeatedly, 'Is this one ours?' At last we slowed down and went left into Village No. 1, Tangmad, at a row of prayer-wheels. We went by a water tap where the villagers were queuing, the only tap for 600 people, Penpa told me. As far as I could see, as we drove through the lanes of traditional mud-brick houses, that was the only sign of modernity, bar some telephone lines and the occasional motorbike or car.

We parked outside a wide corrugated-iron gate. Penpa pulled a rope that opened the inside latch of the narrow side, and we entered the Rikzins' house. Like the others, it has two storeys of the traditional kind, the cows and sheep on the ground floor, and the family on the first floor, with a big courtyard where chickens run amongst the tractor and cart, and cowpats dry on the walls. We climbed up a flight of stairs to the small upper courtyard. Yangdron came out of the kitchen to greet us, smiling warmly. She had a broad oblong face, handsome rather than beautiful, with dark wide-set eyes, and brilliant white teeth – her smile really lit up her face.

'This is our director, Sun, who wanted to find a shaman family,' Penpa introduced me. 'You want to see Tseten,' she said,

11

taking my hands in hers. 'He has someone with him. But let me take you to his room.'

My first sight of Tseten was a little curious. He was sitting on a narrow bed in the family prayer room, in front of a wall hung with *tangkas*, ritual paintings of the Buddha and various deities. On a bench under the windows to his right was his patient, a young woman with a badly swollen face. He leaned over to her and spat on her cheek. After half a minute, he stopped and beckoned us with a smile to sit next to her, and went on with his spitting. I noticed Tseten's smooth, pale skin, unlike any villager we had seen. I supposed he spent a lot of time indoors. His smile seemed to express a benign disposition – no doubt a comfort to the woman. I immediately took a liking to him.

The patient left, bowing with gratitude. We had a brief chat with Tseten about our film, and then he led us to the kitchen to meet the rest of the family. I felt I was taken back to another time. A liquidiser for making butter tea, a solar reflector in the courtyard for boiling water, a telephone presumably for Tseten's activities, and a small black and white TV in a corner – these were the only reminders of the modern world. The family were sitting around the stove, drinking and chatting. Dondan, tall and solid, greeted us with a handshake. Penpa had told me he was forty-six, eleven years older than Tseten; he was a man of very few words, but the pillar of the household who took care of the farm. Loga was sitting in a corner, staring at us with a grin that revealed tiny teeth with big gaps between them. Although the oldest at forty-eight, he was also the slightest. I took a closer look at him. Something seemed to be wrong with him: his complexion was sallow and his hair sparse and yellowish. I looked at Penpa; he whispered, 'He's had some illness all his life, the family does not know what it is.' The two older sons were there, Jigme and Gyatso, looking like younger versions of Dondan, but behaving like typical, bored teenagers.

There were two younger children, Tseyang – the only daughter – and Kunga, but they were still in school that day.

Mila, their grandfather, was away in Shigatse, visiting his wife in hospital. I was keen to find out more about him. Mila has been more than a shaman. He was a lama at the Palkhor Monastery in Gyantse for a decade, but was thrown out in 1959, after the Tibetan uprising against the Communists. He was forced to marry, but that was not enough – he was persecuted right up to the late 1970s. From him I hoped I could learn about the violent upheavals of those times, and how, despite everything, the old traditions have come back, and not just in his family.

I wonder whether Yul Lha did not hear Tseten's prayers. Or was he not pleased with the villagers' offerings? For the next week, whenever the weather looks like brightening up, we go back to the village, hoping to film. But the rain still does not let up enough for them to start harvesting, and if it goes on, the crop will be ruined. Now frustration is turning to fear – the rain might become hail. The villagers say that is Yul Lha's revenge for transgressions against him. Powerful as he is, Yul Lha is also easily offended. Forgetting to say a prayer to him, talking too loudly on the mountain top, making a fire in the forest – these are just a few of the things that displease him. Gale-force winds, thunder and lightning, downpours, blizzards, drought, and hailstones are his other weapons. It is said that Yul Lha has a consort to help him; according to one legend she has lightning in her right hand and hailstones in her left, ready to launch these wherever she is directed.

The Tibetans have a famous story about hail, which dates back to the eleventh century. It is the story of Milarepa, one of their most beloved sages. Born into a wealthy family, Milarepa and his mother and sister were turned out of their own home by an uncle and aunt after Milarepa's father died. Milarepa's mother was incensed, and told him to go away and learn the black arts so he might come back and take vengeance for the loss of their property. Milarepa did as his mother asked, and returned to his village an accomplished sorcerer. First, he made the roof collapse on a wedding party, killing thirty-five members of his clan. But this did not satisfy his mother, who demanded he launch a hailstorm and destroy all their relatives' crops. Milarepa created not one storm but three – and devastated the barley fields of the entire area. He was so appalled by the destruction he had unleashed that he soon turned to Buddhism to find repentance.

Hailstorms do not come around often in Gyantse, but when they do, they can destroy everything in the space of half an hour. Tseten tells me that five years ago villages further up the valley had a disaster. Right before their eyes, the ripened barley was flattened; nothing was left but useless heaps on the ground. They had worked the whole year for nothing. I have read of another hailstorm in 1969 in the County records, more widespread, and even more devastating. All these years later, just mentioning it still sends chills down the villagers' spines.

A hailstorm would be the worst thing for the Rikzin family, especially now. Even in a normal year, they have to be careful. This year, they will need a lot of extra money if Jigme and Gyatso get into university. In other parts of rural China, farmers have extra income from their migrant sons and daughters and from the highly successful 'town and village enterprises', the small local businesses which began with the economic reforms of 1979. I have seen none of them around Gyantse, except for families weaving carpets. The young men in Tangmad village have begun to seek work further away. But they speak only Tibetan and have no skills; they can do manual jobs – building houses for nomads, road construction, menial labour in the city for roughly 15 *yuan* a day (about £1). The Rikzin family do not have even that income, because they want all their four children to be educated.

'Cheer up,' Penpa says to the family one day at lunch time. They – and we – have spent yet another morning waiting for the rain to stop. 'If you are so worried, how do other families cope? After all, you have a hailstone lama under your roof. Surely that is some guarantee?' We all smile.

Indeed, 'hailstone lama' is what the villagers call Tseten, now I think about it. But strangely, since I started following Tseten in August, he has never mentioned his anti-hailstone work. On a particularly threatening day like today, does he not have to say a special prayer? Is there something he is not telling me? Why, when everyone is so worried about hail, is the 'hailstone lama' just sitting here, not doing anything?

'I'm unemployed now. The government brought an anti-aircraft gun a few years ago to disperse the clouds and prevent hailstorms. So I have been made redundant,' he says, laughing perhaps a little too loudly.

'Which is more effective?' I ask him. 'You or the gun?'

'Our family has done anti-hailstone work for six generations. You can ask anyone in this village. Tangmad has not been hit by hailstorms in recent times.'

'What about the one I read about in the County record?'

'That was not us. Our village has never been hit by hail,' Tseten says gently, but confidently. 'One year the hail was particularly powerful. All the trees were killed; even the ground was pitted. But it did not land in the fields. It stopped just outside them because of the power of my mantras. The three villages up the valley suffered for two years in a row *after* they bought the gun!'

'What do the villagers prefer, relying on the gun or placating Yul Lha?' I ask cheekily.

'Some other villages still invite me to do my mantras, but I say no.'

'Why?'

'They say the guns can do it. So let them do it.' He sounds a little peevish.

I ask Tseten if I can film him demonstrating his anti-hail ritual; he agrees. While our cameraman gets ready, Penpa asks if we are going to film the demonstration inside or outside.

'Oh, wherever Tseten usually does it,' I tell him.

'Are you sure?'

'Why not? Is there a problem?'

'I think it is better indoors.'

Is he worried that Tseten might be embarrassed if the neighbours see him doing it?

Penpa shakes his head. 'Suppose his mantra works? If we're outside, it will make it rain and we'll all get wet.'

I burst out laughing – something Penpa has often managed to make me do. He is a tremendous asset to our team. Four years in Beijing and another four years abroad for postgraduate study have given him a broad perspective, and he is wonderful with people, at least when he has not been drinking. I feel so lucky to have borrowed him from the Tibetan Academy of Social Sciences. 'A laugh a day makes you ten years younger,' he likes to tell me. 'Why take yourself, and me, so seriously? You need cheering up.' But sometimes, like now, it is hard to tell whether he is joking.

Inside his prayer room, Tseten puts on a maroon conical hat with stiff wings around its base. The hat is something he wears only for this ritual. In front of him on a tray is a bundle of pointed wooden batons, some short rods, half a dozen clay *tshatshas* which look like miniature stupas, two white conches decorated with stars, and a rosary, all pressed into a heap of barley on the tray. Tseten explains that these items have been much prayed over. The batons stand for male gods, the rods for female gods, the *tshatshas* for the Buddhist message, and the conches for the instrument through which the message is delivered. These, and a robe like the one a monk wears, are his complete equipment for taking on the mighty gods up in the sky.

Tseten says he used to begin his anti-hailstone ritual a full three months before the harvest, shutting himself away to meditate. In June, when the crop was just five inches tall, he would place sticks and rods around the fields – these represented his control over the fields. Then he would conduct a ritual for the whole village, during which he would enter into a trance, invoking Yul Lha and other gods, and asking them not to harm the village. For the rest of the summer, whenever the clouds looked threatening, he would be up twenty-four hours a day, praying and preparing for action. His vigil would last until all of the crops were brought in.

When I listen to Tseten explain the rituals, I am struck by how naïve he sounds. I cannot help wondering if he simply thinks the gods, the mantras, and his communication with the divine are all beyond me. I try to press him for more details.

'What is the first thing you do in the morning?'

'I watch the sun rise and observe how the clouds are moving.'

'Do you pray too?'

'Yes, I pray in the morning and at night. That is to let the heavenly deities know I am keeping a vigil against them.'

'If there are a lot of clouds in the sky, what do you do then?'

'There is a special ritual, but it is a heavenly secret, I cannot read it out to you. I only recite it in my heart. But through the ritual, I can change the way the clouds are moving so they won't form a mass. Or if they do, I will blow this conch at the right moment. As soon as the deities hear it, the clouds disperse. But you can only use this when it is really critical, and you cannot blow it more than five times.'

'What if the weather is really bad?'

'As a last resort, I fan the air with my lama robe, and then throw the robe into the air. That will definitely stop it.'

'How long did it take you to master the whole ritual?'

'I started learning from Mila when I was seventeen, and I've practised for eleven or twelve years. Before then my grandfather was the hailstone lama in this area, and my great-grandfather was also a hailstone lama.'

'Is there anything that the villagers have to do to help?'

'There is a custom that once the shaman controls a field, if a woman or a sheep walks into it, it is a bad omen for hail. That is why, after dusk, women are not allowed to come near the fields and sheep are all kept inside.'

'What is the possible retribution from the gods if you are causing them so much trouble?'

'If my ritual and mantra have worked against the heavenly gods, they will need a rest for several years. This is me committing a sin really, and I will be punished, perhaps by living a few years less.'

I hesitate, but in the end I ask Tseten about the fee for his anti-hail services. He says that when the crops were safe from hail, each of the ninety-six households in the village would give him a portion of their harvest, totalling roughly 500 kilos of barley. I do a quick calculation: a kilo of barley sells for 1.5 *yuan*, which is 10 pence. That means he would have earned about £50 – not much for six months' hard work. He made less than Dondan and Yangdron.

'Oh, but I did four other villages apart from our own, including one seventy kilometres away,' he tells me.

'Do they telephone you when a hailstorm is coming and you go over there?'

'No, I only have to stand on the roof of my house to see the direction the clouds are heading. I am connected to the fields with the batons, remember?'

But does Tseten possess considerable powers, or has the village just been lucky? I cannot help remembering a funny story I read in *The People of Tibet* by Charles Bell, written in the 1920s. Bell was briefly the British trade agent in Gyantse, and later became a confidant of the 13th Dalai Lama. He was informed by a highly placed lama official that hail was not allowed to fall on the Potala, the Dalai Lama's palace. 'Hail is believed to fall chiefly in countries in which the inhabitants are quarrelsome, or in which many illegitimate children are born,' Bell wrote. But while he was in Lhasa, the unthinkable happened – a storm brought hail to the Dalai Lama's palace. The two lamas charged with warding off the hail were immediately sacked – for negligence, Bell claims, too polite to say explicitly that their mantras were not up to the task.[7] Tibetans believe that the successive Dalai Lamas are the incarnations of the God of Compassion. If hail falls even on the Potala Palace, what chance do mere mortals' villages have?

An unemployed hailstone lama? It was slightly hard to fathom at first, but now I can see Tseten has lost a considerable income, nearly 2,500 kilos of barley. I feel for him. We have filmed him treating patients, but in the last couple of weeks very few have come; with the harvest on the way they will only do so in an emergency. And almost all other ceremonies and rituals – marriages or house buildings – are on hold until the harvest is over. Tseten really is unemployed in what used to be his busiest months of the year.

A few days after we recorded Tseten's ritual, the rain finally stops. The Rikzin family and all the villagers swarm into the fields and start the harvest. They are so obviously relieved after all the weeks of tension and anxiety. It is great for us to be filming outdoors again, with the postcard blue sky, everyone singing, the sickles swinging, the grain being tied up, and the tractors and carts taking it home.

Soon Yul Lha seems to change his mind, and the clouds are gathering again over the mountains. I decide to try to film the gun in action. We find it, painted green and mounted on a cart in a big open barley field, its long thin barrel pointing at the sky. It is manned by four gunners, all of them dressed in khaki fatigues. They are farmers from surrounding villages – one of them is Tseten's neighbour. I ask them about their job. They tell me that they have been trained by the Gyantse County Agriculture and Animal Husbandry Department, and that four different villages share the cost of their salaries and the shells they use. Despite the villagers' mounting concern, the gunners have not yet concluded that the clouds are a threat. In fact, not a single shot has been fired all summer. They are only too pleased when we ask them to demonstrate their skills for us on camera.

We pay 240 *yuan*, about £17, for four shells. While they are loading the shells with military precision, we ask them how they feel about the gun. 'It's very powerful,' one says enthusiastically. 'Five or six minutes after we fire it, the clouds disappear, the sky is blue. You'll see for yourself.'

'And how do you feel about a hailstone lama like Tseten?'

'In the old times, before we had the gun, we relied on the hailstone lama. Now we have the gun, we don't need one.'

'It is a good thing, too. The lamas took far too much of the villagers' crop as their reward,' another gunner says.

'But did Tseten or other shamans do a good job protecting the village from hail?' I press them for a clearer answer.

'The gun is definitely effective. Let's watch the demonstration,' the first man replies.

The clouds look heavy and are covering the hills. The gunners turn the wheel to get the right elevation, adjust the direction of the barrel, and fire. The bang is loud, but it is like wailing without tears – no rain comes, and I cannot see that the clouds have noticeably dispersed. Perhaps the aim was faulty, or perhaps we should have waited for the clouds to move closer.

While they reload, my mind flashes back to Tseten demonstrating the hail ritual in his prayer room. He was doing it for our film, but I could not have told that from his demeanour – he was totally immersed in his communication with the gods, whether or not they were listening. His whole life has been spent working for the villagers as an intermediary between the known and the unknown. Now the unknown is being pushed back even here. Tseten has lost his most important job; I wonder what else will be taken away from him.

Tseten said his family is keen to pass on the shaman tradition to one of the children, but I suspect we might have seen the hailstone lama's last performance in this valley.

A second bang interrupts my thoughts. The shell explodes closer to the clouds, but still with no result. Either the gunners need more practice – this is only their first outing this year because the shells are expensive – or the gun is not very effective. 'If you don't believe us, ask the villagers. A few years ago, the gun drove away the clouds, but other villages got hailed on,' they hasten to assure me. 'And the technology will get better. Some countries use planes or missiles now.'

Before we say goodbye to the gunners, something suddenly occurs to me: how did the villagers cope with hail during the Cultural Revolution, when shamans were forbidden to practise and when there were no guns?

'They put dynamite on the mountain tops and set it off, hoping the explosions would disperse the clouds,' one of the gunners says with a laugh. 'Or they relied on Mao's *Red Book*.'

'What? How could that save them from hail?' I ask in disbelief. I remembered seeing a photograph from the 1970s: Tibetan peasants from a production brigade carrying portraits of Mao on sticks, and pushing them into the ground on the edge of a field, while they recited passages from Mao's *Little Red Book*. I had assumed the photo was just propaganda.

'No, that was exactly what they did,' the gunner says. 'They took Mao's *Red Book*, stood around the fields, and read passages aloud; they thought that would stop the hail.'

Later on I did come across a reference to the 1969 hailstorm in Gyantse and its aftermath. The local Communist Party chief did not move swiftly to help the devastated peasants; instead he began a witch-hunt. He suspected a political reason for the failure of Mao's *Red Book* against the hail. Maybe it was sabotage by enemies of the people. Or it was the curses of the expelled lamas and nuns, or the debarred shamans. The witch-hunt went on for weeks. Quite a few of the supposed 'enemies' were severely punished.[8]

But that day on the way back from the gunnery demonstration, I could not get that image out of my mind – Tibetan peasants wielding Mao's *Red Book* against the weather. But perhaps I should not be surprised. When I grew up during the Cultural Revolution, we learned to revere Mao as the great helmsman and saviour; from our earliest years we were taught that we should be ready to follow in the footsteps of our revolutionary forefathers, to lay down our lives for the Communist cause if Mao gave us the order. In the political jargon of the time, Mao's thoughts were carved on our bones and melted into our blood. And many Red Guards really did pin a Mao badge on their flesh.

As I was taught, so were the Tibetans. In the past, they recited mantras, fingered their rosaries, made offerings, and went on pilgrimages to accumulate more and more merit. They set up family altars, built prayer walls, stupas, temples and monasteries to safeguard their homes, villages, and towns. Then monasteries and temples were destroyed; prayer flags were taken from the rooftops. There was no more burning of incense, no votive butter lamps, no praying at all other than to Chairman Mao. Mao's portrait replaced the images of the Buddhas and Bodhisattvas that had once hung in every household. Every family kept Mao's *Collected Works* on the altar. In the first three years of the Cultural Revolution, 7,344,000 copies of Mao's works were distributed, for a population of over one million. Tens of thousands of training sessions in political studies were organised, attended by over a third of the adult population. In 1968 Chairman Mao sent some mangos to the Tibetan people: the massed crowd at the presentation was like a pilgrimage to see the relics of a great lama.[9]

Did the Tibetans ever believe Mao was their new god? Possibly many did. In their harsh environment, they needed a faith, a saviour. We were still driving through the valley on our way back to Gyantse when this idea really came home to me. I had asked the driver to stop so we could take a general view of the valley. There were a dozen villagers working in the foreground. Then I moved away to take a wider shot from a distance. Under the immense sky, the villagers were suddenly so tiny, so lonely and small: an insignificant speck in a vast landscape of mountain and plain. The menacing black clouds looked ready to drop their huge weight and crush them. And this valley is one of the most fertile and densely populated in Tibet. Most of Tibet is far wilder, just boundless barren scrub and grasslands stretching in every direction. I try to imagine what it is like for a nomad with his herds out on those huge plateaus wandering for weeks without encountering another soul – one man against the elements, and completely at their mercy. Is it any wonder that they have so many gods? Mao is gone, and the Tibetans have returned happily to their Yul Lhas, and all their ancient traditions and beliefs.

* * *

After three weeks of backbreaking work, a race against time, the harvest is finally in. The Rikzin family kept at it day and night, whenever it was not raining. It is not a good year for them. They have only reaped half the usual crop. When I come to film them at the end of their labours, I expect to see disappointment or sadness on their face, but there is none. They seem to have been prepared for much worse.

Do they blame the gods? I would think that they might, that after all the offerings they have made they would need someone or something to blame for the bad year. I ask Tseten whether he feels Yul Lha has let them down. He says blaming is not part of the Tibetan culture. The villagers' response to a bad harvest is to perform a 'repentance' ritual, asking for forgiveness. It is they, not Yul Lha, who have not done enough. They promise to do better next year.

I find this hard to take. I know what the Chinese peasant would do: he would shake his fist at the sky and stamp on the ground, railing at the gods for cheating him, complaining about his wasted offerings, and threatening not to pray to them any more. I mention the contrast to Tseten. He smiles gently, 'Our rituals are really just the way we express our faith. We may or may not get anything in return. But that is not what matters most. Buddhism is about giving; it is a virtue in itself and brings its own reward. That is how we will have a better life, now or in the next world.'

TWO

Sky Burial

'Du, Du,' a sharp sound. Another. I fumble about, thinking it is the alarm. But it is too early, only 7 a.m. Then I realise it is my mobile ringing. Who could be calling at such an uncivilised hour? Outside my hotel in downtown Lhasa, it is still dark. It is Dorje, one of our Tibetan cameramen, calling from our house in Gyantse.

'Tseten has just rung. His mother died early this morning. What should we do?'

The news comes as a shock. We have never met Tseten's mother. Since the filming began, she has been staying with her daughter in Shigatse. I was told she had had tuberculosis for a long time, but that she was recovering. Her husband, Mila, went to see her a few weeks ago, and when he returned to the village reported, 'I said to her I would be lost without her, so she has promised to get better.' I was touched by the vulnerability in his eyes. How devastated Mila and the family must be now.

My immediate response is to wonder if we might persuade the family to let us film the funeral rites, especially the sky burial. I know it is the most extraordinary custom, when the dead body is cut up and fed to vultures; I have seen an amateur video of it. To me it seems to embody something at the very heart of life and death as Tibetans see it; capturing it for our film would be incredible.

But I know it is insensitive and crude of me even to think of it, when the family is stricken with grief. How would I react if I were in their position? I would think twice and then probably say no. Grief is so personal, and it is best left in private, with all the love, repentance, regret, or even relief pouring out without being observed or judged. The only reason I have the courage to ask is that we have been following the family for four months and have been treated as part of it.

Of all the people we are filming, the Rikzin family have been the most open with us so far. They have been forgiving both of our intrusions into their lives and our scepticism about what we have seen. Once Tseten allowed us to accompany him on a visit to a pregnant woman, whose body he said had been entered by an evil spirit. He was not offended when we then followed her for a check-up in the hospital, where the doctor told her she was suffering from anaemia. Our doubts did not stop him from offering us treatment either. He tried to cure the spots on our handsome driver's face with saliva. The spots did not go away, and the driver pointed that out, but Tseten was, as usual, unaffected; he was never once defensive.

I discuss the filming idea on the phone with Dorje, who is always thoughtful and sensitive. After much deliberation, it is decided that he should go on behalf of the crew to offer our condolences with a *khata*, the ceremonial white scarf, and 100 *yuan*. He can then judge the situation first-hand. Meanwhile I would rush back from Lhasa, leaving the filming there to our other cameraman.

Dorje was turned away. He left the *khata* and money with a young man who was guarding the door, allowing only close relatives inside. I feel guilty. Am I pushing too hard? Am I as insensitive as the Chinese tourists that I am always complaining about? Just a week before, we were filming an obviously poor pilgrim who was giving money to some monks; they had been praying for his family's health and safety. Behind me, I heard a tourist remark loudly, in Chinese, 'Look at the rags he's wearing! He could buy himself a new outfit with that money.' Quite a few of the monks – who could understand Chinese – stared in disgust.

As soon as I return to Gyantse, I go to see Phuntsog, one of Gyantse's two sky burial masters. I have been introduced to him by the street committee where we rented the house, and found that I already knew him: he comes to our house on a tractor once a week to collect our rubbish. He is a small, hunched man with an extremely dark complexion – possibly a result of the many hours he spends outside. He is friendly, and has a ready smile, but he seldom speaks unless spoken to. His manner is so humble that when I hand him our bin bags, he seems to consider it a favour.

Phuntsog lives just five minutes from us. He has the simplest of mud houses, on the edge of an open space where the neighbourhood's rubbish and waste water seem to have ended up. He is sitting in the small but tidy kitchen, enjoying some *chang* – barley wine – after work while his wife is cooking. My arrival seems to startle him. He stands up, looking at me but not knowing what to say. I explain why I have come: I have told him before that I want to film a sky burial, and all he said was that it would be difficult. Now I really need his advice: how could we persuade the family? Might there be a way round it?

'The trouble is it's a crucial time,' he said. 'The soul of the dead is still in the body. If you come to the house, if strangers come, you will disturb or even frighten the soul. That is why, when someone dies, we put a bunch of juniper twigs on the door to warn people to stay away.'

So when does the family send for him?

'They would call the shaman or a lama first. He works out the location and the right time for the sky burial. Then they let me know. Usually it is three days after the death. They put butter lamps near the body to guide the soul; it must not wander in the dark. The close relatives have to be told, and neighbours help to get a big feast ready – meat dumplings, boiled mutton, and rice with butter and dried fruit. We think this is the dead person's last meal. All this time, there will be a lama reading out mantras beside the body, praying for the soul.'

So we cannot film during these three days?

'No, most families won't want you there,' he said. 'It's too important. The soul has this one chance of finding its next life. They are not going to let you disturb it.'

What about after the three days?

'It is still hard. We do the sky burial and then the soul wanders. It is in the *bardo*, that is the time between death and the next life. If it is frightened, it might get stuck there. That would be terrible.'

How long will the rebirth take?

'It depends. It's all to do with your karma. But normally we think it takes forty-nine days.'

He sees my face fall at that, and goes on: 'Maybe there's a family who will let you. It costs money. They want to do it properly. If they are really poor and you can help them, they might let you film. Even then you will have to do it from a long way off.'

Now I know I will not have a chance with the Rikzin family.

I leave Phuntsog and walk back to the house, passing clusters of old men and women, silent and purposeful. They are doing their evening circumambulation of the whole town: it is to accumulate merit for a better reincarnation. Outside the No. 1 High School, they mingle with students walking up and down, memorising their lessons – their way of taking care of their future. I see the old people every day, and I always wonder whether this 'merit' will really help them; at least they are getting some exercise, I say to myself. But after the big blow I have received, I cannot let go of my disappointment. I find myself, not for the first time, disputing in my head the whole idea of reincarnation, however essential it is for Buddhists.

It all started with my grandmother. Like most Chinese of her generation, she was a Buddhist. Her whole life was one of hardship – seven of her nine children died during a smallpox outbreak in a single year. Her sole consolation was the paradise she believed in. She used to describe it in great detail: the sun forever shining, flowers eternally in bloom, houses made of gold, no sickness, no infirmity – a world where everyone has whatever their heart desires, in which we are all reunited with those we love.

It is the Buddhist 'Western paradise'. To get there, Grandmother was told to pray and do good and no evil. She was eternally kind to everyone, even during the Cultural Revolution, comforting the so-called 'enemies of the people' who no one else dared to go near. When my father, a convinced Communist, told her not to pray or do her superstitious things, she took to saying her prayers wordlessly at night. As a child I always sided with my father, influenced by him, and set against Buddhism by my atheist education. Religion was an opiate; monks and nuns were parasites; the Buddhas and Bodhisattvas were just wooden statues. Mao was the saviour; Communism would bring paradise here on earth. I made fun of her beliefs. As Father said, if her children had been vaccinated, as we were, she would not have lost them. It had nothing to do with her supposed sins.

After her death, I began to find out more about Buddhism. In 2000, I spent a year retracing the footsteps of Xuanzang, a

Chinese monk who travelled in the seventh century from China to India and back, searching for the true Buddhism. I learned that Buddhism had little to do with the version I was made to swallow at school. I was appalled that I had been attacking it without really knowing what it was. For two thousand years, it has given generations of Chinese hope and solace; it has enriched every aspect of our life, our philosophy, our art, even our language. We would have little of a cultural heritage without it. I learned in particular to appreciate the centrality of the mind in Buddhism, and how it can be cultivated. This was not superstition. It was a way to transcend the suffering that is part of life. Things happen; what matters is how we react. I always remembered the story of the Chinese monk who was spat on by the Red Guards in a 'struggle meeting'; he said to himself it was just raining. It might sound extreme, even absurd – but he did not take his life, as many did; he never even hated his tormentors. In the same way Grandmother could rise above her pain and return my ingratitude with love; she took my taunts as just words.

I still have much to learn and understand about Buddhism. But one thing makes it very hard for me to embrace it, and that is reincarnation. I have so many questions about it. What is it that migrates from this life to the next? Phuntsog calls it the soul. But Buddhism denies the existence of a permanent soul because everything is transitory. It says we are merely a heap of five elements: body, feeling, cognition, mental constructions, and consciousness. The five elements are all impermanent; they are constantly in the process of becoming and changing. When questioned by a perplexed young monk, the Buddha said only that 'karma' passes from one life to another. He used the light of a candle as an illustration. A flame passes from one candle to another, but they are two separate entities, neither of which is permanent. It is a beautiful image, and yet, even here, there is *something* that has caused the flame. Something has to reincarnate. When I get back to the house, I look in the *Tibetan Book of the Dead* for an answer. The book comes down to us from Padam, the Indian master credited with bringing Buddhism from India to Tibet in the eighth century. It has the most vivid, thorough descriptions of the soul's forty-nine-day journey through the *bardo*, but its main message is how enlightenment can still be attained every step of the way, from the moment of death.

Once enlightened, we are freed from the cycle of suffering: birth, sickness, old age, and death. In Tibetan the book is called *Great Liberation by Hearing* – it is hearing the book and grasping its teaching that will provide enlightenment after death. Without enlightenment, the only hope is a good rebirth.

The *Book of the Dead* does say that what reincarnates is the consciousness, which is really light and energy. It acquires a 'mental body' that can see, hear, smell, speak, run, comprehend – and all more efficiently than humans can. But I still feel lost. Being told it is light and energy does not help me much, and a mental body with all those properties is even less comprehensible. And if enlightenment is so hard to achieve, how can a ball of light and energy manage it, and just by hearing the *Book*?

I cannot help think of the titanic struggle by Milarepa after he unleashed the hailstorm and turned to Buddhism. He spent years building a stupa at the request of his master, only to be told to tear it down, return the stones to where they came from – and then start all over again. He was not offered a single word from the sacred teachings, but received plenty of humiliation and beating. In the end, the master relented and passed him the secret of attaining enlightenment in his lifetime. But even then he had to spend decades meditating in caves, with little to eat but nettles, which turned his body green, like a caterpillar. He did find his Way, and left thousands of poems, which are recited to this day. They reflect the mind of a remarkable and enlightened man.

> Dwell alone and you shall find a friend.
> Take the lowest place and you shall reach the highest.
> Hasten slowly and you will soon arrive.
> Renounce all worldly goals and you shall reach the highest one.[10]

It is Sogyal Rinpoche, the great Tibetan commentator on the *Book*, who helps me make some sense of it. I have also brought with me his *Tibetan Book of Living and Dying*, and am reading it in bed. I find a good metaphor in it. When you go to meet a stranger off a plane, if you have a picture, you can recognise him. Without it you do not know who you are looking for. The *Book of the Dead* is for the living as well as for the dead. Enlightenment comes with preparedness: you have to rid yourself of ignorance, anger, and hatred, the mind's poisons. Then you have a chance of recognising it when you encounter it in the *bardo*. I do not need to believe in the *bardo* or in reincarnation. I can take his words as advice for this world, even though that is not what he intends. For him, reincarnation is the fact of life, and death.

Dreaming is as near as I can come to understanding the *bardo*. Dreams seem so clear, so vivid, so real, even if we only find them so while we are dreaming. Sogyal Rinpoche in fact compares the 'mental body' in the *bardo* with the dream body we have when we dream. But then, when we wake up, we know we have been dreaming. And we have a mind when we dream. What is it that directs the mental body in the intermediate state? He says it is the consciousness – but is there any consciousness after we die? I am slowly falling asleep; the last thing I read is Sogyal Rinpoche's remark, 'Going to sleep is similar to the *bardo* of dying, where the elements and thought process dissolve, opening into …'

We get a call from Tseten two days later. He sounds calm, and not as sad as I would have imagined. He thanks us for the *khata*, and the money, and then apologises for turning us away. I tell him I understand. I do not even mention filming. The whole thing barely makes sense to me, but I would hate them to think I was getting in the way of their mother's reincarnation. They could not even be at the sky burial themselves. No close member of the family is allowed there; it is said that their sadness would hold back the soul and slow down its journey into the next life.

I am not sure when we can resume our filming with Tseten. Will we have to wait out the forty-nine days, till his mother finds a new life? I am prepared to wait. I should try to think that it is nothing if there is another life to come.

But I am not ready to give up. Phuntsog is now my hope. He knows how keen we are to film a sky burial. Whenever he is going to perform one, he lets us know, and we then visit the family and ask if we can film it. We have three straight rejections. While we are waiting for our chance, I invite Phuntsog, his wife and children to our house to get to know them better. He does not mind talking about his work. 'It has been decided by the Buddha a long, long time ago that this is the occupation of our family. We have been doing it for many generations. Whoever needs my help, I will go and take care of their dead to the best of my ability,' he says with a kind smile, while emptying the *chang* in his cup. He took the job over from his father eight years ago, and says if his sons do not get a place in college, he will pass his skills to them.

Phuntsog enjoys the company of the living, although he has few friends. In Tibetan society, he is regarded as the lowest of the low, along with butchers and blacksmiths. I did not believe it until I was confronted with it myself. We were having some of our film characters over for a meal and I suggested we invite Phuntsog. To my surprise all the Tibetan members of the crew said it was out of the question. 'No one will touch the food from any dish he helps himself from,' Penpa warned me. 'And I think he will be as embarrassed as us. Why don't we give him something instead? Like rice and butter and fruit – something he and his family can enjoy at home.' I tried to plead with them and for the first time almost caused a revolt among my team. I had to give up. Fortunately, though, Phuntsog did not give up on us.

Finally, three months after Tseten's mother passed away, Phuntsog came to us with news of the death of one of the local blacksmiths. He had drunk himself to death and brought ruin on his family. Some years back, he had sold his son for adoption and had promptly got drunk on the proceeds (just £30, Phuntsog told us). His wife had left him and the woman he married later was forced to beg at the entrance to the monastery. He would spend the money she received on *chang*. Phuntsog thought the blacksmith's wife would probably let me watch his sky burial, at least from a distance.

I go to visit the blacksmith's wife with Pantog, our housekeeper, to offer my condolences and to seek her permission. She lives in one of the old parts of Gyantse at the foot of the fort; I like walking there, through its well laid-out lanes lined with traditional houses. But the blacksmith and his wife did not live in one of those. Their dwelling is at the back, where the road stops. It is barely a house, just three mud walls stuck on the side of a stone ruin – there is no door. When I enter I see she has a tiny kitchen area, and a single main room, which is empty except for a small table. On it a few butter lamps flicker wildly. Her husband's body lies on the floor in a corner wrapped in a white cloth. I can hardly believe what I see; I would not have thought anyone in modern Tibet lived this desperately. Pantog hands her a *khata* and a 50 *yuan* note. 'He drank everything away,' she wails through her tears. 'Now he's gone, the easy way. But what am I going to do? How am I going to live?'

I cannot think of anything to say that might comfort her. I leave without making my request. I decide I will just go to the burial, without the cameraman, and trust that she will not mind. If her husband took so little care of this life, perhaps he would not be too concerned about the next one.

When the day comes, I get up very early. I walk from the back of our house under a dark blue sky, past the racetrack and the government grain store, heading for a barren hill. It is about two hundred yards from the sky burial site, but I have brought a powerful pair of binoculars. The site is at a gentle height, standing on its own, surrounded on every side by low meandering hills. Phuntsog has told me that this makes it easy for vultures to see the smoke from his juniper twigs and to land. Aside from two simple shelters and a semicircle of large flat stones made shiny from use, the site is bare. The only colour I can make out is the maroon robe of a monk, sitting and meditating in one of the shelters. I am told that monks often choose such places for meditation: their being places of death helps them to conquer their fears, and to appreciate the impermanence of life.

Just as the sky begins to lighten, the body of the dead man is brought up. Two men carry it, and two others follow behind. Once the corpse is on the ground, the men circle it three times, and then they take a break in the shelter. They drink tea and *chang* and talk; I see that they are even laughing. After about thirty minutes, they re-emerge. One man lights a pile of juniper twigs and *tsampa*, the smoke wafting away. Phuntsog lays out his tools – a huge knife, a pair of hooks, and two hammers.

The body remains on the ground, face down, while Phuntsog

begins cutting it into large pieces, which he hands to the other men. The men lay the flesh on the stones and, using the hammers, begin pounding it into a pulp. Watching them do this, I cannot imagine Tseten and Dondan looking on while it was done to their mother. However they might try to rationalise their emotions and think of what is good for the soul, this would be too much. Perhaps this is the real reason why close relatives are not allowed at the sky burial.

Suddenly I hear singing – a work song, cheerful and rhythmical. I look around to see where it is coming from. The men at the burial site have their backs to me, but one turns in my direction and I can see – it is them! They sing with gusto, as though they are bringing in a harvest, or working on a road gang. Have they forgotten this is a death? No, I realise, for them the death is not the point. The death has already happened; they are charged now with helping the soul on its journey.

When they have finished, Phuntsog rolls some of the flesh into a ball, and walks towards the open space. I can hear him calling 'Come, come!' His deep voice echoes in the air, as he looks up at the clouds. Then he drops the ball on the ground. Everyone looks skyward, hoping for a sign of the vultures. Twenty minutes pass. Phuntsog has warned me that it can take hours for the vultures to come, depending on the weather. Just as he is calling again, a single vulture appears. It circles the site several times, and then straightens its legs and lands. I watch as, with a last flap of its wings, it pounces on the ball – it has the whole of it to itself.

In what seems like no time at all, twenty or thirty more vultures appear in the sky. Their wingspan looks to be more than a metre across. I wonder if my body would be enough to feed even one of them. The men continue to rub their hands with *tsampa* and mix it with the flesh, handing it to Phuntsog, who lays it out for the vultures. In a flash the birds gobble everything down. There is relief on the men's faces. They believe that when the vultures eat the body quickly, without leaving anything behind, reincarnation will be swift too. The intestines are the last to go – perhaps because they are the richest part. Phuntsog has told me that once the vultures have eaten these, they will not take anything else. If the vultures do not finish the corpse – sometimes there are several bodies on a particular day – he will discuss this with the families, and then he will either burn what is left, or take it to the water. Everything must go, he says.

Phuntsog has also told me something else. Vultures have a secret, he claims: whatever they swallow, they leave nothing on the ground, not even their own waste. They defecate in the sky, thousands of metres up, and the waste is immediately dispersed by strong winds and currents. Even when they are dying, they will fly higher and higher, towards the sun, until the sun and wind take them to pieces, leaving no trace. Phuntsog says this is why no one has ever seen a vulture's corpse.

After everything has been consumed, Phuntsog cleans his equipment, wraps up his poles and ropes, and leaves with the others. The vultures are still on the slope, lingering. ('Were they still hungry?' I ask Phuntsog later. 'Oh, sometimes they are just digesting. They are too heavy to fly.') I sit down and wait.

The Chinese have always been appalled by the practice of sky burial. One of the last Ambans declared it to be 'without morals and without reason, and cruel beyond words'. He tried to forbid it and demanded the Tibetans bury their dead as we do.[11] It did not occur to him that the ritual might have practical origins. In the whole Tibetan area, less than 1 per cent of the land is arable, so burial in the ground is hardly practical. The cold winter lasts more than five months of the year, and during that time the earth is frozen. Digging is difficult, if not impossible, in many parts of Tibet. Also most Tibetans live on grassland, and they roam wherever there is water and grass. If they bury their dead, they will be leaving them behind.

But the rituals of death are deeply ingrained in a culture. For us Chinese, who have been so tied to the land for generations, a burial is seen as a way of returning to Mother Earth. Only then can the dead have their final rest. And for my grandmother, such a burial was an event to be prepared for well in advance. When she turned seventy, she announced to us all that she was ready to go and presented my parents with a list of items that she would require: a coffin, four sets of clothes for the four seasons, a house, a boat, a table and two chairs, a wardrobe, a number of animals and plenty of money. I was flabbergasted. How could we possibly afford these things? I remember asking my mother, who laughed and said, 'Don't be silly. Grandmother's treasures will all be made of paper, except for the clothes.'

My father's response to all this surprised me even more. A staunch Communist, he was usually impatient with Grand-mother's superstitious beliefs. Once he had caught her praying in the dark and shouted, 'Your Buddha is not worth a dog's fart. Why don't you pray to Chairman Mao for a change?' But this time, he simply said, 'This is your grandmother's last wish. We should satisfy her.'

My grandmother lived to be ninety-four. For more than a decade, one fixture of my summer vacation was to help her air her burial clothes. We did this covertly, one outfit at a time, so that none of the neighbours would suspect us of being super-stitious. My grandmother would remind me again and again to make sure that, when the time came, my mother dressed her in all four of the outfits while she was still breathing – otherwise, she would be going to the next world naked. Unfortunately, by the time my grandmother died, burial had been forbidden in China because of the population explosion and pressure on the land. Cremation was the order of the day. Although peasants could still get away with burying their beloved in the family plots, Party officials like my father would be severely punished for breaking the new decree. My father had always followed the Party's every command, but this time, he was in agony. He went missing for days and my mother later told me that he was out trying to find a way to transport my grandmother's body secretly to our home village. He did not succeed. The roads were bad, and the trip would have taken too long – the corpse might rot. So Grandmother's meticulous preparations went up in flames.

As I watch the last vulture flapping its wings and flying off, I stand up to leave. It is lifting itself further and further away, into the void. Is it taking the soul of the dead body with it? I wonder. As I walk back to the house, the scene of the sky burial plays over and over in my mind. I had expected something far more brutal, far bloodier. After having seen it for myself, I now understand why there is generally no family present. But for a dispassionate observer like myself, the matter-of-factness of the sky burial is hard to deny. There is something peaceful and dignified about it, and it produces no waste or pollution of any kind. By giving their bodies to the vultures, Tibetans are performing their last offering in this life. I remember what Phuntsog told me: 'Giving is in Tibetans' nature, in life or in death. The vulture only eats dead things. We cannot let it go hungry while we bury or cremate our dead. That would be cruel.' Whether or not the soul is going to a better place, sky burial does seem to me like a natural, and ecological, way to go.

THREE

Journey to the Next Life

Twenty-eight days after the death of his mother, Tseten calls again. The family is preparing for a special fire ritual, the most elaborate they have performed so far. Do we want to film it?

'Are you sure?' I ask, cautiously. I am keen to film it, but I do not want to intrude. In the time since she passed away, I have often found myself thinking of Tseten's mother. Despite my own beliefs, I seem in some curious way to be growing concerned about the passage of her soul.

But Tseten assures me it will be all right. 'Mila has invited you,' he says.

We set off immediately. As we approach the house, we see villagers arriving, carrying baskets of food or large jars of *chang*. One man struggles under the weight of a huge sack full of cowpats. Coming up the stairs by the stable, we find the Rikzins' upper courtyard packed; half the village seems to have turned up. Three shaven-headed nuns in maroon robes are arranging food on a long table: barley and barley flour, butter, sugar, tea, mustard seeds, rice, Chinese dates, spices, and quite a few other things that I don't recognise. Two more nuns are cleaning two five-foot long ceremonial horns. In a far corner of the yard, a couple of men are mixing a vast heap of *tsampa* with brown sugar to make *tso*, small cones of offerings. The heap gets bigger all the time, as new visitors add *tsampa*, sugar, and raisins they have brought with them. I watch a little girl who quietly waits her turn behind the adults. She holds a small bowl of *tsampa* in both hands, with a piece of yellow paper – a prayer for the dead, perhaps – tucked into the middle of it; when her turn comes, she tips it onto the heap.

Mila is standing in the centre of the courtyard. He looks calm and serene, like the rest of the family. Had I not known, I would not have suspected that he had just lost his wife. The only difference I notice is that he seems rather shabby, even dirty, his chin unshaven, the collar and the sleeves of his shirt shiny with grease. I have been told it is the custom for the family not to wash for forty-nine days after a death. He greets us warmly. He is wearing his usual outfit – a crimson sweater and brown vest – and his eyes are crinkling behind the pink plastic rims of his spectacles in the bright sun. He is watching as Tseten bends over a couple of pillow-sized mud bricks. Dondan is pouring sand from a sack. I ask Mila what they are doing. 'We are making a *mandala* for the ritual today,' he says. He points to the small packets of coloured sand on the windowsill. I am surprised. I have seen the famous murals of *mandalas* in the Palkhor monastery – large, gorgeous murals meant to represent the cosmos. They are so intricate, so vivid, and yet also so ingenious. Are we thinking of the same thing? I check with Tseten. 'You just wait.'

Although it is late October the sun is very strong, and Mila invites us to rest in the prayer room. There he introduces us to a young man, Tseten's cousin, who is making *torma*. I have often seen Tseten making them – they are little blocks made of *tsampa* and butter, some painted red, intended to represent both the peaceful and wrathful deities. The good deities will be thanked, praised, and put on the altar for the protection of the family; the bad deities are pacified and then left on the rooftop, at crossroads, or on the outskirts of the village, supposedly taking away with them any bad influences that might trouble the family.

In the midst of the *torma* is a reclining human figurine in red, which I assume embodies the deceased woman. Mila carries it and the finished *torma* to the altar table. He stands and stares at the altar for quite a while. I wonder what he is thinking. I know Mila believes that grieving will distract his wife from her rebirth, so is he trying not to be sad? When he sits down with us, I ask him. 'Imagine you are caught in a storm,' he tells me. 'That is what it is like for the souls of the dead. Our tears would be like a hurricane; our cries would be like thunder. They would frighten the soul. It is best to stay calm.'

I look at Mila long and hard. Perhaps the next life is so important and he is so engrossed in ensuring his wife will have a good rebirth, he simply has no time for grieving. Or does absorption in the ritual give him a natural tranquillity?

I am just about to ask him more questions when he is called to the courtyard to supervise the preparations. I take the opportunity to peek into the next room. There, two nuns are busily refilling empty butter lamps. A huge pot of melted butter is bubbling away on an electric stove, and rows and rows of lamps glow in front of a statue of the Buddha of Infinite Light. The amount of work required to fill and refill all the lamps is daunting, but the nuns seem very happy doing it, chanting while they work.

'Why so many lamps?' I ask them.

'To guide the soul in the *bardo*,' one of the nuns, who is tall and striking, replies.

I ask her to tell me more. She shakes her head, insisting that she is not knowledgeable enough, that she may mislead me. But when I plead with her, she relents. She lists ten functions of the butter lamp; among other things, a butter lamp can help the eyes to see more clearly, illuminate the difference between kindness and evil, dispel the darkness of ignorance, help us to be reborn into a higher state of being, and help us to escape quickly from sadness. Quite a lot for a humble lamp.

But they had a disaster last night, she tells me sadly. A large lump of butter brought by one of the visitors was fake, made of solidified oil, and quite a few of the lamps did not burn at all. 'Even the butter that people offer to the Buddha is often fake these days,' she grumbles. She tells me that even if the fake butter burns, it makes a lot of smoke. It pollutes the air and darkens the old murals and statues in the monasteries. 'The saddest part is that the pilgrims who buy it know it is fake because it is so cheap. But they do not want to pay more for real butter. Money is eating at their hearts. May they not go to hell in their next life for cheating,' she says, sighing.

I sit down to help them, and as I refill the cups with butter, I can't help wondering about the cost: the Rikzins will burn hundreds of lamps, day and night, for forty-nine days. How much butter is that? And butter is only a part of it. Monks and nuns who come to the service have to be fed and paid; food and drink must be served to the relatives and villagers; large quantities of *tsampa* are used to make offerings. Much of the elaborate ritual is repeated every seven days to guide the soul, since it is supposed to experience death seven times. After the forty-nine days, Tseten and the family will go on pilgrimages to the most famous monasteries and temples to make sure the deities there recognise their mother's reincarnation should it appear in their domain. A death can push families into debt.

We have always been lectured in China about the wastefulness of Buddhism. There are endless lists of figures to bolster the message: the old Tibetan government spent 90 per cent of its income on religious activities, while its people led miserable lives; at the time of the liberation of Tibet in 1951, as many as a quarter of all Tibetan men were in monasteries, the highest ratio to the general population of any country; in the two hundred years from the mid-eighteenth century to 1951, Tibet's population increased by just over 100,000, virtually a standstill.[12] No money to invest in the economy, too little manpower on the land, not enough young people to drive society forward. Buddhism drained Tibet's wealth and was a recipe for paralysis.

Strangely, this Communist critique reads almost exactly like that of Austin Waddell, a British medical officer in the early twentieth century; he was just as scathing of the lamas:

> They have induced the people to lavish all their wealth upon building and beautifying scores of temples, and filling them with idols; and through their power over the latter, the priests, as the sole mediators between God and man, are supposed to be able to drive away the hordes of evil spirits that are ever on the outlook to inflict on the poor Tibetan and his family disease, accident, or other misfortune.[13]

A hundred years later, the same view of the dominance of religion and its impact on the old Tibet was voiced again by British historian, Charles Allen, if more mildly worded: 'When a nation's gross domestic product is expressed largely in terms of prayer, meditation, study, pilgrimage and religious art, and its productive population is small, scattered and static, the final outcome can never be in doubt.'[14]

The great 13th Dalai Lama did try to shake Tibet out of its rut early in the twentieth century. He introduced an English-style school for the children of the aristocracy, and sought to modernise the army and reduce the power of the unruly monks.

The monasteries, and the lamas who made up half the government, rose in unison to prevent any reform. More authority for the army, modern and 'atheistic' ideas, and more representative government – these would dent the monasteries' coffers, and break their hold on society. They prevailed. The army commander-in-chief, a favourite of the Dalai Lama, was sacked. Later the leading reformer, Lungshar, was imprisoned and had his eyes gouged out; he died shortly after. The English school was shut down, with the monasteries even threatening 'to send their fierce fighting monks to kidnap and sexually abuse the students'.[15] Football, which had become popular in Lhasa, was banned because it generated too much passion, and was dangerous to social and cultural stability. 'Ironically, by trying to protect Tibet's cherished Buddhist values,' says Melvyn Goldstein, the pre-eminent historian of modern Tibet, the conservative monasteries themselves made Tibet 'unable to defend and preserve those very religious values from the Chinese Communists'.[16]

I emerge from the room full of lamps into the sunny courtyard, and find Mila and Tseten totally immersed in the making of the *mandala*. They sit, bent low, holding pointed iron tubes filled with coloured minerals. By gently tapping the tubes, they let the colours fill in the drawings on the floor. It is painstaking work – one small slip with the coloured sand can ruin the whole thing. Their design is much smaller and simpler than the versions I saw in the monastery, but it is beautiful nonetheless. At its centre is a six-pointed red star enclosed within a blue circle. Around this is a circle coloured black and filled with gold *dorje*, the thunderbolt symbolising the power of the dharma to destroy ignorance. The last and outermost circle is made up of brightly coloured flames.

Tseten and Dondan clear the space around the *mandala*

and Yangdron and some of the villagers lay carpets around it. Mila disappears into the house and then re-emerges wearing a maroon shawl and a crown-like hat of red and yellow silk. He sits down facing the *mandala*. A small settee is brought out and placed near him, and a long black dress – his wife's, presumably – is on the settee. Three nuns take their seats on the carpets to the right of the *mandala* – two of them hold the large ceremonial horns, and the third a smaller horn and a bell. The two nuns who were tending the lamps join the others on the carpet with sutras in their hands. Tseten sits down next to Mila, with his hand drum, a bigger drum on a stand, and a pair of cymbals. At this point, the huge sack full of cowpats I saw on my way in is dumped in front of the *mandala*.

Mila shuts his eyes and begins to pray, and Tseten and the nuns join in. Then the prayers stop abruptly, and the horns and trumpets burst out in the deepest baritone imaginable. The richness of the sound takes me by surprise – it is such a small band, and all women at that. It seems to come from the depths of space, like rolling thunder. Some Tibetans liken this music to the roaring of a tiger. To me it sounds very much as though the nuns are trying to communicate with another world. If the soul *is* listening, I think, it must hear this.

When the playing stops, the man who has been making the *tso* goes to the *mandala* and, much to my dismay, starts laying cowpats on it. Mere minutes have passed since Tseten and Dondan completed it! The cowpats look awful, like warts on the cheeks of a beautiful woman. The man sets the cowpats on fire and soon a huge red flame leaps into the air, lighting up his face. Butter is poured on the flames, and immediately I feel the heat from where I am crouching, some distance away. I wonder aloud at its intensity, and the man who has lit the fire takes a step back and reveals the secret: the cowpats are from the rare red yak, known to produce the fiercest flames, and therefore the most purifying power. 'With the *mandala* at their base, these flames can reach the soul of the dead wherever it is, and purify any sins it might have,' he tells me proudly.

But before the flames can work their magic power, there is something more mundane to be done. The soul of the dead must be fed. In the midst of the nuns' chanting and the crackling cowpats, plates of food are thrown into the flames one by one. Mila says a special prayer with every offering. 'He is pleading for the soul to enjoy its favourite food,' the fire-tender tells me. 'They are giving her the best food because from today on, the soul can no longer taste anything from this world.'

'But can the soul eat?' I ask him, genuinely curious. For some reason, I can imagine the soul hearing the chanting, but not quite gulping down all these dishes, even if they are her favourites.

'You are right,' he says. 'She can hear the chanting, but she can only smell the food being offered in her name, and the incense.' He points to the clay pots hanging on the wall, with juniper twigs burning in them.

I find myself grappling with the gaps between these beliefs and my own. There has to be a soul there somewhere, otherwise what is the point of all this? I smile to myself as I remember a curious story. Hugh Richardson, another well-known British diplomat, stationed in Lhasa in the 1940s, went to offer condolences on the death of a Rinpoche, an incarnate lama. The abbot told him that the 'Rinpoche' would like to receive him in his cell. He wondered if he had made a mistake. He found the Rinpoche sitting in his usual seat. Before he could say anything, the abbot said: 'The Rinpoche welcomes you and asks if you had a good journey, and are you in good health?' It went on like this for some time. 'Everything seemed to be as usual, so that the visitor almost began to doubt his own senses.'[17]

I look around and catch sight of Loga, sitting near the stairs with a bucket of water at his side. What is going on inside that locked head? Does he know that his mother has died and her soul is struggling for rebirth? My experience of the ritual may not be all that different from his. I can follow the process, even enjoy it, but it is like watching a play in a foreign language – fascinating, but mostly beyond my grasp.

In the midst of my distractions, I hear a loud sob. It is Tseten's sister, Samchung, from Shigatse, standing on her own in the corner, her eyes swollen with tears. Soon I see that she is not the only one crying. Dondan has tears welling up in his eyes; Tseten is wiping his face with his shawl. They all gather in front of the burning *mandala* – Tseten, Dondan, Samchung, and Yangdron, all weeping openly now. Mila drops five balls of *tso*, one red *torma*, and a slip of white paper into the fire. Then Tseten walks up to it, and tosses something into the flames. Before I can tell what it is, the fire consumes it. Tseten stands before the fire like a statue, his eyes fixed on the dancing flames. Just then, the sonorous long horns boom out again. The ritual is coming to an end.

I turn back to the fire-tender for an explanation. He tells me that Mila and his family believe that up until now, the four devils who took their mother's life – the devils of air, blood, flesh, and spirit – are still badgering her soul. The devils are represented by the red *torma*. By chanting prayers and feeding them with *tso*, they hope to pacify these devils. In case that does not work, the four wrathful deities guarding the four gates of the *mandala* are also invoked, and asked to bring the devils under control in the flames of the red yak cowpats. At the same time, the soul of the dead, represented by the slip of white paper, is purified of its sins, and readied for its next life.

'But why was everyone crying? Were they no longer worried about distracting the dead?' I ask him.

'Until today, the soul of the dead can remember its previous life. It can smell its favourite food. But from now on, the soul's karma is stronger – what the family does will not matter to it. Also this is the last time that the soul of the dead sees its family.'

The mention of karma makes me ask something that has been troubling me. If reincarnation depends on your karma, what difference does the ritual make? Why all the prayers, all the offerings, the *mandala*, and the fire? A poor family cannot possibly afford them; what happens to their dead?

My questions take him off guard. 'It doesn't matter whether you're rich or poor. What matters is that you do your best. But every little helps,' he says after a pause.

I suppose I should not be posing difficult questions right now. I just ask if he noticed Tseten throwing something on the fire.

He nods. 'Perhaps photographs of his mother. They have to go. All traces of the dead must be removed. Also, after today, the family will not mention her name in the house.'

Tseten's mother has been dead for a month, but, according to the family's belief, it is only now that she is transformed – she is no longer a mother, no longer a wife. Just as the family have tried to make the devils let go of her soul, now they too have to let her go, completely. From this point on, if they wish to mention her, they will refer to her simply as 'the one who has passed away', and never by using her name. It is perhaps for this reason that the Tibetan word for body is *iu*, which means 'the thing that is left behind'.

The ceremony I have been watching marks the final big push to the soul's quest for its next life. The family's faith in reincarnation is absolute, as it is among all the Tibetans we are filming. But my doubts do not want to go away. Does it never even enter their minds that there is possibly no next life? And if there is not, then what?

Perhaps reincarnation can be seen as a state of mind, a mental construct. But I know that is not what the Rikzin family means by it, nor what Tibetans seek when they look for the reincarnate being who will be their new Dalai Lama, their supreme spiritual and political leader. Successors to the important Buddhist lineages are chosen based on the belief of reincarnation, a method that dates back to the fourteenth century. Patterns of water and clouds over a lake, dreams, and of course, wills and instructions of the incumbent incarnation lamas – these are all guides. The present Dalai Lama, the 14th, described his selection in his autobiography: 'The Regent saw the vision of three Tibetan letters – Ah, Ka, and Ma – followed by a picture of a monastery with roofs of jade green and gold and a house with turquoise tiles.'[18] That was during the official search by a party of senior lamas at the holy lake, Lhamo Latso, about ninety miles southeast of Lhasa. The three letters indicated the region and district, where they found a monastery that satisfied the description. In the house with the turquoise tiles they found a two-year-old boy, who was declared to be the reincarnation of the 13th Dalai Lama.

The present Dalai Lama admits that the traditional method of selection has had its drawbacks. In the seventeenth century, for example, a young boy named Tsangyang Gyatso was believed to be the reincarnation of the 5th Dalai Lama, one of the most potent rulers Tibet had ever seen. Born in 1683, Tsangyang Gyatso was chosen with all the usual auspicious signs: his mother drank water from a fountain and it began to pour milk; his grandfather dreamt of two suns in the sky just before his birth, and so on. But Tsangyang refused to accept his destiny. He declined to wear robes and broke all the monastic rules. Wine and women were his passions. He wrote hundreds of poems about them:

If the bar-girl does not falter
The beer will flow on and on;
This maiden is my refuge
And this place is my heaven.

Or again:

I seek counsel from a wise lama
To escape from my predicament,
But my mind remains captivated
By my sweetheart.

If one's thoughts toward the dharma
Were as intense as feelings of love,
One would become a Buddha
In this very body, in this very life.[19]

As tolerant as the Tibetans were, Tsangyang's lifestyle challenged all their beliefs – and some came to doubt that he really was the reincarnation of the 5th Dalai Lama. He was eventually deposed and died when he was twenty-four.

I know better than to discuss my doubts about reincarnation, and especially these thoughts about the Dalai Lama, with the Rikzin family, or even with my Tibetan crew. It is an offence to mention his name or to hang his portrait – punishable by imprisonment. A personal incident made me realise just how risky it could be. Before boarding my plane to come here I had picked up a photo book called *365 Days of Buddhist Offerings*. I turned a few pages and thought the picture and the Buddhist text for each day would be inspiring. I kept it in my room, and looked at the day's page when I woke up, my morning dose of beauty and spirituality. One day a visitor to the house picked the book up. I watched as he leafed through it, interested to see what he made of it. Suddenly he stopped at one page. A look of shock and disbelief ran over his face. He quickly turned past the page as if it was contaminated. After fumbling abstractedly through the rest of the book, he went back to it and stole another glance. Then he put it down and left with the briefest of goodbyes. I wondered what had brought on that look, and went through the entire book myself, for the first time – and found a picture of the Dalai Lama. I learned a lot in that moment. Talking about him might put an end to our film. Even worse, it would put their lives at risk. So I just have to keep these ruminations to myself.

The fire on the *mandala* is now just a pile of smouldering ashes. The villagers and relatives are beginning to gather round it. A young man, impatient, scoops up a handful of ashes, but they are too hot and he drops them quickly. The fire-tender rakes them over to cool them down. Mila is taking off his head-dress and his robe. Everyone is now bending down, and putting the cooled ashes in plastic bags, folded newspapers; one woman puts some in her apron. I ask Mila why they want the ashes. 'They will keep them in their homes or spread them on their fields to bring luck and protection.'

'What will happen now?' I ask Mila.

At the end of a year, he says, the family will ask a high lama to divine what has become of her soul. Enlightenment is one pos-sibility – a rare one; then she will be alongside all the Buddhas and other enlightened beings. Or maybe she will be reborn as a human among their relatives, the next best thing.

I hope the lama will give them the answer they have prayed for.

'We'll be happy either way,' Mila says.

FOUR

The Learning Curve

IT IS 4 A.M., THE STARS in the Tibetan sky hanging entic-
ingly close, when Yangdron wakes her two eldest sons, Jigme,
aged twenty-two, and Gyatso, twenty-one. 'Time to get up,' she
tells them. 'You don't want to be late.' Jigme sits up immediately,
but Gyatso pulls the blanket over his head. When he finally
walks into the dimly lit kitchen a little while later, the rest of the
family is having their *tsampa* and drinking butter tea. Yangdron
hands him a wooden bowl. 'Who wants to eat now?' he snaps.
'I want to sleep!'

Downstairs Dondan starts the tractor, startling the cock,
which begins a raucous crowing as though it too hated to be
woken. Today, 13th October, at 5 a.m. – the hour that Tseten
determined is most auspicious for their departure – the boys
will be leaving for university. Dondan will drive them to the
main road, where they will catch a bus to Shigatse, and from
there travel on to Lhasa. Then Gyatso will take another bus to
his college in southern Tibet, and Jigme will board a train on
the newly opened railway to his university in Xian, home of the
Terracotta Army, in Central China.

Yangdron puts *khatas* round her two sons' necks. Mila places one hand on Jigme's shoulder, counting his rosary with the other. The boys have each packed a couple of small canvas bags, and Loga tries to pick these up, but Gyatso snatches them back from him. Not everyone will be travelling to the station: Tseten was concerned that having too many people on the tractor would invite the jealousy of the local deities. This also explains the early hour: too much gossiping from the neighbours and villagers could irritate the family's protective deities, and so they are leaving well before the rest of the village is awake.

Though I am getting used to the Tibetan way of thinking, I still find myself amazed: two of their sons are going to university and this is something to hide? An event like this is a rare one for the village – if this is not a cause for celebration, what is? When I was accepted by Beijing University, my parents told the whole world. My grandmother was particularly proud. I can still remember her saying to anyone who would listen, 'My granddaughter is going to university – the first in our family to do it. A phoenix has risen from a hen's nest!'

I ask Jigme what he thinks about the early departure. He shrugs – aside from feeling sleep deprived, he does not see anything wrong with it. He trusts his uncle's judgment; after all, Tseten accurately predicted his results in the National Exams.

The National Exams take place in June every year. They determine who will go on to university. They are notoriously difficult and fiercely competitive. Only 4 per cent of secondary school leavers in the whole of China will pass; the number in Tibet is even smaller. They are make or break for Jigme and Gyatso, who are in the same school year, despite the difference in their ages. Success will open up the world for them; failure means they will stay in the village. It is the same for so many young Chinese. Twenty-five years on, I can still remember my anxiety on exam day. When I looked at the sea of heads in the exam hall, I felt not so much intimidated as lost. What chance did I have? Who would be winners and who would be losers? The odds seemed to be stacked heavily against me.

Back in early June, a few days before taking the exam, Jigme had called home from a payphone near his school to ask Tseten to divine his results. He waited an hour for a response, pacing up and down. He looked up at the banners hanging across the street leading away from the school: 'Best Wishes to All Students Taking the Exam!', 'Be an Honest Winner!', 'Report Cheats!'. When the phone rang, he dashed for it.

It was his mother calling him back with Tseten's forecast. Yes, she told him, both he and Gyatso would succeed in the test – they would both be able to go to college, though perhaps not to their top choices. 'Put your mind at ease and concentrate on your studies,' Yangdron said. 'Don't worry. You will pass.'

'Did you believe it?' I asked Jigme, when he told me this story.

'Why not? Uncle has done it many times for others. More than seventy students and their parents have asked him this year. He has got a reputation now.'

Here, Jigme paused, not sure he wanted to tell me anything more. 'I'm not the only one in my class who did this,' he said. 'Most of my classmates had it done too. We also went to the top of the highest mountain outside Gyantse and hung up prayer flags, so the wind could carry our prayers for the Buddha's blessing.'

I had seen something similar one day at the Palkhor Monastery. There I'd watched a smartly dressed, middle-aged woman take half a dozen pens out of a posh handbag and hand them to a monk on duty. I'd thought at first that she was making an extremely unusual offering, but then I watched as the monk climbed the stairs to a thirteen-foot statue of the Sakyamuni Buddha and rubbed each pen against the hand of the Enlightened Being. After that, he touched the pens against the massive volumes of Ganjur (the Tibetan Buddhist canon) stacked along the walls. The woman explained, 'If the Buddha can give my son a little blessing, he will put down the right answers with these pens.' Her faith reminded me of my grandmother, who had prayed fervently to her favourite Bodhisattva, the Goddess of Compassion, in the days leading up to my exams. At the time, I was ungracious and scornful: 'I don't need your goddess's blessing,' I told her. It didn't occur to me that I might have benefitted from the kind of reassurance that Tseten gave to Jigme.

Despite Tseten's divinations, the three weeks spent waiting for the exam results had been acutely anxious. The tension was palpable. Jigme spent most of his time helping Dondan and Yangdron with work around the house, feeding the cows, making cowpats for fuel, or carrying bricks for neighbours who were building houses. He worked until dark and went straight to bed. Very occasionally, when Jigme and I crossed paths, he would ask a question or two: 'What's Xian like? Do you think I will be able to fit in with the Chinese students if I go there?' But he never seemed to expect an answer; before I could respond, he was off.

Meanwhile, Gyatso slept a lot. Only Loga could not understand why the family was leaving Gyatso alone – why he was allowed not to work while everyone else slaved away. Loga tried every morning to wake him, pulling at his blanket, gently whispering his name, then shouting at him. Invariably, Gyatso howled back, 'Get lost, you stupid idiot!' Often when Gyatso saw us, he shot us looks like daggers of hate, muttering curses loud enough for us to hear: 'What a shameless lot! Why do they keep bothering us? Don't they see they aren't welcome?' And perhaps it was more than just a teenage grudge. Perhaps by following his family, we were drawing unwanted attention to them, even bringing maledictions. Or perhaps Gyatso simply felt exposed – it might be embarrassing for him to have friends and classmates watch our series on television.

Yangdron was very worried. She tried to be positive, but she told me this was the most anxious time of her life.

'More anxious than your wedding day?' I asked.

'Yes, at least then I knew my family would find me a good match. And I knew the Rikzin family would treat me well. But with Jigme and Gyatso, if they can go to university they will have jobs and salaries. And that will be for life. If not, they will be stuck here with us.'

'If they stay here, will they marry like their father and uncles, and share a wife?'

'I think so. Everyone does that here.'

'What if they do go to university?'

'People with official jobs take only one spouse. They aren't allowed to share. So that's what Jigme and Gyatso would do.'

'Would they choose their own wives?'

'I think Tseten has to decide who is suitable.'

At last, at the end of June, the results arrived. Gyatso scored 203 out of a total of 750 for seven subjects, and Jigme scored 12 points higher, 215. This year, Tibetan students needed to score above 200 in order to pass. It is uncanny how accurate Tseten's prediction turned out to be – even Jigme and Gyatso are surprised. They had passed the most important exam of their life by a hair's-breadth. It could so easily have gone the other way. How did Tseten do it? I could not help asking him.

'It is not just me. I have the help of my spiritual master who guides me,' he said humbly and evasively.

'Where is this master?'

'He has passed away. But he guides me from above.'

There was hardly time to celebrate before the boys had to start worrying about choosing a college, and their parents about money. Jigme's first choice was the Tibetan Medical College in Lhasa, so he could carry on the shaman tradition. 'My family has been doing it for six generations. One of us has to do it. Gyatso hates the idea, but I have loved it since I was a child. At least I'll be useful to people. At medical college you learn about astronomy and about making calendars – the science of it. You have to know all that for fortune-telling and divination.'

It was the first time that Jigme had spoken seriously to me since we started filming. He told me that he doubted he would get in. 'Medical colleges require top grades. And I've just barely passed. There is no chance for me. Still I will put it down as my first choice,' he said firmly. 'But it is only a dream.' After the dream came three very practical choices: agriculture, veterinary studies, and aircraft technology. This last one was almost an afterthought.

'Medicine is a load of crap,' Gyatso told me, nonchalantly. 'Find me an honest doctor. They are all cheats. You have a better chance of survival if you don't go to hospital. Doctors are greedy – they'll squeeze the last penny out of you. But they rarely know what they're doing; they cut you open and sew you up and solve nothing. If you're unlucky, they'll leave a knife inside your stomach by mistake. You read about this sort of thing in the papers every day.'

'But what about Tseten?' I asked Gyatso, tentatively. 'Couldn't someone say the same thing about his treatments?'

'If he does no good, at least he also does no harm. He never sets out to cheat people.' Gyatso spoke curtly, offended by the comparison. 'You see the villagers coming to our house. Uncle tries to help them. Does he charge them? Most just bring a thermos of butter tea, or even nothing at all. Does Uncle throw them out or refuse them treatment? Never! More importantly, he comforts people and puts their minds at peace. Sometimes that is more important than medicine.'

Perhaps Gyatso should do law. He could make a passionate and persuasive litigator. He laughed off my suggestion. 'You hardly know me. How can you talk about what suits me?' He had already made up his mind to study agriculture, because he loved to work on the land. He applied, as his first and only choice, to Lingzhi Agriculture and Animal Husbandry Polytechnic in southern Tibet. 'Anyway, my score does not give me too much choice,' he conceded.

Dondan, Tseten and Yangdron did not care which college their sons chose, as long as it would land them a job with the government. I do not blame them. Government employees in Tibet enjoy the highest pay in the whole of China, while Tibetan farmers have one of the lowest incomes in all of China, and little if anything seems to be happening that will make them richer. A recent graduate working for the local government earns approximately 3,000 *yuan* a month, more than Dondan makes in a year. In 2006, the average annual income per person in Gyantse, according to the county government figures – doubtful as they are – was only 2,361 *yuan*.

And it is not just the pay. The work is light, sitting in offices, reading papers, and the occasional inspection trip, normally accompanied by a lot of eating and drinking. Above all there is a guaranteed salary, medical care, and a pension for life. It is a world away from the farmer breaking his back in the fields, anxious about the weather, and worried about falling sick. No wonder Dondan, Tseten and Yangdron wanted their sons to 'sharpen their heads', as our expression goes, to pierce their way into the burgeoning bureaucracy.

But finding the money to support the boys through three years of college looked beyond them. The combined annual fees and living expenses for the two boys would be roughly £1,000, or 15,000 *yuan*. Shortly after the boys learned their exam scores, Tseten visited the Karmad *xiang* government office to ask for help. He wanted a note detailing the family's financial difficulties, which he would use to support an application for a loan from a commercial bank. The official listened briefly to Tseten's request and then cut him short. Yes, he said, he would write and stamp the note. But it was unlikely that Tseten would get a loan. Had he not heard that government policy had changed?

It had been a tumultuous year for Tibetan educational policy. Just before Jigme and Gyatso took their exams, the Tibetan government announced that it would no longer take responsibility for employing Tibetans who graduate from universities each year. (This same policy change was made more than a decade before in the rest of China.) The announcement did not go over very well. Some students protested in Lhasa, and their protests worked. There were numerous demonstrations against the Chinese government in the late 1980s and the 1990s. Most were led by monks, but many students participated as well. As the Tibetans and their leaders are reminded almost daily, stability is the number one priority, and has to be ensured at any cost. So it still fell to the government to solve the problem of employing its graduates: in 2006 it absorbed almost 1,000 into its already swollen ranks.

But job allocation by the government has to stop sooner or later; Tibetan students will have to fend for themselves, as they now do in the rest of China. Without the certainty of employment, banks in Tibet have cut back on their loans to students. As usual, the poor and the powerless are affected most. When Tseten returned home that day with the stamped note, and the news that it was as good as useless, Yangdron reacted badly. 'What if the boys do not get jobs after they graduate?' she wanted to know. Was it really worth spending 15,000 *yuan* every year, and for three years? Tseten, Dondan and Mila were firm: 'Give the boys a chance. We will sell our grain. We can borrow from relatives. We will find a way.'

But in early September, Jigme received a blow. As he feared, he did not get into the Tibetan Medical College in Lhasa. He was offered a place by the Aircraft Technology Polytechnic in Xian to study airplane ventilation – the last choice on his application. Gyatso was successful in his choice: he would be majoring in agriculture and animal husbandry. He was not sure what he would do after college – the best would be working for the agricultural department of the Gyantse county government. Jigme was downcast for quite a few days, almost totally silent. We tried to cheer him up by saying that at least he would find work after graduation; the government was investing in a new airport in Tibet, and would need young people with his skills.

'But my family does not know anyone important,' he responded. 'In Tibet, you need connections for everything, particularly when you are trying to find a government job. Our parents are so worried about the money. They will probably have to borrow a lot. If I'd got into medical school, I'd always be able to practise, whether I got a job or not. Aircraft technology is useless if you don't have a job.' He said this so quietly that I had to ask him to repeat himself.

'Airplanes can't be maintained by people with connections,' I said, trying to reassure him, and myself. 'You're going to get a qualification few Tibetans have. You'll have really good prospects.'

Jigme smiled weakly, but I did not think he was convinced. His dream really was dashed, and Tseten's hope for a shaman to succeed him now rested on Kunga, the youngest boy in the family. Kunga is fourteen years old and, for now, he studies in the Junior Secondary School in Gyantse, a brand new school with impressive facilities built with aid money from Shanghai. He hangs around with us a lot at weekends when he is back from school, quietly observing what we are doing, always with a smile on his face. Whenever we need any help, he is there. Compared with Jigme's silence and Gyatso's hostility, his demeanour is angelic.

Kunga had no problem getting admitted to the junior

secondary school, but he has struggled since he's been there. '*Hen nan*,' Kunga said slowly in Chinese ('It's very hard'), when I asked him how he was doing. I thought he was finding it difficult to adjust to being a boarder among all the other children, after living with his parents in the village. Then I realised it was something more fundamental: Kunga was having trouble understanding what his teachers were saying in class, because everything was taught in Chinese. In primary school, he had studied in Tibetan; Chinese is a second language. Tibetan students are required to learn at least 2,500 Chinese characters, but very few manage to do so. In 1989, a survey conducted in primary schools in Lhasa – schools with some of the best teachers and facilities in Tibet – showed that, on average, students had mastered only 800 characters, less than a third of the requirement.[20] I asked Kunga how many Chinese characters he knew. He thought for a long time, and said, 'Not enough.'

During my time in the village, I have heard very few people speaking Chinese. The village doctor, a People's Liberation Army veteran, two school teachers, the vet, and a couple of young farmers who spend most of their time up in the north as migrant workers – that's about it. Chinese is, for all intents and purposes, a foreign language, even though the government insists that all Party documents and government instructions are issued in Chinese. In urban areas of Tibet, Chinese is used more frequently, but more than 90 per cent of Tibetans live in villages and speak Tibetan. Coming from such an environment, students like Kunga are suddenly expected to absorb subjects in Chinese. It's close to impossible, like trying to look at a green field through red spectacles.

Kunga told me that he found his maths lessons in Chinese nearly incomprehensible. The first time the teacher wrote one plus one on the blackboard in Chinese instead of the usual way most of the students in his class were lost; more complicated calculations had them completely mystified. It was hardly surprising that the average score on their first maths test was under 20 per cent. 'I even took the exam questions from their exercise book,' a maths teacher told me, with a sigh. 'But they still didn't understand. Many of them got a zero.'

But it is clear that the teachers have a lot to learn too. An English teacher from Kunga's school sent me a note she had written about what could be done to improve her students' spoken English. This is exactly what it said: 'When I went to teaching practice, student didn't use what they studied word, and they didn't think their using or their differences. Sometimes, teacher asked something to students, they knew their meaning, they didn't say.' What on earth was she teaching them?

The teachers are the first to admit they may be lacking: for many of them, teaching was a last choice of profession. But they insist that, if they taught in Tibetan rather than in Chinese, the students would learn far more. Over the last twenty years, there have been three separate pilot programmes conducted in Tibet, designed to compare the results of teaching in Tibetan versus teaching in Chinese. Gyantse No. 1 High School took part. The students taught in Tibetan scored an average of 80 per cent on their year-end exams, compared with 39 per cent for those taught in Chinese. And, most tellingly, the students taught in Tibetan even scored slightly higher on their Chinese language exams. A top Party official in Lhasa confessed that there was 'conclusive evidence that nothing could substitute for the effect of using the Tibetan language to raise educational quality... Therefore it is apparent that we should use the Tibetan language for communication more than ever.' [21]

But the pilot programmes were never expanded. The government claimed this was because the National Entrance Exams were in Chinese, and, by their reasoning, studying in Tibetan would only make it harder for students to integrate into the mainstream, both at university and in the job market. The government also cited the prohibitive cost of printing new text-books and training new teachers. But perhaps, like most things in Tibet, the real reason was political. As the Party chief in Tibet bluntly told a gathering of Tibetan teachers:

> The success of our education does not lie in the number of diplomas issued to graduates from universities, colleges, polytechnic schools, and secondary schools. It lies, in the final analysis, in whether our graduating students are opposed to or turn their hearts to the Dalai clique and in whether they are loyal to or do not care about our great motherland and the great socialist cause. This is the most salient and the most important criterion for assessing right and wrong.[22]

So it is part of Kunga's patriotic duty to learn his lessons in Chinese, even though he may not understand what is being taught. Unsurprisingly, many Tibetan students find this unre-warding and simply drop out. Rarely do their parents mind. They see no point in their children spending so much time in school learning so little, and learning nothing practical at all. Worse, because the secondary schools are located in town, the children often pick up bad habits – drinking, smoking, fighting, spending all their spare time on the internet, and acquiring a disdain for village life. 'Hot at the beginning, lukewarm in the middle, and cold near the end,' is how a teacher at Kunga's school described his students' attitudes to their education.

Nine years free education for all children is the Chinese gov-ernment's goal, but the attendance at junior secondary schools in Tibet is less than 20 per cent. Gyantse has done better than the average, but keeping students in school is a constant challenge. One day, while I was waiting outside Kunga's school to pick him up, I saw a small crowd of men in suits standing at the gate, having a heated discussion. They didn't look like parents. I walked up to them and struck up a conversation with a man who told me he was a Party official in charge of education, from a remote district in Gyantse. He had just been rounding up drop-outs from the twelve villages in his area because there was a government inspection.

'Was it hard to find them?' I asked.

'Nearly impossible,' he said. 'Most are out working. I have to plead with the parents, "Please, it's just for this week. After the inspection, I don't care where you hide them." I have to threaten them with fines.'

He told me that one of the girls he rounded up was five months' pregnant. When her boyfriend objected that she could not go to school like that, the man said, 'You want to come too? That's fine; you'll help to make up the numbers.'

'What happens if you don't reach your target?' I asked.

'I didn't last year. I was due for a promotion, and I didn't get it. I didn't get a bonus either.'

The man's story reminded me of an anecdote I had read, about the British experience of setting up a school in Gyantse. At the beginning of the twentieth century, the famous Colonel Francis Younghusband entered Tibet, forced his army unit into Gyantse, killed 3,000 Tibetans, blasted the Gyantse fort, and pushed on to Lhasa – all in the name of protecting the British Empire in India. When the dust of the battles had settled and the ink on the Treaty of Lhasa was dry, the British left an agency in Gyantse, ostensibly for trade but really to collect intelligence. This agency established a school for the children of local Tibetan aristocrats, and invited a British schoolmaster named Ludlow to run it. It opened in December 1923, with thirteen children.

Ludlow kept a diary about the experience. One day, when he proposed expelling two students aged fourteen and fifteen who were found to be suffering from venereal diseases, the Tibetan authorities intervened. They told him that if he expelled those students, other boys would voluntarily contract the diseases in order to escape having to attend school.[23] Until his school was closed in 1926, Ludlow managed to keep attendance up by introducing the boys to football.

But there is one kind of secondary school that many Tibetan children dream of attending: the Tibetan Inland Schools in Central China. These schools were established in 1985, during a more liberal period when China's economic reforms were in full swing, when people were rehabilitated after the Cultural Revolution and allowed to criticise its mistakes openly, and when there was even talk of political reform. Hu Yaobang, the Party Secretary, went to Tibet in 1980 and apologised in person for the failings of the previous thirty years. He promised more autonomy, more economic assistance, and less direct Chinese rule in Tibet. He wanted to repatriate the Chinese officials who were there, and to put Tibetans in charge. A new generation of young Tibetans needed to be trained – so new schools were built in Beijing, Tianjin, and Chengdu expressly for this purpose; classes for Tibetan students were also added to the best Chinese schools in two dozen cities.

Competition to enter these schools is fierce, not least because all expenses are taken care of by the government. Each year, there are only 1,830 places in the junior secondary schools, and 1,600 places in the senior secondary schools. Kunga had wanted to go, but his marks were not high enough. The family hopes that his sister still has a chance. Tseyang is seventeen and in her third year at Shigatse Experimental Secondary School. Next year she can apply to finish her senior school education at one of the Tibetan Inland Schools.

Of the four Rikzin children, I find Tseyang the most striking. She has a beauty that grows on you; she is petite and compact, with a gentle nature, and unlike her brothers, she is articulate and sure of herself. Usually when I ask the boys a question, I get at most a few syllables in reply; Tseyang answers with four examples and three subsidiary considerations. She is keen to get a good job and help support the family, and she works very hard. While in school, she stays with an aunt in Shigatse, and so I rarely see her. 'It is just study, study, study with her,' Yangdron tells me. 'I don't know where she gets it from. She is turning into a bookworm. I hope she succeeds because she won't know anything about running a home, or doing farmwork.'

I decide to accompany Tseten the next time he visits her, so I can ask her about her plans. To my surprise, she tells me that she might not apply to study in the Tibetan Inland Schools. She knows that attending one of those schools will give her a better chance of going to university; it will also save her family the school fees. But she thinks it would be best for her to stay in Shigatse. Does she think she might not get in? I wonder.

'No,' she says. 'If I go away now, I won't be using Tibetan much – I'll only have studied it up to junior secondary school level. That's not good enough.'

'But what about your Chinese? Won't that be improved?' I am thinking of Kunga and the trouble he is having.

'There are so many Chinese in Shigatse. They run most of the shops, and they don't speak Tibetan. It's not like being in the village. Here, if I want to practise my Chinese, I can go to the shops. I just have to make the effort.'

I am amazed at how mature she is for her age. And she's right that this is one of the biggest dilemmas facing students who choose to attend the Tibetan Inland Schools. If Tseyang were to choose one of those schools, apart from three or four Tibetan lessons a week, she will be studying in Chinese for the next seven years, including four years in university. This is the experience of Roten, one of our Tibetan researchers and assistant cameraman. He went to the Tibetan Secondary School in Beijing when he was twelve. For his entire secondary school education, he had only one Tibetan lesson a week, and because there were no tests, he often skipped them to play football or watch television. He almost forgot his Tibetan and could not even write home in it.

And language is not all they forget. The elite young Tibetans in these special schools spend their most formative years away from home – they are only allowed to visit their families once – and their grasp of their own culture stops at primary school level. What did I understand about Chinese culture when I was eleven? As I was, they are immersed in an atheist Communist ideology, the very antithesis of Buddhism, the foundation of Tibetan society. They get an effective, modern, very Chinese education, which gives them a head start over their brothers and sisters who stay in Tibet. But they lose touch with the values, outlook, etiquette, attitudes to marriage and the family – everything their parents and grandparents cherish. And they are going to run Tibet one day.

At the sparkling new Lhasa railway station, Tseten, his sister Samchung and Gyatso are putting Jigme on the train. Tseten has lost his usual calm and is fussing like a mother hen. 'Don't forget to eat well. Remember your books and don't leave anything on the train.' He turns to the other students sitting next to Jigme and says, 'You've all got to look after each other.' I can understand Tseten's concern: Jigme is leaving home for the first time and will be on his own for the next three years. But Jigme just seems embarrassed. He sits looking down at his knees, impatient for his aunt and uncle to go. Tseten gives him a last piece of advice: 'Take it easy. Don't put too much pressure on yourself.' Then he gets out of the train, continuing to gesticulate to Jigme through the sealed window.

Jigme is going to face new challenges from a world that Tseten knows little about; Gyatso too, to a lesser extent. Will he be able to exercise any influence? After all, their lives will be so different from his. Tseten can hardly imagine how travelling to Xian and studying aircraft technology for three years might change a boy. Will the boys still ask Tseten to divine things for them? Will they marry according to his reading of the signs? Will they share a wife? Will one or both of them fall for a Chinese girl? Will they come back to the village at all and work on the land? Will they be lost to him? Tseten wants what is best for them, but I know that he can't help but fear the consequences.

I can see Jigme through the window, trying to be the cool teenager. I suspect he is anything but. In the past few days he has been increasingly anxious. He showed me the college's acceptance letter with all the information for freshmen, including how he would be met off the train. He still asked me to call the college and make sure someone would be there. He worried whether he would understand the dialect in Xian. Would he be able to keep up with the other students in his class, many of whom had scored close to 500 on their National Exams, more than twice his mark? Would they look down on him, think him a barbarian? 'Look, I'm taking this,' he told me, holding up a book of colour photos of Tibet. 'I would like to show them the beautiful land I come from.' I wanted to tell him that the King of Tibet in the eighth century, Chisongdezan, sent his troops and looted Xian for a whole month – and Xian was then the metropolis of the world, with almost a million residents. He did not have to apologise for being Tibetan. But I thought it would be best for him to find it out himself.

The whistle blows, the guard shouts for people to stand back, and the train pulls out. Tseten runs alongside it as far as he can go, still waving to Jigme. For some time after the train has left, he remains with his back to us at the end of the empty platform, seemingly lost in concentration.

When I view the rushes of this scene later, I find myself touched by the image of Tseten standing on the vast empty station, alone, watching the train disappearing, carrying Jigme away. But then I hear the words, '*Om mane padme hum, Om mane padme hum ...*', louder and louder. It is Tseten's voice, recorded by the microphone on his robe – the most private, and the most instinctive reaction of this profoundly religious man. He is praying for Jigme's future.

FIVE

Cold Feeling

MY FIRST REAL HINT of the Tibetan winter comes when I notice it getting harder to breathe. We are filming Tseten on a house call in early November. I have trouble keeping up with him, which has never been a problem before. He slows down and waits for me. 'Remember, do quick things slowly,' he says enigmatically.

'Do you think I'm catching something?' I ask.

'It's just the season changing.'

Then the wind suddenly arrives from nowhere, whipping up a fierce storm. Every afternoon, it picks up the dust from the fallow fields and barren mountains and pours it all over us, and all over the houses. The bare trees are bent to the point of breaking; the white fort above the town recedes into a grey mass; the empty streets seem haunted. The swirling dust sticks to the lenses, and tends to give everything we shoot a grey pallor. Sometimes, the Tibetans say, a dog eats the sun, and the day is as dark as night. That is when I remember the warnings from my Chinese friends who heard I was to spend a year in Tibet.

'It's okay for a couple of weeks, but for a year? You must be mad. The heart has to work twice as hard at that level, it can collapse. Even if you don't die immediately, it will affect you later.'

'Your IQ will go down.'

'I think you should see a psychiatrist. You are already suffering from oxygen deprivation.'

My Chinese producer of long standing refused to join me in Tibet. 'I always help you in any way I can but this time you are on your own,' he said emphatically. 'Two cameramen from my studio went to Tibet for only a month, and a few years later they dropped dead. I want to live a long life, even if you don't.'

But Tseten says I must have been a Tibetan in my previous life. He lists my accomplishments: I have not suffered any altitude sickness; I have picked up some of the language fairly easily; I don't mind eating raw meat, which few Chinese can bear; and I'm familiar with Buddhism. While most of this may be true, at least in part, I'm struggling much more than Tseten realises. Every word, every action, every ritual I witness is a small puzzle, and seldom means what I think it does. And with the winter coming, I'm struggling physically too. The air is thin at 13,000 feet; now that all the leaves, crops, and grass are gone, there is even less oxygen. Every evening, after the news on the Tibetan channel, the weather girl gives out the level of oxygen in the air that day. From November, it begins to drop to less than 50 per cent.

What really worries me, though, is the sudden drop in our characters' activities. We had a big bang with the start of our filming in the autumn. The Palkhor Monastery was a major focus of our film. Our three monks there, Tsultrim, Tsephun and Dondrup, were thrown into hectic preparations in September for a visit by the 11ᵗʰ Panchen Lama, the most important spiritual leader after the Dalai Lama. The continuing disquiet over his appointment, in 1995, by the Chinese government made the grand visit more nerve-racking. But it filled the film with tension, a dream for a director.

Elsewhere in town, forty-four-year-old hotel manager Jianzang had a record week during the Panchen Lama's visit as Tibetans crowded into Gyantse for the occasion. Rincheu, our builder, took on his first government contract – a canal – as well as building half the Tibetan houses in Gyantse; money was pouring in like water. Life was not so easy for Lhakpa, the rickshaw driver. It was quite painful to watch him struggling up the hill every day for only 15 pence a time.

The harvest in the village was anxious and all-consuming, not only for the Rikzin family, but even for our village doctor, Lhamo, and Pasang Butri, the local head of the Women's Association. They had to join in with their own families, rushing to get in the barley before the weather broke. Lhamo was not seeing patients; Butri gave up her Party work, except for lecturing the villagers not to get too drunk, to little avail.

With the onset of winter, Gyantse seems to have gone into hibernation, and so have our characters. Rincheu, the builder, has seen his brisk business slow down. He now spends a lot of his time schmoozing with officials in order to get more government contracts, but he does not want us to follow him on his 'mission'. As he suavely puts it: 'This is all behind closed doors, how can we do a deal with a camera crew there?' Jianzang is also having a lean time. He has an empty hotel and has sent his staff home. He decides to change all the beds in his hotel from Western style to Tibetan painted ones. There is only so much you can film of beds being painted.

Lhakpa is tired of spending hours waiting for a customer and then battling the wind when he gets one. He hits the bottle and talks about leaving home and finding work in northern Tibet, somewhere on a construction site. He was sent there three years ago by the Gyantse County government, to take part in the construction of the new railway line. It was hard work, eight hours a day, at 16,000 feet. But it was good money by his standards, 80 *yuan*, over £5 pounds a day.

Even the monks have time on their hands: Tsultrim works on the end-of-year accounts for weeks on end; Tsephun drops in frequently with a group of young monks to use our internet connection and ask us about the latest electronic gadgets they are thinking of buying.

In the village, after the hectic harvest, comes the real relaxation, drinking *chang*, sitting in the sunshine, early nights – hardly the dramatic stuff of the autumn. Butri tries to take advantage of this leisurely time and plans a series of meetings to give the villagers the latest Party instructions: law and order, women's issues, health policies. But one meeting will be quite enough for the film. Dr Lhamo seems the only one who is really busy: in the cold weather, the old and the young get sick, but the filming is limited there too; her treatment is nearly always the same, whatever the complaint, put them on an intravenous drip. I know a wedding is coming at which Tseten will preside, and I look forward to it. But that is about it.

I wonder if our research is not thorough enough, but I do not think it is a problem now. Penpa and Roten, our two researchers, are wonderful with all the characters. The only problem is that things can be too familiar for them and seen as not worth filming. They come back from a long chat with the characters and I ask them what leads they have come upon. 'Oh, nothing new, just the same old things.' I have to sit them down and go through the conversations bit by bit, and then find a story. Still we miss an interesting story now and then. A few weeks back, in a desperate attempt to find work, Lhakpa, the rickshaw driver, went to the No. 1 High School, his old school, asking if he and his two brothers could clear its cess pool. Roten mentioned it in passing when it was all over. I asked him why he did not tell me in the first place. 'I don't think it is interesting, do you, Teacher Sun?', he replied.

For once I felt annoyed with Roten. A young man clearing out the shit from the school he had to give up after his father died? With some of his former classmates now teaching there? What would be going through Lhakpa's mind? Only desperation would have made him think of doing such a job. From then on, we started having daily meetings; everyone talked about what they had discovered about our characters and it was all written down.

I begin to think that if nothing too much is going on, I can leave everything else to the crew, while I go back to Beijing with the rushes we have shot so far. Maybe I am having the winter blues. But after a particularly virulent dust storm which rages for twenty-four hours, I wake up to our first snowfall. I rush out of the house like a child, shouting to everyone to come out and see. It looks so pure and brilliant, with the blue sky returned to us completely cleansed. I am in heaven – we have had the golden autumn and now we will have snow to usher in the new winter season.

We rush to the hills to film Gyantse from above, and then the monastery. Then we start at breakneck speed towards the village. As we get close, my spirits drop. There is almost no trace of snow: just the slightly damp road and the odd patch of white left in the fields. Only the mountains stand out with their majestic winter glitter.

When we reach the village, we find the Rikzins' courtyard almost dry. Yangdron sees our disappointment and tells us that when she was small, the winters used to be much colder. Snow fell for days on end; the wind was so strong birds would take off and be swept backwards. 'The crows turned white with the dust,' she says. She offers us some butter tea to comfort us. Tseten is busy with patients suffering from the cold. But he comes out of his room to ask if we will wait so he can get a lift into town.

While we are waiting in the kitchen, I think about what Yangdron just said. Certainly the winters were tougher a hundred years ago. I had been re-reading books about the Younghusband expedition to Tibet in the winter of 1903-04. Lord Curzon, who was then Viceroy in India, wanted to extend British influence in Tibet, but had had trouble persuading the British government. When they finally gave the order, he sent Younghusband off before they could retract it. 'The idea of crossing into Tibet in midwinter of course seemed horrible at first and had never been dreamed of till I put it before govt.,' Younghusband wrote to his father. 'But I knew that cold...does not really knock over so many men as heavy rains and malaria will.'[24]

His optimism was short lived. Soon his men began to be worn down by altitude sickness, and by the cold. Edmund Chandler, the *Daily Mail* correspondent with the expedition, recorded: 'Twenty men of the 12th Mule Corps were frost-bitten, and thirty men of the 23rd Pioneers were so incapacitated that they had to be carried in on mules. On the same day there were seventy cases of snow-blindness among the 8th Gurkhas.'[25] One officer wrote, 'The cold was so great (57 degrees of frost) that the bolts of the rifles froze, and the Maxims would not work, in spite of the oil having been carefully wiped off both previously...Everything was in favour of the Tibetans if they attacked.'[26]

The British could have suffered worse casualties. At least the snow was light that year; the local Tibetans put that down to the flashing of the expedition's heliographs. They begged the British to stop using them, so that more snow could fall, to provide water for the springs and the next year's crop.[27]

Back in Gyantse, we drop off Tseten; he is looking for materials for a stupa the family is going to build to commemorate their mother. He is going to stay with us for the evening. I call our cook, Mr Li, to ask him to prepare special food for

Tseten – no garlic, no onions, which Buddhists are supposed to avoid. 'Don't you believe him,' Cook Li tells me. 'Even the monks eat onions and garlic in my restaurant. I'm sure your shaman will be no different.'

By this time, I have grown used to the near-daily groaning from Cook Li – mainly about the laziness, drunkenness and hostility of the Tibetans. Cook Li came to Tibet from a village in east Sichuan as a young man with nothing in his pockets. He took menial jobs, and slowly worked his way up, saving every penny to open his hotpot restaurant. His success story is the same for many of the Sichuanese in Tibet, and he is proud of himself. We were lucky to find him: he treats us to delicious food, and spices it up with his impressions of the local people, Chinese as well as Tibetan. The information he culls from the conversations round his tables is not necessarily to be trusted, but he hears a kind of talk that I never would, talk that is all the more frank when his customers are drunk, as they frequently are.

At 5.30, Cook Li arrives on his bike, with his preparations in neat plastic bags in the basket. He always wears a suit and tie, something the crew and I never quite get used to – a man in a suit in a smoky kitchen with sparks and oil flying in all directions. When guests come for dinner, they always ask if he is the big boss inspecting our work. He looks the part: he is short but upright with a military haircut, big intense eyes and precise movements.

I go to the kitchen to see what treats he has prepared for us: chicken with peanuts, cured beef, twice-cooked pork belly, steamed pork with preserved vegetables, eggs with cucumber and wood-ear mushrooms, and a whole chicken in broth – a rich and balanced selection from the best of his repertoire. I thank him for his thoughtfulness.

'Do you think you can become friends with the people in

your film, even after all the kindness, help and gifts you have given them?' Li asks, as he dropped chilli in the hot wok.

'Yes, they are already our friends,' I say.

'They are characters in your film, but I don't think they will regard you as their friends. The Tibetans hate the Chinese. If you heard what they say about us it would make you cringe. They think I don't understand Tibetan when they talk among themselves in my restaurant, but I have learned enough over the years.'

'So why do you stay?' I ask him. Doesn't the harsh environment, the isolation, and the locals' hostility bother him?

'As long as I can feed my family and make money, does it matter if they don't like us?' he replies. Then he adds: 'The important thing is, they need us.'

With that declaration, he is done. He has prepared six dishes in half an hour, and he is off on his bike, back to his hotpot restaurant, where his assistant is cooking for any early customers for the evening.

We serve dinner in the sitting room, which is also the room for all the women on the team. Tseten sits at the head of the table. He likes every single one of the dishes, particularly the clear chicken broth for the cold winter evening. I ask him to help himself and I do a bit of helping too, piling things in his bowl. Finally he begs me to stop, saying, 'Please don't give me any more. Otherwise Dondan will make me pay excess baggage for the ride home.'

Suddenly the electricity goes off, as has been happening increasingly often with winter here. I suppose people are using more electricity and the system is overloaded.

'Do you want me to perform an energising ritual for the Electricity Board?' Tseten jokes.

'Why don't you skip the Electricity Board and do it just for us? That would save a lot of trouble,' I say.

'It would be a waste. You should think of all the people who are sitting in the dark.'

But we have to do something quickly. The driver and the cameraman decide to start our small generator. Instantly the bulbs come back on.

'See how powerful compassion is,' Tsedan says, laughing.

With the power back on, Penpa and the driver decide to play chess, with a case of beer on the table as a 'disincentive' – whoever makes a wrong move has to drink one glass, and three if he loses a game. Amidst the noisy tapping of the chess pieces, and the squabbling between the tipsy players, Tseten sits there quietly, doing a drawing. I am amazed that he can concentrate in the midst of all the noise. When I look over his shoulder, I see a woman kneeling on a lotus under a ceremonial canopy. The picture is delicately drawn, and perfectly finished, like an illustration in a book. Tseten says it is used in rituals for women who are beset by evil spirits; he is so busy at home, he has to take every opportunity to get things done.

Once he has finished his drawing, I ask him what people in the village do in the winter.

'Lots of things,' he says decisively. 'Going on pilgrimages is very popular. The winter's the only time there's no work on the land. People visit the holy mountains and lakes, and the sacred places; they also accumulate merit. Then lots of weddings and celebrations, villagers helping each other build houses, making babies, or simply sitting in the sun. I'm sure one of the people in your film will go on a pilgrimage. Otherwise where do you think all those pilgrims in Lhasa come from?'

So far none of our characters has mentioned pilgrimages, except for Jianzang, who is thinking of going to Nepal. But that is to find a chef for his restaurant, though he will also be visiting Lumbini, the birthplace of the Buddha. Perhaps Penpa and Roten did not ask them directly. Perhaps they are not keen on being filmed? The government does not stop people from going on such pilgrimages, but it does not encourage them either.

The next day I go with Penpa and talk to each of our characters again. Tseten was right. Three of them say they are thinking of going on a pilgrimage, but they are not sure when, so they have not told us. Rincheu is planning to take his wife and infant son to Lhasa to see the Potala Palace and prostrate at the three great monasteries there. The novice monk Tsephun and his master are thinking of going to Lhasa too, but they have to ask the monastery first, and then the police, for permission. Since Lhakpa has not got much money, he and his family will probably go somewhere nearby – perhaps on a day trip to the Tashilunpo Monastery in Shigatse, to repent their sins, and to pray for health and wealth.

Lhakpa needs his prayers to come true. Roten first found him after taking a ride in his rickshaw. He was impressed by his honesty, his frankness, and his fighting spirit. With no land or skill, he is the poorest of all the film's characters – I can see he does not eat enough, from his thin frame, and his lined, gaunt face and straggly hair. He told me he bought his first and only pair of leather shoes two years ago, when he turned twenty-five. But he did not want to be filmed at first. 'I'm not proud of being poor. Why should I allow you to laugh at me? You can't help my family. You can't find me a job. You won't pay me. You tell me why I should let you make money out of my misery.' He almost shouted at the official from the street committee whom Roten took along to help persuade him: 'How dare you come to this house? You say you work for people but you don't really give a shit about us. Tell me, where has all the relief for the poor gone? I bet your cronies and relatives got most of it. Shame on you!'

Lhakpa finally agreed to appear in the film after observing

us at work for two months. 'You are not making fun of these people,' he said to me one day when he dropped in to have a meal with us. 'And you do not get in their way. I'll have a go.' He soon became one of my favourite characters, bringing so much force and emotion to the film. He stops at nothing to make ends meet: apart from his rickshaw, he paints houses (50 *yuan*, or £3, for a house, and he does three a day with his two brothers and sister-in-law); unloads trucks (a twenty-ton truck takes the three brothers four hours; they get 28 *yuan* each for that, less than £2 pounds); cleans cess pools, and buys and sells puppies.

But he is also difficult, liable to flare up at imagined slights. He stopped us filming once because Penpa asked him why he was still not married at twenty-seven. 'Can't you find a woman good enough for you?' He stormed off protesting, 'You think I am too poor to attract a woman!'

'I'm sure lots of girls find you attractive. Get one, show Penpa he is wrong,' I called as he left. Sure enough, he soon met Dadron, a delightful and hardworking young woman, a waitress in a tea house in Gyantse. The Lhakpa soap keeps running, though since I do not, of course, write the script, I do not know what will come next.

Two weeks after we discussed the pilgrimage, Lhakpa drops in and says he has now finished his three weeks of house-painting, has saved 700 *yuan* (£50), and is ready to go. We offer to drive him and his family to Shigatse. On an auspicious day chosen by his mother, they put on their best clothes and pile into our Land Rover – Lhakpa, one of his brothers, his sister-in-law, his two nephews, his mother, and the new girlfriend, very excited and chattering like monkeys.

We head for Tashilunpo, the seat of the Panchen Lama and one of the most revered Tibetan sites. We can see it from a long way off, stretched out over a large hill, the many gold roofs marking the holiest shrines. As soon as we pull up, Lhakpa and his family jump out of the car and immediately start prostrating themselves. They clasp their palms together in prayer, then bend down, touching the ground and sliding their hands forward until they are lying flat with the whole of their bodies stretched out, from toes to fingertips. Then they stand up, walk three paces, and do it again, repeating the process over and over, along with hundreds of other pilgrims, until they reach the monastery gate.

Lhakpa leads the family straight to the temple of Maitreya, the Future Buddha. Its gilded copper image is one of the main things the family, like many of the pilgrims, has come to Tashilunpo to see and to pray to. At twenty-six metres tall it is the biggest of its kind in the world – just one finger is more than a metre long. The giant statue fills the whole temple, looking down on the faithful, serene, compassionate, and merciful, its eyes holding you in their gaze. Ozer, Lhakpa's five-year-old nephew, stands staring at the statue for quite a while. I am about to ask him a question, but he holds his finger to his lips and shushes me. Without being told, he throws himself on the floor and prostrates, like the rest of the family. When he stands up, a monk who is looking after the hall fluffs his hair and pats him on the shoulder; Ozer smiles radiantly.

Outside the temple, I ask him what he has prayed for. 'To be healthy,' is all he says. It might seem a strange wish for such a young boy, but I know he has a defect in his heart and needs an operation that the family cannot afford. Without it he will probably die before he reaches adolescence. I wonder whether we should try and find some way of raising the money for the operation. It will not be easy, but I do not like to think of him just waiting for his prayers to be answered.

Next we follow them into the temple for the 10th Panchen Lama. I watch Lhakpa and his family prostrate in front of his statue and the stupa that holds his body. Then they read out from a plaque about the cost of the stupa: 64 million *yuan* (about £4.5 million pounds), 614 kilos of gold and 275 kilos of silver. The stupa is indeed like a pile of gold, eleven metres high and covered with precious stones. Inside it is filled with offerings, barley, rice, tea, salt, dried fruits, sugar, sandalwood, medicine, silk, horse saddles – but also the Buddhist canons and statues. In the midst of the treasures is the embalmed body of the Panchen Lama.

I ask them what they know about the Panchen Lama. 'He is a god,' Lhakpa's mother says meekly, in a hushed voice. 'But he spent most of his time in Beijing,' Lhakpa adds. Then they file out of the temple. I was hoping for more, but I knew I would not get it. I tell the cameraman to follow the family while I linger just a little longer. Lhakpa seems to be reverential, but I think he is ambivalent about this Panchen Lama. Many Tibetans think he was a traitor. Unlike the Dalai Lama, they say, he stayed behind and compromised himself by working with the Chinese, and also by marrying a Chinese woman.

I must confess I had thought similarly of him. I used to see him on Chinese television, in the company of Chinese leaders, and wearing a brocade gown, not his monk's robe. He did not look like a lama to me. But the more I learned about him, the more I began to think he has been wrongly censured. Perhaps staying behind was the harder path. As the incarnation of the God of Infinite Light, the 10th Panchen Lama, Choekyi Gyaltsen, was indeed a light in the Tibetan people's time of darkness. He gave them hope when everyone else despaired; he spoke out when no one else dared; he stood up when he knew that he would suffer for his audacity.

In 1962, the Panchen Lama used the testimonies of people and officials he met on his tour of Tibet and the neighbouring Qinghai and Sichuan provinces where many Tibetans live, and compiled his *70,000-Character Petition* – a record of his people's grievances. He was just twenty-four-years old. He concentrated on the three issues that concerned them most: religious life, impoverishment, and imprisonment. After the Tibetan uprising in 1959, 97 per cent of the monasteries were closed, and 93 per cent of the 110,000 monks and nuns were sent home. Buddhist sutras were used for compost; *tangkas* of the Buddha were used to make shoes. As the Panchen Lama put it: 'Religious activities were as scarce as stars in the daytime.'[28] Anyone suspected of even the most remote connection with the uprising was put in prison. 'Where the total population is only 1.2 million people,' the Panchen Lama wrote, 'a prison population of about 10,000 people is too great.'[29]

And for those outside the prisons and camps, the physical deprivation was just as appalling. The Panchen Lama pointed out that 'in the past, although Tibet was a society ruled by dark and savage feudalism, there had never been such a shortage of grain'.[30] As a result, he observed, 'dregs of fat, grain husks and so on which formerly in Tibet were fodder for horses and donkeys, bulls and oxen, became hard to get and were considered nourishing and fragrant foods'.[31]

In May 1962, the Panchen Lama sent his *70,000-Character Petition* to Prime Minister Zhou Enlai to pass on to Mao. Mao was incensed and called it 'a poisoned arrow'. Almost immediately, the Panchen Lama was put under house arrest, and then imprisoned for the next fourteen years as 'an enemy of the Party, an enemy of the people, and an enemy of socialism'. He was subjected to long interrogations and humiliated. At one mass struggle meeting in a sports stadium in Beijing, his sister-in-law was persuaded to accuse him of raping her. His seat at the Tashilunpo Monastery became a target of the Red Guards in 1966. In a frenzied onslaught, they led a crowd to break statues, burn the scriptures, and open the stupas where the 5th-9th Panchen Lamas were entombed, and throw their remains into the river. If the Party could allow this to happen to the Panchen Lama, whom Tibetans regard as a god, what would it not do?

After his release in 1977, the 10th Panchen Lama picked up where he had left off. He never gave in to pressures to denounce the Dalai Lama, and continued to be the public conscience of his people. He worked to save and restore Tibetan culture. In 1985, he started his most important act of homage and restoration, building a stupa for his five predecessors. Astonishingly, some of their relics were rediscovered; even in their wild rage, for some Tibetans in the crowd destroying the stupas had been a step too far. They had hidden away some of the remains, either out of fear of retribution for so barbaric a crime, or in a momentary onset of reverence. On 22nd January 1989, he consecrated the completed stupa for his predecessors. Six days later, he died in Tashilunpo aged fifty-one. It was as if he was saying now he could rest.

We get back to Gyantse in the early evening, and drop Lhakpa and his family at their house. I leave the crew at home; earlier in the day I have arranged to have a meal out with a Tibetan couple from Shigatse I know who live in Gyantse. I want to talk to them about the visit to Tashilunpo. I meet them in Dzong Square, the latest modern addition to Gyantse, and walk with them down Hero Road. This is Gyantse's main street, and it is full of restaurants: 'Old Li's Barbecue'; a Sichuanese restaurant called 'Sliced Lungs by Husband and Wife'; a new chain owned by a Sichuanese family called 'Overflowing Noodle Bowl'; 'Dumpling King'; the 'Hand-Picked Mutton Restaurant', run by Muslims from Gansu; and two Tibetan-Nepalese restaurants for tourists. Nestled in among the restaurants is 'People's Portrait', the only photographer's in town; 'Trivial Profit', a stationery shop; the 'Outlook' and 'Big Thumb' internet bars; 'Western Patisserie'; the 'Sainted Buddha Clinic'; and half a dozen fruit stalls. After walking up and down wondering where to eat, we choose one of the Tibetan-Nepalese places.

It has a relaxed atmosphere, so relaxed that the pizzas we order take nearly an hour to come. We joke that the chef has gone to Italy to ask for the recipe. When the pizzas finally arrive, their crusts are as hard as rock. You could crack a tooth on them. I ask the waiter, a shy Nepalese boy, if something can be done. He nods, and takes them to the kitchen, but returns quickly with the same pizzas. 'Sorry, Ma'am,' he whispers. 'The manager says this is how pizza should be.'

I call for the manager, a strongly built Tibetan woman in her thirties.

'What is your problem?' she asks us sharply. 'All the foreigners eat my pizzas happily.' She points to a group of tourists sitting at the next table. 'Why are you making a fuss?'

I explain that I do not know what they are eating, but the pizzas we have been served are inedible.

'If you haven't got money, don't come here,' she replies. 'There're plenty of cheap Chinese restaurants around. Even better, why don't you go back where you came from? Nobody invited you here. We don't want you in our country. Get lost.'

When the manager has finished her harangue, there is a deathly silence in the restaurant, and then crude laughter from two Tibetan men sitting in a corner. The foreigners at the neighbouring table are stunned by the outburst. My friends sit there, looking at each other but not saying anything. I am shocked and saddened – not so much by the manager, as by the response, or lack of it, from the Tibetan couple. I did not expect them to defend me, but at least they could have told her not to turn a request about a pizza into a political fight. But neither of them said a word.

When we get up to leave, I pay for the drinks and the rest of the food, but not the pizzas, which we have left untouched. The manager launches into another tirade, this time in Tibetan. The awkward expression on my Tibetan friends' faces tells me it must have been particularly rude. For once, I am glad my Tibetan is not good enough.

We leave the restaurant in silence. I tell them I am going to wander in town for a while. Where can I go? I often visit Jianzang's hotel for relaxation and for a chat. But I do not feel like it tonight. As I walk down Hero Road, I catch sight of the big sign outside the Luxury Public Shower at the lower end of the road, run by a Muslim family from Gansu, northwestern China. I decide to go in. As usual, it is busy. The owner is cleaning the used cubicles; his oldest child, an eight-year-old girl, is glued to a gangster movie from Hong Kong on the television; the middle child, a boy, pees on the floor; the youngest, just over a year old, is screaming his head off on the sofa. The wife is trying to keep them in order while she takes the customers' money. I am glad to get in quickly. I pay my 5 *yuan*, about 35 pence, for my own cubicle with shampoo and a pair of slippers, and 2 *yuan* extra for a towel.

As the water washes over me, I let my tears roll down as well. The scene in the restaurant plays over and over in my head. I know what many Tibetans feel about us, but when it becomes personal, it is hard to take. I feel chilled to my bones and the hot water is a relief.

Perhaps the manager assumed I work for the county government, which does nothing to stop the flood of migrants pouring into Gyantse; perhaps she thought I owned one of the shops down the road. Either way, she holds me responsible for taking business away from Tibetans like her. I know that most of the shops along Gyantse's two main streets – Hero Road and Shanghai Road – are run by Chinese. There are some small Tibetan tea houses, mostly with just three or four tables, scattered about town, and about two dozen tailors', run by Tibetans.

Along the street leading up to the monastery, there are small shops selling traditional Tibetan goods – stoves, carpets, prayer flags, incense, *khatas*, *bamdian* (traditional aprons) and Tibetan-style shirts, jackets and coats. But even these shops are under threat. It's hard to believe, but most of the butter, *khatas*, and *bamdian* available in Gyantse are made outside Tibet. Why do such simple and fundamentally Tibetan objects need to be made elsewhere? If I were the Tibetan woman with her precarious restaurant, I might be just as hostile.

I'm sure it wouldn't make much of a difference to her to know that none of the Chinese workers are here because of government promises. It's not like in my student days, when young people were encouraged to go and work in Tibet, mostly for the local government. 'We did not need any encouragement,' Cook Li declared. 'Just seeing the cash other villagers were sending back home was motivation enough.' Asked how he thought the success of people like him impacted on the Tibetans, Cook Li was characteristically blunt. 'We do what the Tibetans are unwilling to do. We do not make trouble. We do not rob. We do not break the law. We pay our taxes. They make money by renting shops to us. We provide a service they need. Otherwise we'd go out of business. It's as simple as that. They have a choice. It is not as if we are forcing them to eat in our restaurants at gunpoint.'

I did once ask Cook Li why there were not more Tibetan entrepreneurs, and he replied without hesitation: 'They are lazy and they should get their heads screwed on! I hired a Tibetan girl for my restaurant. I gave her food and lodging. You'd think she would have saved some money. Not a chance! She squandered it like water. Even worse, any time a man bought her a bottle of beer or some chewing gum, she would drop her trousers and let him fuck her. Why did she allow them to exploit her like that? She could have made the men pay.'

Above Ploughing near Tangmad.

Below Mila making ritual objects.

Above far left Three brothers and Yangdron.

Above left Fire ritual for Tseten's mother.

Above Sky burial master with vultures.

Left Summer when the mustard seed is flowering.

Left Mountains around the lake.

Right Old houses in Gyantse.

Below Gyantse in winter.

Lhakpa on his new autorickshaw.

Rincheu, the builder.

Rincheu's wife.

Above The bride.

Below The Bull Race before spring planting.

Above Tseten curing toothache

Below Dr Lhamo on a house call.

He must have been thinking of all the Sichuanese girls in the beauty parlours, karaoke bars, and hairdresser's down the road from his restaurant. When we first arrived, I walked into one of these places by mistake, thinking it really was a hairdressers'. There wasn't a single pair of scissors to be found, but plenty of mirrors. A tiny girl wearing heavy make-up and a pink mini-skirt asked me what service I would like. I fled.

These girls from Sichuan have surely brought new business to Gyantse and are making plenty of money out of the men, Chinese and Tibetan alike. They have plenty of the shrewdness, toughness, and entrepreneurial skill that Cook Li appreciates. Not long ago, a senior Gyantse policeman, a Tibetan in his late forties, visited one of the girls, but refused to pay afterwards. She reported him and he was demoted. No doubt, Cook Li approved of that too.

But the success of Li and people like him does put pressure on Tibetan businesses. Lhakpa feels the pressure too. He wants to learn to drive and then work as a taxi driver – a job hotly con-tested by young men from Sichuan and Gansu. At least five out of the ten taxi drivers in Gyantse are Chinese; and they arrived qualified and experienced. Lhakpa has little chance. In Shigatse and Lhasa too, young Tibetans are losing out – they cannot compete with better-qualified migrants, and they are angry, like the restaurant manager.

She might have even deeper reasons for her hatred. Her father might have been killed in the Tibetan uprising of 1959; or he might have been thrown out of his monastery when the govern-ment closed them all down in the same year; or he may have been persecuted in the Cultural Revolution. She might have had a cousin who was jailed and tortured for supporting the Dalai Lama. I often find myself rehearsing in my mind an apology to the Tibetans I meet. There are many things I could point out. The destruction of Buddhism and the insanity of the Cultural

Revolution were not aimed at Tibet alone. In the rest of China there were a quarter of a million monasteries and temples in 1949; by 1976 barely a hundred remained.[32] But how could any opinion of mine carry weight in the face of the sufferings of the people and the almost total destruction of Tibetan culture?

With everything the Panchen Lama suffered and bore witness to fresh in my mind, I can understand Tibetans who do not forgive the Chinese. Any repair or restoration of monasteries, any new road or dam, any school or hospital – these are seen as atonements for our sins, but there is so much that can never be atoned for. Perhaps Cook Li is right: the Tibetans will never be our friends. This might explain the silence of the Tibetan couple in the restaurant; at the very least, they did not want to be seen to be taking my side.

But then I think of the Rikzin family and the people in their village. They did not escape the horrors of the past. I have yet to find out the whole of Mila's story, but I think he suffered greatly after the uprising and during the Cultural Revolution. I do not imagine the villagers will forget or forgive the past, but they have been warm and kind to me. In the village there is very little contact with the Chinese; the people do not experience the daily friction that is inescapable in Tibetan towns and cities. Perhaps that is why they can take me as I am – perhaps they really do like me. I can only hope so.

I leave the Luxury Public Shower with some reluctance. The owner has knocked on the door twice, wondering if I am sick. I have been there over an hour; if everyone was like me, they would be out of business. I give them some more money, and walk home along Hero Road as night falls. In Dzong Square, I pass the Museum for the Anti-British Martyrs, which honours the men who defended Gyantse against the British invaders in 1904. I had paid it a visit when I first arrived. It has the maps and weapons the British used, and the matchlock rifles, knives, spears, and daggers that the Tibetans had to reply with; their cannons were equally primitive. They were no match for the British Maxims, Lee-Enfields, ten-pounders and light guns. There was a bloodbath at Chumik Shenko, a hot spring a hundred miles south of Gyantse, where 628 Tibetans were killed and 222 wounded.[33] It was their first experience of machine guns; they were mown down like a field of barley.

'Why, in the name of all their Bodhisats and Munis, did they not run?' the *Daily Mail* correspondent Edmund Chandler asked. 'They were bewildered. The impossible had happened. Prayers, and charms, and mantras, and the holiest of their holy men, had failed them … They walked with bowed heads, as if they had been disillusioned with their gods.'[34]

It is hard to credit, but the Tibetans actually thought their prayers would be enough to protect them. They believed that the talismans the lamas had given them to wear on their chests would stop bullets from harming them. When they heard the British were coming, monks from the three big monasteries in Lhasa came out in force to chant special invocations for the protection of a host of deities. 'Arrows were fired and imprecations hurled at life-size effigies of white-faced men in solar topees, which were then immersed in cauldrons of boiling oil.'[35] That would be enough to frighten the invaders. The idea that they might reach Gyantse, let alone Lhasa, was too fanciful to be taken seriously.[36]

The white fort, the Dzong, accompanies me all the way home, towering above Hero Road, above Dzong Square, above the museum, above the houses that curve away from it to my street. Against the black sky and glimmering stars, it does look impregnable. I can see why the people of Gyantse felt protected by it. But it fell in barely more than a morning. On 5th July 1904, seven months after the expedition led by Younghusband began, Gurkhas whose ancestors had twice almost brought Tibet to its knees, took it, under the cover of pounding British artillery. Many of the locals had gone there for protection. An officer cheered as he watched shells exploding and the gate caving in: 'The Tibetans were escaping [by the] hundreds, climbing and jumping down the far side.'[37] When the senior lamas of the Palkhor monastery came to ask Younghusband not to fine them 36 tons of barley for the role the monks had played in resisting the British, he refused. 'A more cringing lot I never came across. They are not worth powder and shot. I have them in great awe of me though ... I remain obdurate: and they retire still bowing profoundly and stepping backwards like we do before the King ... It is great sport.'[38]

A hundred years on, the Museum in Honour of the Anti-British Martyrs serves as a reminder of imperial brutality against the brave Tibetans. The message is repeated across Gyantse: 'Welcome to Hero Town', then Hero Road, Hero Square, the Hero Monument. Video shops sell a film called *Red River Gorge*, a romanticised account of the battle against the British and the fall of the Dzong. Its theme song is the town's anthem; the museum guide sings it as she takes the visitors round.

That night, I decide I will take a break and return to Beijing after all. I do not want to let my bad experience colour my feelings or my judgement. I need distance and a little time for things to get back to normal.

In a way, I am doing what the Chinese officials in Tibet do – after eighteen months' service, they are entitled to four months' paid leave, sometimes more. The exodus starts in November and lasts well beyond the Tibetan New Year in February. Maybe the physical demands of life in Tibet require it. Maybe it is the only way the government can entice senior officials to come to Tibet and help run it. These positions have other perks too – accelerated promotion, subsidised housing, jobs for spouses, schooling for children, or a lump sum as high as 300,000 *yuan*

(£20,000) for those who come from a rich province like Canton or Shanghai.[39] Because I have been here so long, I am often taken to be one of them. The Chinese taxi drivers often say: 'You're one of the lucky ones, not like us, working like serfs.'

Once in Beijing, I keep in touch by calling the team every day to see what our characters are up to. One of the messages from the team is: 'Tseten was asking after you again today. "When is Teacher Sun coming back? Please tell her we miss her."'

I feel a surge of warmth when I hear it.

When the time comes for me to return three weeks' later, I am loaded with gifts for our film's characters and the production team. Boarding the plane, I look like a beast of burden, and wish I was the Bodhisattva of Compassion with a thousand arms. The other passengers cast all sorts of disapproving glances my way. Why am I carting all this stuff around, when it can be found easily enough in Lhasa?

I am doing it because the quality of goods sold in Tibet is so poor. Almost everything we bought for our house in Gyantse fell apart. We paid £550 for a high-definition TV, which had to be exchanged because it had no picture. In stores where there are hundreds of porcelain cups and bowls, I could not find a dozen without blemishes. The zip on my makeshift wardrobe came off on the first day. The drawer of my computer table collapsed and all the edging came off after a week. The thermos fails to keep our water hot. The washing powder has no effect on grease. The pressure cooker refuses to open unless we thump it really hard. Light bulbs last as long as chewing gum. The sticky tape does not stick, and the pills for tummy trouble do not stop me from having to run to the toilet. Of the eleven electric blankets we purchased for the winter, only four still worked after a month; we bought three electric heaters – one went dead after a week, while another only works when we take the back cover off. Tibet seems to be a dumping ground for shoddy goods from the rest of China. And everything costs more here too.

I have bought one big gift for Tseten's family – a DVD player. I have also made a copy of the trailer of our autumn filming. They want to watch it straightaway. The trailer opens with Yangdron, Dondan, and their two older sons in the field, bringing in the harvest. The bright blue sky above their heads, the golden barley, the rhythmic swish of the sickles, and the forceful bursts of song. 'Ah!', Yangdron cries out, laughing, her eyes wide open, her hand over her mouth. She stays like that for a few minutes, frozen in surprise and wonder. Then tears well up in her eyes. She is laughing and crying at the same time. It is the first time I have seen her let her guard down. Not even death in the family did that.

SIX

I'm Getting Married?

TSETEN IS SITTING IN HIS USUAL position on the bed, surrounded by a pile of scriptures and brightly coloured wool. He is making Tibetan good-luck amulets, folding small pieces of white paper into tiny squares and entwining them with red, blue, and green threads. His slow, deep chanting fills the room. He is so involved that he does not look up when a man and woman enter, holding two large casks of barley flour and white wool. These are their offerings for his services.

Tseten finishes an amulet and tosses it into a small bamboo basket. He turns to me, explaining, 'These two people have come to see if his son and her daughter are suitable for each other.' The man and the woman, both in their forties, place the casks on the table in front of Tseten and sit down at his feet. He brings out a pen and a piece of paper, and asks for the hour, the day, the month, and year of birth for the boy and the girl, and then for every single member of the two families – grandfathers, grandmothers, aunts and uncles, brothers-in-law and sisters-in-law, nephews and nieces.

I can understand why Tseten might need dates of birth for the boy and girl (he is nineteen, born in 1988, and she is three years older). But why does he need to know about everyone in the family? It is hard enough to find someone you love who shares your tastes and values. What chance is there to find someone you love who matches not only your horoscope but those of all your family members? And does it *really* matter if one of the girl's nephews is not astrologically in tune with her prospective husband?

Tseten can see that I am bursting with questions. 'It will take me an hour or two to work this one out,' he says 'You retire to the kitchen for some butter tea. I'll explain later.'

I find Yangdron in the kitchen, stoking the fire. I offer to help, and go to collect more dried cowpats from the courtyard. We have a cowpat stove in our rented house, and I have grown rather fond of it. In this vast land, animals outnumber people by thousands to one, and their manure provides both fertiliser and fuel for the home. And at an altitude of 13,000 feet, it is a struggle for bacteria to survive, so the cowpats have no smell. The ashes from these stoves are dumped on human waste in the outdoor toilet, which is then used as manure for fields. Nothing is wasted. I find myself marvelling at Tibetan ingenuity every time I make a fire.

In a little while the girl's mother joins us in the kitchen to help Yangdron prepare a special lunch of stewed yak meat and potatoes. Yangdron has told me her name is Droma. She has a warm beauty, which she conveys through her smiling eyes. Her smile is something else: like many Tibetans from the villages, she has hardly any teeth. She is long and lean, and is wearing a red silk blouse and a floor length black wool dress. Droma has five daughters; it is her middle daughter whose fate is being decided today. Yangdron tells me, 'Her daughter is the smartest girl in the village. So far, there have been so many suitors we've lost track.'

'Only a dozen or so,' Droma says humbly.

'None of them were good enough for your daughter?' I ask.

'Some were rich, some were handsome, some have gone to university, some work for the government. They were keen, but each time we asked Tseten's opinion, he said they were not suitable.'

But did she think some of the boys were suitable? After all, she knows her daughter better than anyone. And what does her daughter think?

'It doesn't matter what I think,' Droma says quickly. 'It all comes down to Tseten. My daughter does not know about the suitors. It is not our custom to inform her.'

Yangdron nods in agreement while peeling the potatoes.

'Your daughter doesn't know you are choosing a husband for her today?'

Droma shakes her head. 'If Tseten works out that this boy is good for my daughter, we'll accept the marriage proposal. If he says no, we won't.'

She is not sure what Tseten will say today, but she already knows the boy and his family well. The village is small, with only ninety-six households. She has watched the boy grow up. 'He is a good boy, shy but kind. If he is anything like his father, the match will be a good one. His father's the hardest-working man in the entire village.' What Droma does not say is that the family is also the richest in the village.

'But what about your daughter's feelings?'

'Those come with time. If she is lucky enough to marry the boy, she will be the envy of everyone in the village. What more could she want?' She pauses, and then tells me: 'The two were classmates in secondary school, so they are not total strangers. I don't think she'll object.'

'Why is Tseten's opinion the only one that matters?' I ask, aware that Yangdron has stopped peeling potatoes and is listening closely.

97

'Without Tseten's approval the marriage is doomed,' Droma says simply. She pours me another cup of butter tea from the thermos and then takes the rest to Tseten and the boy's father.

Astrology and fortune-telling have been central facets of Chinese life for centuries. *The Book of Changes*, which dates back to 1,000 BC, is the classic text of Chinese astrology, and a repository of the profound knowledge gathered by the Chinese about celestial changes and their effect on human lives. For centuries, methods of divination have been used in declarations of war, in peacemaking, and in all aspects of private life – marriages, births, aging, illness and death.

Where Western astrology allocates a different sign to every month, Chinese astrology allocates a different animal to every year. There are twelve animals – the rat, cow, tiger, rabbit, dragon, snake, horse, sheep, monkey, cock, dog and pig – and then the twelve-year cycle starts again. Some animals are believed to coexist happily: my grandmother was a sheep and I am a rabbit, and the two animals are said to be sympathetic. But others are doomed to conflict: pigs are frightened by snakes; rabbits irritate dragons.

The Chinese also believe that the world is made of five elements – gold, wood, water, fire, and earth. These five elements represent five directions: gold is west, wood is east, water is north, fire is south, and earth is the centre. Harmony is the essence of the universe, and therefore of astrology. There is the sun and the moon, hence day and night, masculine and feminine. Of the five elements, gold gives rise to water, water to wood, wood to fire, fire to earth, earth to gold; at the same time, gold trumps wood, wood trumps earth, earth trumps water, water trumps fire, fire trumps gold. *The Book of Changes* synthesises all these different but related strands into something called the *Eight Diagrams*. The *Diagrams* are at the heart of Chinese astrology; they are deceptively simple looking, but to master them requires a great deal of study. Almost every aspect of your life, according to believers, can be accurately foretold by reading them.

The Book of Changes was banned during the Cultural Revolution. The Yellow Ridge Temple in my hometown, Handan, famous for its fortune-telling, was burned to the ground, and the priests were thrown into prison for spreading 'superstition'. I thought they deserved it. I even wondered whether with all those tricks up their sleeves they had foreseen their own fate. But the temple was rebuilt in the 1980s and the priests and fortune-tellers are once again in great demand. When I was about to marry an Englishman in 1988, my mother wanted to know whether I would be happy; my sister asked if my nephew would pass his university exams; a girlfriend was desperate to find out whether her marriage would survive her husband's love affair. The predictions were so ambiguous you could interpret them almost any way you chose. I do not believe that my family and friends take the words of the fortune-tellers literally. They might like to, but they know their lives are also in their own hands. At most, they are hoping for a little assurance. It is nothing like the absolute ruling which Tseten has given in the past and is about to give again.

When lunch is ready, I sneak into Tseten's room to see if today is Droma's lucky day. Tseten is still counting on his fingertips and murmuring, but I see that Droma is barely suppressing a smile. Tseten puts down his pen and paper and declares, 'The wedding will be on 13th November.'

Over a celebratory lunch, we discuss the upcoming event. 'At least you have given Droma's daughter some time to prepare herself,' I tell Tseten. I have no idea how the young woman will take the news.

'Oh, she won't know about it until near the big day,' Tseten responds, with a characteristic chuckle.

At first I think Tseten might be teasing me. He is good at that. Before I went back to Beijing, I asked him what presents I could bring for the family. 'A mountain of gold and a mountain of silver,' he said, and then added: 'If you come back safely, that will be a good present.'

But right now, he's serious. 'Ask Droma,' he says. 'She probably won't tell her daughter until the wedding day.'

Droma nods.

'Why not?' I'm dumbstruck.

'Because she might run away,' Droma says.

'But she might be in an unhappy marriage for her whole life,' I lower my voice for fear of offending the happy parents.

'She will have a good marriage,' Tseten says. 'The boy is a dragon and she is a cow. They have the matching earth element; they even complement each other in their life directions. Both will be quite good at making money.' Tseten talks as though it all made perfect sense.

I am always fascinated by how his system works. I want to know how he reached this conclusion, and whether his method differs greatly from one used by the fortune-tellers my mother consults. But I have a more burning question: What about love?

'Young people do fall in love,' Tseten admits. 'But in Tibet, it is the custom that they listen to their parents. The parents consult a shaman. If the lovers' stars signs are crossed, they have no choice but to give up the relationship.' Tseten pauses, thoughtfully. 'Once the foundation for a good marriage is laid, you can build on it with love and affection.'

'Do you think that Jigme and Gyatso would give up girlfriends if you found them incompatible?' I ask him.

Tseten is firm. 'I think they would, yes. They would have to.' Then he adds after a long pause: 'If it is a minor conflict, I can fix it by saying a prayer for them, or making them wear an amulet. But if they are just incompatible, there is not much I can do.'

Back in Gyantse that evening, I ask the Tibetan members of the crew what they think of all this. My tone must have betrayed some of my sense of indignation.

'Calm down. It is not your marriage. What is the problem?' Penpa teased me

'I hear the boy is gorgeous,' our driver, Tashi, declares. 'With his looks and his family's money, surely he deserves someone better than a peasant girl?'

I could have expected that their attitude would be slightly more cavalier than mine, but our translator Shilok's reply comes as a shock to me. Like our researcher Roten, he has spent over a decade studying in Beijing. His Chinese is better than his Tibetan, and he has a confident and street-wise way about him, unusual among young Tibetans in Gyantse. I imagined he would think differently. But I was wrong. 'I owe my life and everything to my parents. Without them, I'm nothing. Obeying them is my duty,' he tells me solemnly.

'What about your duty to yourself?' I ask.

'It comes second.'

He says that he is even willing to consider sharing a wife with his two elder brothers if that is the wish of his parents, who will no doubt consult a shaman on the matter. He says he can't speak for his friends in Lhasa, but those he knows in Gyantse and in the villages would probably say the same thing.

I have asked Tseten, many times, why it is that Tibetans, rural and urban, educated and uneducated, seem to accept their fate more readily than the rest of us. He laughs and says, 'That is how we are. We are Buddhists.' As Buddhists, they believe in karma. Your life, just like your horoscope, is set. Denying this is futile, like one man fighting an army.

I am sure that the girl, Dolkar, will marry the boy approved by Tseten. Even if she gets wind of her impending marriage now, I doubt she would run away; where would she go? The furthest place she has visited is Gyantse, twenty miles from her home. Until recently, with the introduction of a minibus, most villagers relied on carts to take them there, and the journey took half a day. Other than for weddings and funerals of close relatives, an illness that needs hospitalisation, or pilgrimages to holy places, people rarely venture far. Some of the young men in Tseten's village may look for work up in the north during the winter because there is little to do back home. But girls mostly stay put – otherwise they will be gossiped about: who knows what they get up to when they are away? Eligible men in the village will avoid them. I am told that, although Dolkar and the boy have been in the same class and live in the same village, she has never been alone with him, and has perhaps never spoken to him directly.

I am keen to find some way of filming the bride at home with her family, but obviously Droma does not want me to come to the house in case Dolkar suspects something. 'We will be sending her away to her sister who lives in Gyantse ten days before the wedding. That way she won't see the preparations. You can come then,' Droma says apologetically.

I do not want to wait that long. Every time I am in the village, I have a strong urge to see Dolkar and tell her everything. To hell with the custom! It is so cruel. But I know this would mean the end of our filming in the village – trust is everything here. Then I have a flash of inspiration: Tseten is going to invite a well-known lama to say a special prayer for their late mother. Many of the villagers will be coming to be blessed by him. Why not ask Dolkar to come and help out? At least then I can see her myself. Tseten gladly agrees.

Dolkar looks much as I expected. She steps into the kitchen, somewhat stocky and wearing a traditional dress – long and black, and made of coarse wool with a matching jacket. It is bulky on her, even a little matronly. She has her hair in long plaits around her head like most Tibetan women do. Her cheeks are reddened from the cold and wind in the valley, giving her a healthy glow. After a brief word with Yangdron, she sets about helping with the lunch. She puts more cowpats in the stove, fills the thermoses with hot water, makes dough for Tibetan noodles, chops up the meat for the sauce, washes bowls, and then takes the waste out to feed the animals. All the while, she keeps up a soft flow of conversation with Yangdron and the two older women who have also come to help. She has a gentle smile that never leaves her face. I can see why the boy's parents are so keen for their son to marry her: she is strong, capable, demure, and pleasant looking, surely an asset. I understand why they want to snap her up so soon, before someone else does, even though their son is only nineteen.

I watch her furtively, trying to gauge whether she knows about her impending marriage – it is less than three weeks away. Yangdron thinks she may have guessed something from the gossip in the village. She must also be wondering why our camera is following her. Is this my way of warning her? I wonder too. But if she does know something, she does not show it; whatever she might feel about it, she gives nothing away. She is a picture of serenity. I get the impression that she is a woman of some strength, someone who will hold her ground and make the best of her life.

And then, a week before the wedding, we get a call from Tseten. 'Droma says her daughter has gone to visit her sister in Gyantse, you can come and film her in the village.'

I cannot see anything special going on in Droma's house. She is just making some *chang* in the kitchen when we arrive, but there are no decorations, no new furniture, no big cooking pots steaming. Penpa explains it is the groom's family who provide the celebrations. Droma just has to feed them when they come to fetch her daughter. 'I'm getting ready for that,'

Droma says cheerfully, pointing towards the staircase, where I had seen two sheep's carcases hanging from a rope. 'This is my third lot of *chang*, and I have to make one every day till the wedding.'

After a while, I get around to my main question: has she told Dolkar yet?

'No,' she shakes her head lightly. 'Her brother-in-law will tell her near the day.'

But does she not need to prepare Dolkar for the biggest day of her life? She will have a lot to learn – about the man she is marrying, about sex, about dealing with her in-laws. Otherwise, how will she know what to do?

'My oldest daughter will be with her and her husband on the wedding night, and for the three days after. She will teach her what she needs to know.'

'Her sister will be there on the wedding night?' This shocks me more than anything else I've heard so far.

'More or less,' she says, unperturbed. 'Would you like to see the dowry?'

I really want to sit her down and talk to her, but Penpa wags his finger, signalling that she is not going to say any more. Reluctantly we follow her to the family's prayer room, where the two dowry chests are on the floor next to the altar table. She opens one and shows us what is inside: shirts, scarves, blankets, a beautiful traditional dress, a Chinese brocade jacket. She unwraps one of the scarves so we can see the one piece of jewellery: a silver pendant set with lapis lazuli, something women in Gyantse wear a lot.

'Didn't Dolkar see you getting all this ready?' I ask.

'No, we bought the things and hid them away. There isn't that much, as you can see. We are not so well off.'

Luckily, the groom's family is rich. They will not be concerned at the slimness of the dowry. I am sure Dolkar herself will more than make up for it. I just pray that she and her husband will like each other.

On 13th November, the first day of the wedding, I get up early and wake the whole crew. 'You won't see the bride until tomorrow. What's the hurry?' Penpa grumbles in the morning cold.

Tashi, the driver, teases me, 'You're keener than the bride. Maybe you should take her place. She doesn't know what's happening anyway.'

'Have some compassion, please!' I snap. I'm suddenly very irritable at their insensitivity, and feeling sad for the girl.

We drive straight to the groom's house. The gate leading to the house is being decorated with a white curtain with bands of red, blue, and green across it: it is to bring good luck. Inside, men are struggling to carry the marriage gifts down a narrow set of stairs – three sacks of barley, a newly slaughtered cow, two sheep, ten jars of barley wine, five large bricks of tea, seven tubs of butter, a set of clothes for every member of the bride's family, and a small mountain of white scarves. When we enter the house, it is like being backstage at a theatre, all the actors donning their finery, with the help of a retinue. The groom's father is lost in a heap of snow-white suede decorated at its edges with leopard skin; his daughter, his wife and another man are trying to assist him. The groom's uncle stands there passively while the groom's grandmother ties a belt around the waist of his long gown.

At the edge of it all, a young man leans against the window, looking pale and sullen. He's wearing jeans, a black leather jacket and a khaki hat – so trendy he would blend in perfectly on the streets of Shanghai, New York, or London. He is handsome but has the air of someone who would like to be somewhere else, with his pals, listening to rap music or watching a kung-fu movie; anywhere but here. He is twirling a stick in his hand absent-mindedly, dropping it and picking it up. He does not so much as glance at the high-spirited wedding party. I turn to Roten. He nods, and whispers, 'That's the groom.'

I know Tseten thinks he and the girl are a perfect match, but I must confess I cannot see any sign of their compatibility. As the Tibetans say, they look as different as milk and charcoal. She is more of a mother figure, and he looks so much like a child – far too young to be married. Judging from his sulkiness, I don't think that he is too keen on the idea either.

I try to interview him. His name is Gyatso, the same as the Rikzin boy. I ask how he is, and how he feels on his wedding day. What is his impression of the girl? He takes little notice of the questions. He tells me his age, then drops his head and does not utter another word. A few minutes later, he abruptly walks out. Through the window, I watch him walk away from the house in the direction of the mountains, taking the family's flock of sheep with him.

'Gyatso does not want the bride,' Penpa tells me, after a short conversation with the groom's father. 'But his parents have insisted, so he's agreed. Poor fellow.' I have never seen Penpa so concerned for anyone. He is as sorry for Gyatso as I was for Dolkar. Of course, I also feel sorry for Gyatso; it is just as unfair for him. But at least he knows about the wedding, even though his protest is futile. This is why he took off for the mountains, as far from the wedding as possible. But then he will have to come back, change, and wait for the wedding party to bring him his bride. Or will he? Will he run away? I wonder to myself.

We trail behind the wedding party to the home of the bride's family, who are waiting eagerly. After presenting their gifts, the groom's family proceed to put on a show of pleading with the parents for their daughter's hand. They drink endless cups of *chang*. I cannot see the bride anywhere. I ask her younger sister, who says Dolkar is staying with a relative nearby; she was told the news by her brother-in-law three days ago, and since then, all she has done is cry. She does not want to eat or talk. Still, I want to go and see if we can film her. Can she take me to her?

'You don't need me to take you. Once you get outside, just listen. You'll hear her crying.'

I go outside, and sure enough I can hear Dolkar's wailing from a hundred yards away. The dog barks non-stop, as if to keep her company. I stand by the gate, listening, but not knowing what to make of her heartbreaking cries. I am thinking of Gyatso, alone in the mountains, kicking a stone, slashing the ground with his stick. Is she wailing because she is sad about leaving her family? Because she has not chosen him herself? Or is she crying because this is what tradition expects of a girl on her wedding day? Whatever it is, I do not think I can talk to her now, let alone film her. I go back inside.

At eight o'clock in the evening, Dolkar is brought back to her family's house. Hearing her cries, I go out to watch her approach – she is doubled up with grief, dragged along by her two older sisters, a scarf covering her face. She is ushered into the tiny storage room where they keep firewood and grain. A flow of women, from the village and beyond, go in to comfort her. One of them, the bride's aunt, has been there since the morning and I have got to know her a little. I ask her what advice she gave Dolkar.

'I told her to stop crying,' the aunt says. 'It's fate. As a woman, the only way she can get out of marriage is by going to university. But she is not clever enough. So she just has to accept it. She will soon get used to it. Her husband is quiet, and if he is anything like his father, he will be hardworking and obedient to his wife. Besides, she is marrying into a rich family. What better can she ask for? So no more tears, I told her.'

'Then why does she keep crying?' I ask.

'It is the custom,' she explains with a kind smile, perhaps sensing my bewilderment. 'She has to cry otherwise people will think she cannot wait to leave her own family. I was like that too on my wedding day.'

I must say if I were in Dolkar's shoes, I would be crying for real.

Now the wedding guests are arriving in a steady stream, bringing sheep, sheets for the bride and groom, barley and *chang*, tea, and butter. The courtyard and the house fill with the sound of their laughter. But Dolkar is still wailing; no one seems to pay any attention. Then I notice an old woman going to the storage room. To my surprise she switches off the light inside and locks the door on Dolkar. Perhaps they still fear she will run away.

I join Mila in the prayer room, the only room with no visitors, where I can rest for a while and warm up. Mila asks me to sit next to him, and gives me a very welcome thick blanket – it was minus fifteen degrees outside. He has been praying and performing rituals since the afternoon. He has explained to me what they are for. He has to ask the god of the house and various other deities to bless the bride and her family, and not to be angry because the girl is leaving. He begs the god not to follow the bride, although he is very fond of her, and abandon the family, who cannot do without him. He even warns the god that the groom's family will not look after him as well as they do. I could hardly keep from smiling as I listened to Mila. What sort of god was this? He sounded very petty and jealous. I hope Mila manages to placate him. Dolkar will have enough to contend with in her new home; she will not want the groom's family to complain that her god has followed her, conflicting with theirs. For the same reason Tseten at this very moment is performing a similar ceremony in the house where the groom lives. The gods of each household must be cajoled into staying put.

It is almost midnight. Mila will take another three hours to finish the prayers. Only then, at three o'clock in the morning of the 14th, can the groom's family take the bride away. This is the auspicious hour calculated by Tseten – an hour which does not conflict with the horoscope of any family member on either side, so no harm can be done. It has been a long day, and while Mila chants, I fall asleep.

I wake up to the now familiar sound of Dolkar's wailing. I look around: Mila is gone, the room is empty, and the courtyard is in a commotion. The groom's family is finally taking the bride away, and I nearly miss it all. Fortunately, our Chinese camera-man Zhao Dong is vigilant and captures it on film. We make our way in the dark to the groom's house. There is a long delay while we wait for the groom's father and his party to bring the bride back. Custom demands that she stays in the open fields outside the village until dawn – despite the extreme cold, they have to carry out this ceremonial remembrance of the old times, when the bride could travel for days to reach her new home.

Finally the sun struggles up over the mountains and casts a pink glow over the frosty fields. The wedding party must be relieved to come into the warmth of the sitting room. The two families take their places on either side of the bride and groom. They sit there rather regally, receiving offerings and blessings from friends and relatives. The bride lies in the lap of her older sister, covered with white scarves; the groom stares absently about him. By the side of the groom's father, Tseten guides the ceremony step by step. Despite the long night, he retains his usual animation and grace. Once or twice, I catch him looking at the young couple. I wonder what he makes of the bride's silence and the groom's aloofness, but it does not seem to concern him.

A cheerful teenager in jeans and a silk jacket runs in and out of the room to see if he can be of any help. He is all smiles. I ask an old woman standing next to me, presumably a relative of the family, who he is and am told that is Gyatso's younger brother.

'He looks so happy – as though he were at his own wedding,' I say.

'How did you know?' the woman looks at me in surprise. 'It *is* his wedding.'

I am confused; I hadn't heard about this.

'He will share the bride with his brother when he finishes high school,' the woman tells me.

'Do you know whether he likes the bride?'

'You can see for yourself. I think he is very happy that his parents have found him such a good woman.'

'Suppose he goes to university?'

'That will be that. Then he will take another woman. This one will stay in the village.'

How complicated can a marriage be in this Tibetan village? I look at the bride, the groom, and the boy in jeans. Maybe they are perfect matches for each other, maybe Tseten is right. But to me this hardly seems like a happy start. No doubt everyone here would tell me I just don't understand.

SEVEN

One Wife, Three Husbands

I T IS TWO DAYS AFTER the wedding. I have recovered from thirty-six hours of continuous filming, but I am still in a state of mild shock. Is the marriage really going to work, as everyone keeps assuring me? Two brothers sharing a wife, and all three of them so young? I decide to go to the village and talk to Yangdron; after all, she has been through it herself. Perhaps she will set my mind at ease. We leave the cameraman at home. He is exhausted, and I am not sure she will answer our questions in front of the camera.

I have a long list of questions to ask, so I decide to bring some thing special for lunch, as well as an antibiotic for Yangdron's toothache. At the vegetable and meat market on Hero Road we buy a huge bull's head, complete with horns and hair, and put it in the car, all 14 kilos of it.

The sky is clear and blue, the trees are bare, and the farm animals are inside. The fields have been ploughed and watered – they are now glistening with ice, which keeps the ground moist and prevents the soil from being blown away. It is mid-November, and although it is warm in the day, the temperatures can drop to minus twenty degrees at night – punishingly cold, and particularly hard on the old and infirm. There have been three funerals in the valley so far this month.

I always enjoy the drive to the village. With the busy harvest over, other tasks and celebrations have started up again. We frequently stop to make way for carts carrying brightly dressed women and children, heading probably to yet another wedding. They wave to us cheerfully, as do a number of men and women building houses by the roadside, some making bricks, ankle-deep in mud.

'Would you mind asking the questions today? I'll translate,' Penpa says beseechingly. 'I'll be too embarrassed. Tibetans don't talk about these things. They just do it.' I say I will try my best. But I feel the same. So far, I have not asked our characters about their shared marriage – it seemed too personal. I have had to sit on my curiosity, and have tried to hide my amazement. How does it work? Why has shared marriage survived in Tibet when it has vanished almost everywhere else?

On previous visits to Tibet, I had seen little of rural life. I knew that polyandry existed here but I thought it might have been suppressed during the Cultural Revolution. The first law the Communist government passed in 1950 was a new marriage law. It forbids men taking more than one woman – a tradition that dated back over a thousand years. The official Chinese attitude to polyandry was summed up in a recent study: 'In polyandrous families women's status was embarrassing. They were physically ruined by primitive and barbarous habits and mentally tortured by feudal patriarchal authority. They did not have any equal rights because each of their husbands could dally with her, abuse her, and even beat her.'[40] The study used the past tense, as if polyandry had vanished. I thought, if anything, these marriages would only be found among older people, in a few isolated villages.

Yet here I am, seeing the Rikzin family almost daily. Not only that, nearly all the characters we have been following live in these multiple marriages – the sole exceptions are the three monks from the Palkhor Monastery and Lhamo, the village doctor, though our novice monk has four fathers and one mother. Shared marriages, I have learned, come in many variations. Lhakpa's two brothers share a wife, but he has found his own woman. Our hotel manager, Jianzang, and the builder, Rincheu, both left the woman they shared with their brothers in the village and each found a woman of their own in town. Some of the Tibetans in our crew – our housekeeper and our translator – also live in families of shared marriages. Even Pasang Butri, the head of the Women's Association in the valley, a Communist Party member, has four sons who share a wife.

We find Yangdron in the kitchen, stirring a huge pot of barley for *chang*. She is wearing a high-necked red shirt underneath her long black wool dress, with a black cloth over her woven apron, striped in shades of brown and pink. Loga is by her side, occasionally dipping his fingers into the pot and grabbing a few grains of barley. 'Are you celebrating something?' I ask Yangdron. 'If you are, here is our contribution to it.' Penpa and I lift the bull's head and hand it over to her.

She smiles. 'Tseten is out performing an exorcism for a new house, and Dondan has gone to a neighbour's. Dondan will prepare this for your lunch when he comes back,' she says. 'I'm making *chang* as a gift for the groom's family. They will be celebrating for fifteen days. We will go and share their happiness and we have to take them a proper gift. Normally, we would bring fifteen jars of *chang* and half a sheep, but because of the death in our family, I'm not sure how much is expected. I will have to discuss it with Dondan and Tseten. But it is going to be a lot so I have to get started now.'

I do not have to worry about finding the right moment to

ask my questions. Yangdron brings it up naturally: she asks me how I enjoyed the wedding.

I tell her I didn't find it very joyful, with the bride crying her heart out the whole time, and the groom looking so uninvolved, while another groom-to-be was waiting his turn. 'I wondered how happy they were going to be,' I say. I know this is not the right thing to say, that it will sound ill-omened to her; but I can't help myself.

'You worry too much,' she says, gently. 'It was just the same for me. Nobody told me who I was marrying or what the family was like. I was even younger than Dolkar, just seventeen. I can't even remember who was at my side during the ceremony, Loga or Dondan. I cried throughout the wedding. But it all worked out.'

I ask whether anyone had told her that Loga was not normal.

'No, no one said a word. You can imagine my shock,' Yangdron says. Nobody told her she was going to marry Tseten either, who was twelve at the time. 'But it is the custom for brothers to share a wife,' she says, matter-of-factly.

When did she and Tseten become man and wife?

'When Tseten was nineteen, Dondan asked me whether I objected to the idea that Tseten join us,' she explains. 'I did not say yes or no. So Dondan took it as a yes.' Yangdron looks a little flustered. She gets up to take some barley out of the pot and let it cool. But she does add that there was no ceremony or celebration, nor did they get a marriage certificate. Dondan conveniently went away for a week to visit some relatives.

'What is it like to be married to the three brothers?' I ask, going straight to the point.

'You can see Loga is different from us,' Yangdron says, gesturing to him. Loga watches us as though he were hearing an interesting story, with no idea that we are talking about him.

'There are many things he can't do. When we're harvesting,

he might cut himself on a sickle, and he can't plough straight. He can't really be trusted with any tools. We have twenty sheep, but he can't recognise them. If our sheep get mixed up with others, which happens easily, Loga is completely lost. He took them out a few times, and came back home with only half a dozen. Sheep are just too complicated for him. But feeding the cows he can just about manage when I get the fodder ready. We have ten and they stay in the yard. There is no chance of their getting lost.'

Loga lifts the lid of the pot again to grab a handful of barley, but it's too hot, and he drops it on the table. Yangdron speaks to him softly, perhaps remonstrating with him, and tells him to go and fetch water. This is the task we have most often seen him occupied with. He sometimes returns with water soaking his sweater and his trousers, and I think he must feel the cold, but I have never heard him complain, not once. But today he wants to stay with us rather than fetch the water. Yangdron talks to him sweetly, and he reluctantly stands up, takes the brass barrel from under the water container, grins at us, and goes out.

'I'm grateful that he does this, as it is quite a lot of work. We need about fifteen barrels of water a day for the household and the animals. It took the family three months to teach him how to do it. At first he nearly fell into the well, and then he often dropped the barrel into it; or he would splash most of the water on himself, and there would be hardly any left in the barrel when he got it home. But finally he mastered it.'

'Do they talk to each other much?' I ask her.

'He likes talking, but not always to me, and sometimes about things you'd rather keep in the family,' she says. 'He repeats things he hears at home, the arguments, the discussions, money matters. He is like a child really. It can be embarrassing.' I knew the sort of thing she meant. A week ago some visitors came to the house, and Loga was excited by the crowd. In the kitchen

Yangdron poured them butter tea. Loga wanted to give them *chang*, but *chang* is only served to relatives and close friends. It was hard to explain this to Loga in front of everybody, so Yangdron just said the *chang* was not ready. He got agitated, insisted Yangdron was wrong, repeating, 'It is ready, it is!' It was all very awkward.

There are so many things I'm curious about, though I'm not quite sure how to ask. Does Loga know who Yangdron is? That she is his wife? Do they have a sexual relationship? Has he ever asked for sexual favours? Does he have the capacity? Just then Loga comes back with the water. Yangdron gets up, takes the barrel from his back, and tips it into the huge brass container that stands behind the kitchen door. I ask him to come and sit near the stove so he can warm his hands. Penpa moves closer to Loga, and teases him, 'You've been very good today. Yangdron is going to let you sleep in her bed tonight. Do you like the idea?' Loga just laughs, though I doubt he knows what Penpa means.

'What are you all laughing about?' Dondan asks. He comes into the kitchen with his hair and his khaki jacket almost completely white with dust. Everyone looks up. Yangdron helps him off with his jacket and fills a plastic basin with soap and water. While he washes himself, he tells us that their neighbours are building a new house. They've run out of bricks due to a miscalculation and wanted his advice about how to speed up their work. Yangdron listens attentively, and they talk for a while. Then she pours him a cup of *chang*, his favourite drink, and points to the bull's head on the floor: 'They brought this specially for you. So you are in charge of preparing lunch today.' Dondan gulps down the *chang*, and takes the head, a chopper, and a board outside to get it ready. Yangdron follows him with more *chang*, and Loga trails after her with a huge metal platter.

When she gets back I decide to broach the subject of Dondan with her.

'Dondan was my first man,' Yangdron says happily. 'Two years after the wedding our first boy arrived. The second came not long after.' Twenty years on, they seem very content. He does most of the work on the family's six acres. She helps him whenever she is needed, mostly during the planting and the harvest; the rest of the time she cooks, cleans, washes, looks after the children, serves Tseten's patients, feeds the cows, milks them, makes butter, makes cowpats for the stove, makes thread from the sheep's wool, and weaves blankets. 'There's no need to tell Dondan what to do or to pester him. He always does what has to be done,' Yangdron says appreciatively. 'If we need to buy something for the household, we discuss it between us and then ask Tseten for his opinion. When it comes to work, Dondan and I make the decisions.'

Like all Tibetan men, Yangdron says, Dondan drinks, and gets drunk sometimes. 'But he has never lost his temper with me, not once, and he has never raised his hand to me. When he's drunk he simply curls up and falls into a deep sleep,' Yangdron says. Occasionally they argue about small household details. 'I'm sure you do too, even in your educated families,' she says, pointing at me and Penpa. 'We argue now and then about the children, the way they behave, or what they should do. But it never gets bad between us. He is a good man, a good father.' After a pause, she murmurs, 'I suppose Dondan and I are very close. I don't have to stand on ceremony with him.'

Sometimes I get the feeling there are only the two of them in the marriage. There was a moment between them not too long ago that has stayed with me. Dondan was sewing the soles for a pair of shoes out of six layers of felt, the only work in the house women do not do; the soles are simply too tough. Yangdron was sitting next to him, spinning wool from their sheep. Watching them gave me a warm feeling; they seemed to be in complete harmony, chatting away and laughing. I had brought them some oranges, and Dondan peeled one, sniffed the skin, and ate a segment, savouring it, licking the juice from his lips with a look of great pleasure – fruit of any kind is a rarity in their household. But then this hefty, six-foot-three man broke off another segment in his big hands, and passed it to Yangdron. She took it with a tender, grateful smile.

Perhaps I'm reading too much into these small scenes. I want to ask her more, but just then Penpa says he is hungry. Yangdron picks up the kettle with more water for Dondan and we go out to check on his progress with the bull's head. The horns have been taken off, and put aside. They will be made into snuff bottles for someone. The skin has been removed carefully too – it can be used later for mending, or dried to cover straw baskets, turning them into the handsome containers I've seen women carrying in the village. Now Dondan carefully inserts the knife along the cheekbones and drags it around the skull. He is meticulous, even pulling out the grass that was stuck between the bull's teeth, and rubbing off the black stains on its gums with an old toothbrush. Yangdron pours water for him while he washes the blood off each piece of meat and bone. She suggests she cook the half he has cleaned, while he continues with the rest. She's worried that otherwise lunch will take too long.

Suddenly I hear a cart clattering to a halt down below. 'It's Tseten,' Dondan tells us. 'The owner of the house he went to bless has brought him back.' Sure enough, Tseten climbs up the stairs in his pink robe and trilby hat, carrying his drum and cymbals. 'What's this big lunch for?' he asks. 'No occasion,' Dondan says. 'Except that they have brought it specially for us.'

I take the drum from Tseten and follow him into the kitchen. Yangdron gets out his wooden cup with its silver lid, wipes it with a towel, pours him some tea and hands it to him. She is very respectful, even reverential towards him, as if she were a servant with her master. I chat with Tseten about all the goings-on we had encountered on the road. 'You're right,' he says. 'I have two more weddings to preside over this week.' And every new house in the valley will need his blessing before the construction can start. And the winter weather always brings more funerals. But now he must take a rest as he was up early in the morning. He heads to the prayer room.

Tseten always seems so relaxed with us, but I mention to Yangdron that she is rather formal with him, not like she is with Dondan.

'Tseten is different from us. He is a shaman, more knowledgeable than us. I respect him.'

'Do the two of you argue?'

'No, he treats me well. We never quarrel. Sometimes he tells me off though.'

'Why?'

'Oh, just little things. He has patients coming to see him every day. He might be bothered if I'm too busy with housework to bring them tea right away. Other times I cannot find the things he asks for. He gets annoyed. Apart from that, we get on fine.'

'Now that he is here, why don't you ask him to treat your toothache? Do you not trust his healing?' I ask her, thinking of the antibiotic she requested this morning. As often as not, when we enquire whether the family wants us to bring them anything, Yangdron asks for medicine.

'You can see how busy he is. When he is home, he is often tired.'

'Not too busy and tired to hold your beautiful face in his hands and kiss you,' Penpa says, joking. He's referring to Tseten's most common method of curing toothache – reciting mantras and spitting on the patient's face.

I asked Tseten once whether he treated Yangdron. He said, 'I give her my pills. Often she won't wait for them to work. Once when she was in pain from a wisdom tooth, she went and had it pulled and her face swelled up like a balloon. The whole village laughed at her.' Perhaps he was also thinking of his own reputation. Then he added, 'Sometimes you do not have the same power with people close to you, especially if they have doubts.'

While the pressure cooker with half the bull's head is hissing away on the stove, Yangdron visits Tseten's room several times to refresh his tea cup. And then she goes out and puts the water from the boiled barley into the vat where they throw left-over food, and mixes some more barley in. She asks Loga to take this out to feed the cows. When she returns I ask if she thinks she could live with just one husband. Penpa nudges me, to warn me that I am pushing my luck.

Yangdron is direct. 'In the village, if you want a decent life, it is better to have more than one man,' she explains. 'If Loga could handle them, we could have more sheep and take them to the mountains in the summer; we would have more meat and wool, and also have some to sell. Then you need several pairs of hands for planting and harvesting. That falls to Dondan and me. We have Tseten making a bit of cash. That takes care of a lot of our expenses. A family with one man will find it hard to get by.'

Yangdron takes the lid off the pressure cooker, and there is a burst of steam. It's 3 p.m. and the bull's head is finally ready. Loga jumps up and down, clapping his hands like a child. Yangdron tells him to go and call Tseten and Dondan. She hands us all small plates and bowls, and dishes out the meat. I take a piece in my hand, and dip it in a bowl of chilli sauce she has made. The meat was cooked just with water and salt; I cannot believe how delicious it is. Yangdron does not start eating herself, but begins making *tsampa* for us – squeezing it into sausage shapes in a small leather bag and handing one to each of us.

Just watching the men sitting around her to get their food, it is clear that Yangdron is the central pillar of the household.

There is a Tibetan saying: 'A good family is one where the brothers share a woman; a good wife is one who unites the brothers.' I still have to ask Dondan and Tseten what they think of her, but clearly she holds them together. She is the strong one.

My first introduction to the unique status of Tibetan women was the popular fifteenth-century novel *The Monkey King*. It tells the adventures of a monk, in the company of a monkey, a pig, and a novice, on his journey to India and back. They have to go through a female kingdom, supposedly in Tibet, where there are no men, and where women conceive by drinking from a river called 'Mother and Child'. The queen falls in love with the humble but erudite monk Xuanzang at first sight. She offers him her beauty, her kingdom, and her love. But he has to turn her down in order to continue his search for the true teachings of the Buddha.

I was a child when I heard the story. I wished I was in that kingdom. The Chinese view of the opposite sex was poles apart. My Communist father, despite the official creed that women are 'half the sky', believed they could not be the equal of men. He accepted Confucius's dictum: of the three worst failings of a son, not producing an heir is the most grave. When I was born, the third daughter in a family with no sons, my father did not even bother to collect my mother and myself from the hospital, in the freezing cold month of December. I was a girl, and unwanted. My father's neglect, and his constant beatings, made me want to run away. I even started collecting the tiny sum I got for the Chinese New Year, along with the hair my mother cut, scrap metal – anything I could sell to the rag-and-bone man. I wanted to be in a place where I was appreciated and loved.

Later I read many travellers' accounts which record the high status Tibetan women enjoyed. Kawaguchi, a Japanese monk who spent three years in Lhasa in the early twentieth century, was particularly impressed by what he observed: 'The condition of Tibetan women with regard to men, especially in the provinces, may be considered to surpass the ideal of Western women, so far as the theory of equality of rights between the sexes is concerned.'[41] The rights that Kawaguchi noted included: that to a share of her father's property, which she could keep if she left her marriage; compensation from her husband for the work she did for him; and the right to marry again without stigma. Such things were unthinkable in the China or Japan of a hundred years ago, or even today; no wonder Kawaguchi was so struck by them. At the same time, as a Japanese, he thought that Tibetan women's freedom made them 'loose'. 'They lack weight and dignity, such as command respect from others,' he wrote, patronisingly. They 'are prone to flirt and to be flippant … one [might] say they are more like ballet-girls than ladies of high station'.[42]

I mention to Penpa and Tseten what the Japanese monk had written. 'Perhaps our women were too strong for him,' Penpa replies.

Tseten wants to know what a 'ballet-girl' is. When Penpa explains, he bursts out laughing. 'You said he was a Buddhist?' he asks, of Kawaguchi. 'A cheerful woman makes a cheerful family. What's wrong with that?'

I have always wondered why Tibetan women enjoy such respect. I ask Tseten and Dondan. 'You know, many of our important deities are women,' Tseten says. 'Tara for example – she is our favourite goddess, you see her in all the temples, the monasteries, in people's houses – we believe she can answer all our prayers. We recite her mantra all the time. Ghosts and devils don't dare to harm us – as soon as they hear the mantra, they think the deity is descending, and they run away.'

'Palden Lhamo is another important female deity,' Tseten

adds. 'You know we have guardian gods to protect the dharma. She is the only female deity entrusted with the task.'

I have seen her statue in the Jokang Temple in Lhasa, covered with cloth. The guidebook says she is frightening to look at, but is extremely powerful. Reading up about her later I discover she really had special powers: she was the protector of the old Tibetan government, of Lhasa, and the Dalai Lama. She was even allowed to criticise the old government. Once a year during the New Year celebrations a woman sang in the streets of Lhasa, songs full of dirt about the rich and powerful: who was taking bribes, who was courting whom. Then the songs spread, and the dark secrets of the hated elites that ran the country were exposed; the people had their moment of power, however limited. This woman was regarded as an oracle, possessed by Palden Lhamo, so no one could harm her.

'But Palden Lhamo is a bit naughty,' Penpa grins, adding 'she has a lover, though she can only see him once a year. The day is coming up in two weeks' time.'

I am not sure I can trust Penpa, so I look to Tseten for confirmation. He nods his head.

'So what will happen when she goes to see her lover?'

'Palden Lhamo – or at least her statue from the Jokang Temple – will be carried by monks to the bank of the Lhasa River,' Penpa explains. 'Thousands of people will have gathered there. On the opposite bank will be a statue of her lover, carried by monks from another temple. They are allowed only a glance at each other before they are hurried away and returned to their "palaces". Remember, on this day, I guess we can call it Tibetan women's day, like Valentine's Day, a woman can ask any man for a present, even a stranger, and he cannot refuse. My wife and her girlfriends collected nearly 4,000 *yuan* last year from the men in their office alone, and they had a great time.'

It is hard to imagine that such a deity could ever exist in the vast Chinese canon of Buddhas and Bodhisattvas, gods and goddesses. It would be scandalous, they would think her place was in hell. In temples across China, I see stone tablets, no doubt very Confucian interpretations of the scriptures, telling women how the Bodhisattvas want them to be good and obedient daughters to their fathers, wives to their husbands, and mothers to their sons. The ones who are really good, those who follow their husbands to the grave, or never so much as look at other men, will go down in their clan's history as 'virtuous women' and be rewarded with a place in the Western Paradise. If a man required a woman to bind her feet in order to please them, she should do it willingly. If he wanted several wives, she should be pleased for him. These practices have gone from China now, but their shadow remains. And nowhere have I read of Tibetan women ever being subjected to such subordination. They were always more liberated than we have ever been.

Yangdron listens to the conversation with the greatest of interest, and then says: 'But still our word for woman, *skye-dman*, means "low birth".' I look up at her. She is serene as always, but I notice how deep the lines are on her forehead. With her responsibilities comes an endless burden of work. I must say I feel ashamed listening to Yangdron talk about managing three husbands, four children, six acres of land, ten cows, and twenty sheep. We are roughly the same age, and I find it hard enough to manage my work and one husband, let alone two or three. Perhaps in my keen admiration for her freedom, especially when compared with that of my fellow Chinese, I am forgetting that like any society, Tibet is still male dominated.

In fact it is not hard to find Buddhist texts that put women down. 'Women's bodies are vessels of pain, and women's minds are vessels of suffering.'[43] That is why women are cursed with thirty-two extra illnesses that men do not have. Women are

124

seven lifetimes behind men: they must accumulate the merit of seven additional lifetimes before they can be reborn as men.[44] A survey among Tibetans living near Labrang, one of the most important Tibetan monasteries in Gansu, revealed that the locals still look at nuns as having 'inferior intelligence, excessive attachment and uncontrollable desires, therefore they are less efficacious in performing ritual services for the laity'.[45]

'You must know the story of Nangsa. Her village is not far from here, by the Nyangchu River. You see it on the way to Shigatse,' Yangdron says, handing me a cup of Chinese tea and the others their butter tea.

I indeed know the story and love it. I first saw it performed as a Tibetan opera, with half a dozen actors in masks, in a monastery outside Gyantse soon after I arrived. I could not understand it, but the expressions on the audience's faces showed how moved they were, laughing, crying, fearful, jubilant – one old woman even prostrated half-way through. Afterwards, talking to some of them, I understood why.

The story is set in Gyantse in the twelfth century. Nangsa is a young woman 'as pretty as a peacock, as melodious as a song bird, as radiant as a rainbow'. She catches the eye of the powerful lord of the region named Dagchen, who forces her to marry his son, Dakpa Samdup. His sister is very jealous and invents a malicious lie – that Nangsa has taken a beggar as her lover. Her husband believes it and nearly beats her to death. Nangsa decides to renounce the world. Her son pleads with her not to leave him:

> Without you mother,
> I am like a bird with clipped wings;
> Trying to soar high,
> It plummets to the ground.

To which she replies:

> Do not cling to me as the swift fish does to the lake,
> Like the lake I will dry up in the drought.
> Better you rely on the ocean.[46]

Finally Nangsa leaves home and finds a lama who will take her on as a disciple. Even then there is a fight – Lord Dagchen brings his army and attacks the lama's monastery, killing many monks; but the lama's supernatural skills make him submit. Finally Nangsa can do what she had always wanted: devote her life to the dharma.

Nangsa is one of the most popular Tibetan operas. It is also told as a story at home on long winter nights, or by storytellers in market places. I can see why – the beauty of Nangsa, the injustices, and eventually, redemption – but now I also see it must reflect the experiences of many Tibetan women, then and now. It gives them an example, something to help them transcend their lot. As ever, Yangdron has deftly given me her perspective.

'Why are women thought to be so inferior?' I ask the men.

'I don't know,' Penpa says, shaking his head. He turns to Tseten. 'Do you think it might be our creation legend?' he asks, hesitantly.

The creation legend is very familiar to me. I have always thought it was like a mixture of Darwin, and Adam and Eve. It begins with a monkey who is the incarnation of the Goddess of Compassion. He is kind and idealistic and vows to be celibate. There is also a female incarnation, a she-devil, cunning and selfish, and uncontrollable. She cannot live in solitude so she wants the monkey to be her husband. She begs and begs, until the monkey consults the Goddess of Compassion, who tells him that Tibet should have its own children. The monkey marries the she-devil, and they have six children; these children are said to be the ancestors of the Tibetans.

So even in their creation story the male is virtuous, the female unruly and devious. But at least, if that is where Tibetan women have come from, they have proven themselves to deserve the kind of respect that they enjoy today, even though it is far short of equality.

I still have more questions for the family, but after such a big lunch, and my long interrogation, they want a rest. Well, except for Yangdron. She sits down in the courtyard with a big pile of dirty clothes – a week's worth of laundry for the whole family. She just does not stop. No wonder the Tibetans have a saying: 'Children's feet have calluses from following the sheep; men's bottoms have them from sitting too long and drinking; women's hands have them from working.'

I decide to use the lunch break to go and see Pasang Butri, the head of the local Women's Association. We get into the car and head off for Village No. 4, the headquarters of Karmad *xiang*, which includes all twelve villages in the valley. Butri has told me about a coming Women's Association meeting, with each family in the twelve villages sending one woman. They hold it every year in winter, when the villagers have more time. She has not told me what it would be about, but I imagine it will be fascinating to film.

I chose Butri, a tall, forceful and cheerful woman of fifty, to be in our film. I wanted someone in government but also someone working at grass-roots level, so that we could see how rural Tibet is run. I have not been disappointed. So far we have filmed some very strong stories with her. We caught her mediating between two drunken men who came to her office after a fight, one with blood still dripping from his scalp. She took them to the *xiang* clinic, scolding them like a mother, rather than a Party official: 'Why can't you be like a man? Stop this stupid nonsense. You have given me so much trouble. If you don't listen, I will send you to the police.' In another she was in charge of getting a school built. The contractor tried to cut corners by mixing a lot of sand in with his cement. 'Have you ever thought your greed could put the children's lives at risk? You could go to hell for it,' she shouted in his face. Her biggest headache, however, is keeping an eye on the six nunneries and monasteries in the valley. The monks and nuns are supposed to ask her for leave every time they travel for more than three days, but they do not. 'Why are you so troublesome?' she ranted against the frightened nuns. 'Why don't you think of me? You give me more worries than all my other work put together. You're supposed to have compassion.'

The *xiang* headquarters is fifteen minutes' drive from the Rikzin house. Amidst traditional houses stands a compound with two brand new buildings, covered with pink and white tiles, and enormous glass windows. The reflections are blinding. The offices are for meetings; the one-storey building at the back houses the twelve officials who run the *xiang*. It is deserted today, as usual. Half the officials, including the Party Secretary, live in Gyantse and only come down when they have to. The others follow their example. But someone is always on duty in case something crops up, at least on weekdays. Butri is often the one, because she is low in the hierarchy. She does not seem to mind – especially when she has company.

The man is there today. He is the headman of Village No. 3, and former Party Secretary of Karmad *xiang*. He is quite elderly, short and ruddy faced, and always eyes us with suspicion. He and Butri are drinking together in her office, and Penpa gives me a sidelong glance, as if to say, 'See, I told you.'

'Oh, come and join us,' Butri says, not at all embarrassed. 'Let me get you a cup.' She goes over to the cupboard, takes out three cups, and polishes them with her apron, and pours out *chang* for me, Penpa and the driver.

I ask her if she has decided on the theme and the date of the women's meeting. 'Oh, that is nothing for a capable woman like her,' her companion replies. 'She could be really high up if she had been educated.' He looks at her with affection, and then adds: 'I'm going to leave you. I have to pop into the clinic to get some medicine.'

'We could come back another time,' I offer.

'Don't worry, he'll be back,' Butri says with a smile, and goes on to tell me her plan for next week's meeting. She has invited a senior woman official from Gyantse: 'I've asked her if she could bring leaflets and some presents to give the women activists in the villages. That would make my life easier.'

'Will she be speaking at the meeting?' I ask.

'Yes. Telling them not to have too many babies. And when they are having one, they should go to the clinic to deliver it. We have the largest number of newborn babies this year in the whole of Gyantse County. Not good.'

I ask her why.

'We are the poorest *xiang* in Gyantse, with the highest infant mortality. The families need to be sure.'

Is there a target for her? In the rest of China she would have to achieve the one-child family by whatever means – it would really make her a hate figure. Escaping that must be a relief.

'Yes,' she nods. 'Birth control is advised here, not compulsory. But three children are what we recommend.'

'Three for each husband or the whole family?' Penpa asks.

'For the family, of course. What do you think?'

But the marriage law does not permit more than one husband, I say. I can see the law does not seem to hold around here, although Tibetans working for the government and as Party officials are not allowed shared marriages – they can lose their jobs.

'It is our tradition, and people are happy with it. They don't

129

register with us anyway. So we let them be.' Butri does not seem troubled by what the law says. She goes on: 'In the old days, we could control them by cutting off their rations. In my generation there were very few polyandrous families. They were not allowed, but there also was no need. Everything belonged to the commune, the land, the cows, and the sheep. However hard you worked, you didn't get more. You got just one ration from the commune, so you were no better off in a shared marriage. Brothers began to share a wife when the land was given back to the farmers in the economic reform in the 1980s. Now they all feed themselves and they don't always listen to us.'

I do not know how Butri expects people to listen when she does not set an example. Her own four sons share a wife; it was she who told me – though she also told me two of them have found women they love and that they want to move out. 'They fight like tigers; the house is like a battlefield. I cannot really keep them all under one roof any more.' I do not know whether to sympathise or not. Her sons have only followed their hearts, like she did herself.

But I have heard many similar stories. Our housekeeper gives me regular updates about her troubled family. Her three brothers have a wife in common, and the wife prefers the middle brother, a successful trader. The older brother has gone off and found another woman; he rarely comes home. According to our housekeeper, their aunt told the wife: 'I warned you; you should not be picky. You should have jumped into bed with each of them and kept them happy. Now he is sleeping with someone else, and nobody says a bad word about him. They all blame you for driving him away. You have made the whole village laugh at us.'

I ask Butri my last question before I go, very conscious the former Party Secretary is waiting impatiently in the clinic for us to leave. 'How many women will be coming to your conference? And when should we turn up?'

'Every family must send one woman, or even a man. If not, they will be fined 5 *yuan*,' she says firmly. For a moment she reminds me again how tough she can be. It seems that if it is clearly Party business, she can impose her will. Otherwise she will let it go. Drinking with her lover in her office, her sons sharing a wife? No problem. I wonder what Yangdron and the women at the meeting next week would think if they knew.

As we say goodbye to her, she takes Penpa aside and talks to him in a hushed voice. I tell him I will wait for him in the car.

'You know what?' says Penpa when he joins me. 'She wonders if we can help her find some money. She's got to build two houses for her breakaway sons.'

I can see it will put a huge strain on Butri and her family. She has worked for the Party for years, but her salary is only 1,000 *yuan*, or £70, a month. The locals have a saying: 'A broken-up family will be two beggars.' But it is really hard for us to help. We must not appear to be 'buying' her; it is professionally unacceptable and also it would change our relationship with her and make filming very difficult. I tell Penpa I will have to think about it.

Yangdron still has not reached the bottom of the dirty-clothes pile when we get back to the house. I tell her a bit about Butri and her coming meeting. 'She's told the village about the meeting already. She is good.' If she has her own thoughts about Butri, she is not going to tell me. She does not gossip and she does not like to speak ill of others. The morning's conversation showed me how discreet she is. I am sure that is a crucial skill for balancing husbands.

I leave Yangdron in the courtyard and go into the kitchen. Dondan is by himself, spinning thread. With some apprehension, I start on my last questions, the most sensitive ones. Is he happy with Yangdron as a wife, and how does the sleeping arrangement work? And the children? As if he has been expecting the questions all along, Dondan answers without hesitation: 'I think she is good,' he says, and pauses. 'I think she is *very* good.'

'What is their relationship like?' I ask.

'She loves me very much. She is very close to me.'

'How do the sleeping arrangements work?' Penpa asks.

'Mila is over there,' Dondan says, and points to the bed furthest away, near the line of cupboards along the wall. 'Loga is here, and I am in between the two of them.'

'Where are Yangdron and Tseten?' Penpa and I ask, almost in unison.

'Tseten sleeps in the prayer room,' Dondan says. 'Sometimes Mila sleeps there too. Yangdron is in a separate room. In the winter she sleeps in here sometimes, because it is warmer.'

'Is there a way you and Tseten will discuss whose turn it is and let Yangdron know, like leaving a shoe outside?' Penpa asks vaguely. He is trying to be sensitive for once, or else he is embarrassed to ask. In some families, he has told me, the wife has a separate room; one of the brothers visits each night – or they all do, one after another, but that is rare. Others share a room with the eldest husband and can go and spend time with one of the brothers, but return to him.

'There is no such question,' Dondan says emphatically.

'But won't there be clashes otherwise?'

'We don't have such problems in this house. You just have to use your head.'

I do not think we are likely to get more from Dondan so we go into the prayer room, where Tseten is making amulets. No one is ever idle. To my surprise, Tseten's answers could not be more different. 'What do I think of Yangdron?' he says. 'Let's say she is somewhere in the middle as a wife.'

'But you spend so much time away from home,' Penpa puts

in. 'Won't the two of them be the husband and wife, leaving you out?' Tseten has told us that he was even thinking of moving his practice to Gyantse, where he could earn more money and do more to help pay for the children's college fees.

'That is fine with me, as long as they are happy,' Tseten replies.

'Would you find another woman then?'

'I have no such plan.'

I ask him about the children. Do they know who their father is? It seems fairly obvious in Dondan's and Tseten's case, as there are only two brothers, eleven years apart in age. Jigme and Gyatso must be Dondan's, while Tseyang and Kunga are Tseten's. Still I ask him whether they do know.

'Ask Dondan,' he says. 'He is the one they call father. They call Loga and me uncle. But we are the same with each of them, as they are with us.'

Clearly this question hardly arises for them. When I put it to Yangdron in the morning, she even sounded slightly irritated for the first time in our conversation. 'Dondan and Tseten treat them all the same. There is no difference. You see how hard Tseten worked to get loans for Jigme and Gyatso to pay their college fees.' She is right. Whatever Tseten has to do for whichever child, he does it with a smile. He is only twelve years older than Jigme, the oldest of the children, but he is like a father even to him, and is respected as such.

When we leave the house, Penpa turns to me and says: 'You owe me quite a few bottles of beer tonight.' I know what he means. That conversation was among the most delicate and potentially difficult of the whole year, but also the most interesting and intimate. Before this talk, Mila, Dondan, Tseten and Yangdron had always been helpful and responsive to our questions, but still I felt we were on the outside of things, just observers. Now we have been through a lot of experiences with them – their mother's death, the harvest, seeing the two boys off to college – and we have gained their trust enough for them to begin to open their hearts. It is like a mountain off my back.

When we come back to film the same interviews later on, the family retains the same openness in front of the camera – remarkable, on such sensitive matters, for people who had probably never voiced these thoughts before, even to themselves. After the filming, I decide to take some still photographs. In the kitchen, Yangdron and the brothers sit side by side – Yangdron on a stool on the left, then Dondan on a higher one, winding some woollen thread round a spindle, then Tseten and Loga on a bench in front of the green kitchen cupboards with a mirror above them. The cameraman shoots in bursts, chatting with them the whole time. More often than not, Loga grins too hard, or covers his face with his hands or looks unnaturally sombre, so we have to repeat the shots. Finally, we get a really good one – everyone is smiling, Yangdron stares straight at the camera, Dondan looks down at his spindle, and the other two look up towards him as though he has just said something funny. They are happy together, natural, serene, and at ease with each other, a harmonious family.

I suggest we take some more pictures outside in the yard; everyone agrees, and we all stand up and file out of the kitchen. As we head down the stairs, Yangdron tugs at my shirt and I stop. She comes up close to me, and whispers shyly in my ear: 'Do you think I could have one just of Dondan and me?'

EIGHT

The Woman, the Goat, and the Chang

T HE TIBETAN NEW YEAR, the Year of the Golden Pig, is drawing closer. I ask all our characters about their plans. Rincheu, the builder, will buy four whole sheep to entertain his big extended family and business friends. Lhakpa, the poor rickshaw driver, can only afford sheep's heads, but he says they symbolise an auspicious start to the year, and he has invited us to watch him and his two brothers clean nine of them, three white and six black. Jianzang, the hotel keeper, is preparing the most elegant *chiemar*, a basket filled with barley, *tsampa*, candies and dried sweet yoghurt. If I take one item from it, I am supposed to enjoy a year of abundance. Tsephun, the novice monk, will join half a dozen others to make 540 fried naans, their offerings to the Buddhas and Bodhisattvas, and treats for themselves.

I asked Dondan what are his family's plans to celebrate. He said their New Year would be quiet due to the death of their mother, but they would come to Gyantse for the Winter Fair. 'We have to come. We will buy everything we need for the new year. You will like it too,' Dondan said, adding that the fair was particularly good last year. People from the neighbouring counties packed the three major streets of Gyantse. The County Singing and Dancing Troupe kick-started the day by putting on a big show at the foot of the fort. After the entertainment came the buying and selling: prayer flags, incense, cow and sheep heads, carpets, *pulu* (woollen cloth) for making Tibetan jackets, posters of the late Panchen Lama and various Buddhas and Bodhisattvas, DVDs of Tibetan and Chinese pop songs, firecrackers, plants, butter and yoghurt, sweets and biscuits, fruit. Everything was there, fun and food.

Immediately I see the Winter Fair will be wonderful for our film. It will bring all our characters together, which does not happen often. I set about organising things, calling everyone up, finding out their exact days at the fair, taking on an extra cameraman to cover the show. We just manage to get everything ready on the day the fair is supposed to open – ten days before the Tibetan New Year. But there is no sign of any show, just a few more stalls than usual in the streets. We ask around, but nobody seems to know what is going on. Wandering in the street, I run into a crestfallen Lhakpa. This time last year, he said, he made 80 *yuan* a day, carrying a stream of customers and their mountains of purchases. So far, he has only had four people and made 8 *yuan*. 'I have been looking forward to this since the summer. Now what do I do? I haven't got any money for the new year. What is going on?'

I wish I knew.

Finally, a week later, an official, perhaps tiring of our persistent enquiries, tells us that the Gyantse Winter Fair has been called off. He does not say why. I guess the gathering of such a big crowd is always considered a risk because of the sporadic riots in Lhasa and elsewhere in recent years. I clearly remember my unease two weeks back: the monks at the Palkhor Monastery were bringing down a great pole covered with prayer flags amidst loud fanfares and scuffling – everyone wanted a piece of a flag to bring them good luck. Our cameraman was on the ground following the action; I was on a roof top, taking a general view of the scene. Even from a long distance, the policemen were conspicuous. It seemed the entire Gyantse police force had turned out. They kept coming into shot in their dark blue overcoats with 'Police' written in English on the back, and carrying walkie-talkies. When there was the slightest pushing and shoving over a prayer flag, a couple of policemen would appear instantly and stop it, as if it was a spark that might set the whole scene on fire.

I am really disappointed that the fair has been cancelled. Not just because of my plans, but because I feel for all the people, all the traders who are banking on it, all the families who are looking forward to it. Somewhere some official feels his job is safe because whatever incident might have been threatened, he will be blameless. If people are resentful, he does not care. But I wonder whether he has not just stored up trouble for the future.

With no fair in prospect, we hit the shops and stalls in a panic – we had hoped to buy really nice presents for everyone. Instead, we are stuck with little choice and the usual substandard goods. I look for things our characters do not have, sweets in pretty boxes, smart clothes, special food in bottles, exotic fruit. But my assistant comes along behind me, examining what I look at, rejecting everything piece by piece, out of date, falling apart, rotten. Penpa watches us wearily, 'Why don't you listen to me? You're wasting your time. Buy beer.' I was not so keen on the beer; people drink it all the time, while they never see fruit. But Penpa insisted. In the end, we opt for some traditional but safe picks: butter, rice, sugar, tea, fruit. And thirty cases of beer, bottled and canned from Lhasa, and imported Budweiser – Penpa's advice. 'New Year is about making people happy. Fruit is what you want, not what they want. Take my word for it. As we say, goats love willows; Tibetans love *chang*.'

Still I raise my eyebrows: *thirty* cases of beer? 'Just you wait a couple of days,' he says. 'You haven't seen real drinking yet.'

Penpa knows. He is our resident drinker. I remember the first time he came home drunk, late on a winter's night, with no shoes on, mumbling that I should not worry about him, he would always do his job. It was true; he has never let me down. By now I am used to his hard drinking. And drinking is everywhere. So often I see groups of men and women sitting on the pavement in Gyantse, helping each other to *chang* or bottles of beer, chatting away, bursting into song now and then, or offering a drink to passers-by with a smile. A few cups of *chang*, the sun coming out, friends gathering together – that is enough for them. They are oblivious to the traffic, the dust, the plastic bags dancing around them in the wind. We pass them in the morning on our way to the village and when we return in the late afternoon, they are still there, drinking, talking, and singing.

If they want to drink indoors, they go to the tea houses, usually dirty places without any decoration, with just the bare necessities, simple tables and benches. In Gyantse they are small, with three or four tables; in Shigatse and Lhasa they can be huge, with hundreds of people crammed into one dim, smoky space. Sweet milky tea in the morning, and beer in the afternoon; if they are hungry, there are noodles and *momo* – Tibetan meat dumplings. People exchange gossip and news, but they have to be cautious. There may be plain-clothes police and informers around. I rarely object when Penpa goes to the tea houses. He says he is bonding with our characters and learning more about them, and asks me to pay for his beer. But the next day when I want him to tell me what he has learned, he usually says he cannot remember, and they cannot either, because they were all drunk. He often comes back singing this song in his slurred voice:

The bars in Lhasa are filled with people,
Except the girl I desire.
A glass or two is nothing,
Because we are all drunkards.

I see what Penpa meant by 'real drinking' when we join Dondan and the whole village to film them making offerings to their mountain god. The place where the god is said to live is disappointingly simple: a small white stupa-like structure two miles from the village on a slope, but with a good view of the surrounding fields. The offerings are simple too: a handful of *tsampa* and a few juniper twigs inside the stupa, which Dondan lights; and a prayer flag to go on top of the stupa – a large branch with blue, white, yellow, green, and red squares of cloth printed with mantras. The smoke from the *tsampa* and juniper will send a message to the god about their visit and their offering; the flags will broadcast their prayers far and wide on the wind. Then everyone stands in a line and throws *tsampa* in the air, shouting 'Victory to the god! Victory to the god!' That is the food offering. Next comes the drink. Dondan pours a small cup of *chang*, dips his index finger into it, flicks it three times in the air – to heaven, to earth and to the deities – and then gulps it down. Now the drinking can start in earnest.

We sit down in circles of a dozen people or so. A young woman starts pouring *chang* for everyone, three cups each. Dondan swallows his as if he has been dying of thirst. When it is the Chinese cameraman Zhao Dong's turn, he declines, saying he has to film them. 'Drink, drink, today you don't work, today is for drink,' the young woman demands in Chinese. Zhao Dong tries to avoid having to drink by turning the camera on her. She does not shy away. Instead, she looks straight into the camera, and bursts into song, this time in Tibetan:

I offer you a cup of chang,
Made from the best barley after the harvest,
I only wish that you drink it,
And please do not say no.

When she finishes singing, she offers the cup with both hands to Zhao Dong again, but he still declines, remembering Penpa's golden rule: do not start if you do not want to continue. But hardly has he said no when a white cloud of *tsampa* lands on him, thrown by a woman in the crowd, turning him into a snowman. The camera is completely covered with *tsampa* too. 'Now you can't work any more,' laughs the woman.

Zhao Dong grabs some *tsampa* himself and throws it at the crowd. This saves him, and me, from drinking because now a playful *tsampa* fight has started. Everyone is throwing it. A man standing next to me almost pours it down my collar. Everything is blurred. The ground is turning white, all the men and women beginning to look like snowmen. I thought of the Tibetan saying that drinking is like a battle where brother and sister do not recognise each other. I certainly can hardly recognise anyone. I might as well be drunk. But I do not even drink: just one mouthful of beer turns me into a red rooster.

I shake off the *tsampa* on me and turn to Dondan, asking him about his family's New Year. He says if it was not for the death in the family, he would be going around, calling at every house. 'As you know, it is quite a big village and it takes more than one day to go around, especially with all the drinking.'

'Is there a lot of drinking?' I ask.

'Absolutely. Every family offers you at least three cups or ladles of *chang*. Usually they insist on you drinking more. If you don't, they have a needle ready to prick you. I'd rather have the drink than the needle. One year I drank so much I fell asleep in someone's house while I was doing the rounds. Yangdron had to come looking for me the next morning,' Dondan says with a smile.

I ask if that is what he does after drinking too much? Sleep?

'You should ask Yangdron that question. She knows best. She is the sober one. But I don't get drunk often. I can drink that much without any problem,' he says, pointing to a 7-litre container in the middle of the circle. Yangdron has already confirmed what he says. Dondan is strong enough to drink without losing control.

'You are better than my brother,' a young woman says from behind our circle. 'When he drinks too much, he beats the first person he sets eyes on. I wish they would put him in prison.'

Another woman listening adds, 'My man is odd: when he is drunk, he checks the name of everyone in the family – first his mother, his sister, two brothers, then the children and the grandchildren. Everyone has to report for duty, otherwise he gets stuck calling out the names, again and again. He keeps doing it till he falls asleep.'

Dondan seems the only one in his family who drinks seriously. Why is that?

'I need it,' he says. 'I work the hardest. It makes life easier. And I enjoy it, especially now, with everyone drinking together.' As always Dondan is his honest self. Then he asks me if I have heard the story of the woman from the sea. The legend goes that long, long ago, a beautiful woman walked out of the waves in the sea that is now Tibet. She was so gorgeous, every man wanted to make love to her. After her death, there appeared a grass called *groma*, the ingredient used as a catalyst to ferment the barley and make *chang*.

'That's why the more we drink, the more we want to drink.'

'You must have heard of the argument between the *Chang* Fairy and the Tea Fairy?' an old man sitting across from Dondan chips in. His eyes are cloudy and red; his skin is dark, almost the colour of a monk's maroon robe – a sign that he has had quite a lot to drink in his life. 'That tells you why we drink. See if I can still remember a few lines by the *Chang* Fairy.'

> I am the offering to High Lamas, to peaceful and wrathful
> deities;
> I am the glue between the king and his concubines,

he pauses, trying to remember more, then goes on:

> I am joy for ordinary people;
> I am a trap for seducing lovely girls.
> I help you sing more joyfully;
> I help you dance more vigorously.

I was intrigued, and later found some more lines of the *Dialogue Between the Chang and Tea Fairies* in a book by one of the most popular Tibetan writers: Phuntsog Tashi. His caricature of a drunkard called Lhakpa is well known; perhaps many Tibetans see something of themselves in him. The poem, written in the seventeenth century, describes a debate before a Tibetan king who has to decide which is better, *chang* or tea. The *Chang* Fairy gets plenty of good lines:

> I comfort you when you cry
> I am the key to making the dumb speak;
> I am the brain for the clever;
> I help the brave wipe out their enemies;
> I guide the coward through barren mountains and hills.
> I am the lamp that exposes the hypocrites;
> I am the gift that makes wise men talk.
> How in the world can they achieve all this without me?[47]

But the Tea Fairy makes out a good case too:

> I am the lamas' favourite, they love nothing better;
> When they drink me, their memory sharpens, their
> > knowledge increases and their desires are reduced.
> I am the king of drinks.
> I am the hammer for crushing ignorance;
> I am the saw that cuts through laziness.

The *Chang* Fairy has the better of it today. The weather is perfect. The grey winter clouds hanging over Gyantse have given way to a pure and brilliant sky. The sun is big and powerful, bathing everything in warm golden light, as though it is already spring. Only the wind is still playing tricks, but that is a good omen in Dondan's view: the gods will hear their prayers more clearly. I am sure if it was cold, that would be a good reason for drinking too.

It was not long before three women were sent home to get more *chang*. The rest started singing. As the Tibetans say, drinking and singing are twin sisters. *Chang* is just cold water without singing. I had no idea what they were singing – the songs were slow, rhythmic and hypnotic like a lullaby – and I did not ask for a translation as I normally do. I do know they sounded as beautiful as any I have heard in my time here: the monks' prayers in the monastery, Lhakpa singing as he paints houses, or Jianzang and his six-string guitar, Yangdron and Dondan's joyful chanting while they harvest the barley, or the sky burial master's slow and deep droning as he pounds the bones and flesh of the dead for the vultures. Today, as often, singing is an offering to the god, while the singers enjoy it too. And they are very good at it: song flows from their hearts like water from a pitcher. But songs for drinking are the most magical, as if the composers came up with those ingenious lines and tunes when their imaginations were ignited by *chang*. The crowd start with what they call the Tibetan marching song of drink:

> We gather here,
> Praying we will never part company
> Praying every one of us
> Will be happy and healthy.

The singing flows on: one person stops and another picks up, as effortlessly as the flow of *chang* down their throats. Suddenly I think I hear the word 'Buddha' in the lyrics. Maybe I am mistaken. I ask Penpa. He listens, and then nods. 'It is the Buddha. The song goes something like this.'

> The Providential Buddha within me,
> Like the warm sun in the sky,
> Dispels the darkness in my heart.
> Ignore the size of the bottle,
> Notice the quality of the chang,
> As sweet as nectar,
> And good enough to be offered to the Three Treasures.*

How does alcohol find a place in Tibetan Buddhism? I am intrigued. I thought alcohol was one of the five things that monks renounce in their vows, together with killing, stealing, sex, and lying. I ask Dondan. He gulps down a cup and shrugs his shoulders. I should put the question to Tseten. But in his humble opinion, the gods are so powerful that no amount of alcohol can do them harm.

A friendly young man, whom I have met in the Rikzins' house several times, asks me if I have been to the Zhachi Temple in

---

* The Three Treasures are the Buddha, his teachings, and the monastic community.

Lhasa. It is devoted to Vajrayogini, the Goddess of Intoxication and Money. She is one of the most popular protective deities in Tibetan Buddhism. I tell him I have heard Penpa mention it, but I have not been there yet.

'I go there quite often and help out. You should visit it. It is quite something, not like any other temple,' the young man says. 'Visitors bring their own *chang* or buy a bottle of Chinese liquor from the stall outside, they cost anything from 3 to 600 *yuan*. Inside the temple, you have to queue to make your offering. The goddess is inside a glass cubicle. She is a bit scary, she has a black face and bulging eyes and her tongue is hanging out. You go in and touch her with your forehead; that gets you her blessing. Then you hand your bottle to the monk who's waiting there. He takes your bottle; if it's *chang* he pours it in one vat, if it's white liquor he puts it in another; and if it's really expensive he puts the bottle aside. The liquor ends up back on the stall – they sell it again! But the *chang* doesn't keep, so they give it away or throw it away. I do whatever work they ask me to, sweeping, clearing away the empty bottles or the cartons they came in. When I've finished, I can drink as much *chang* as I like, and go home with as much as I can carry.' He looks up at the sky for a moment. 'It is heavenly. The temple is so popular, it makes a lot of money. With the goddess's blessing, maybe I will too.'

I wonder how the goddess can bless your drinking and make you rich at the same time. Another Tibetan paradox. Later I ask Tseten about it. He reminds me that when Padam subdued the demons and devils, he did not make them give up their unBuddhist habits, including their drinking. Perhaps Padam knew he would not have much of a following if he took away people's greatest pleasure. According to legend, he himself drank copiously, and could manage 500 jars of *chang* at a time. That is why Ningmapa, one of the oldest Buddhist schools in Tibet, allows its followers to drink.

Gelupa, the sect founded by Tsongkhapa in the fifteenth century and headed by the Dalai Lama, thinks the old sects were too lax. Its name means 'good at discipline'. Tsongkhapa asked how monks who broke their monastic rules could possibly help others. His reforms, the biggest in Tibetan history, proved extremely popular, and Gelupa soon overtook all the other sects, and has dominated Tibetan religious and political life ever since.

But it seems that even the Gelupa monks could not escape the power of *chang*. When the Japanese monk Kawaguchi sneaked into Tibet, he spent a few months in the Tashilunpo Monastery. He was shocked by the monks' indiscipline. He noted their drink problem in particular:

> A curious rule was enacted in order to prevent the habit of drinking. Every priest returning from the street was bound to present himself before the priestly guard at the gate of the temple, who examined his breath, and any disclosure of his drunkenness was followed by an immediate punishment. Some impudent priests often attempted to conceal their inebriation by eating a good deal of garlic, the strong smell of which impregnated their breath and thus might prevent detection.[48]

Perhaps the majority of monks can resist. But it is near impossible for the ordinary faithful. I have been told a famous story by many Tibetans about the dangers of alcohol. A woman approaches a monk leading a sheep, and carrying a jar of *chang*. She tempts him with her body, with meat, and with drink. He thinks long and hard and says to himself: 'I should not kill the sheep, which breaks my first vow. I should not touch the woman, which breaks my second vow. *Chang* is the safest of the three.' The next morning, he wakes to find he has got drunk, killed the sheep and eaten its meat, and raped the woman. Everyone knows the story, and yet...

The crowd has been drinking and singing for six hours; women have been sent back twice more to the village to bring more *chang*. It is getting late, the sky is suddenly grey, and from nowhere the wind blasts in, whipping up dust and draining the warmth from the ground we sit on. I begin to shiver, regretting that I was fooled again by the brilliant sun during the day. Nobody else seems bothered in the slightest by the sudden cold. Some are slumped in a heap, drunk and oblivious to it, while others are singing away. They do not want the party to end. We decide to leave, and say goodbye to Dondan. He is coherent, but only just. I am sure the party will go on.

On the way back from the drinking party for the mountain god, we decide to drop in at the village clinic to wish Dr Lhamo a happy New Year. She picks up the big ladle from the pot on the table and asks us to drink straight from it, three ladles each. Penpa swallows them down like a fish, but Zhao Dong has a real problem. He asks if Penpa can drink for him, but Lhamo will hear nothing of it. Zhao Dong gives in but I resist. Lhamo asks her husband Tashi to go and get a needle from the surgery next door. 'We have a custom: anyone who does not drink will be pricked with a needle,' she says seriously.

I get a little prick. I thought Dondan had been joking when he told me of this tradition.

Next morning Zhao Dong woke up with a bad headache; he had never had so much *chang* before, although by Penpa's standards he had hardly drunk anything. I was glad we were going to call on Rincheu, the builder we have been filming. He is one of the very few people I know in Gyantse who does not drink. I thought sweets for his young son and a case of tangerines for the family would be the right gifts to take. 'Absolutely not,' Penpa said. 'Too cheap. We've got to give him two cases of beer, the Budweiser.'

I looked at him, shocked. 'How can we be so insensitive?' I said.

'What do you mean?'

'After what happened to his son?'

'Oh, you're worried about that? He is still a Tibetan. But you can give him the tangerines too.' He went out and told the driver to put the gifts in the car and drop us at Rincheu's house.

I do not want to argue with Penpa about the gifts, but I completely disagree. Penpa himself had told me what happened to Rincheu's son, Pasang. Ten years ago, when he was sixteen, he was helping to load a truck Dondan had rented from Rincheu. He had been drinking, got into a fight, and stabbed a man eight times in the chest, killing him. Rincheu told us Dondan should have intervened and stopped the fight; he could not forgive him. Now Pasang is half way through a twenty-year sentence in a prison in Lhasa. How could we take drink to the family?

To my surprise there is a big copper pot filled with *chang* on the sitting room table when we arrive, and a string of cans of Budweiser. Rincheu sticks out his tongue to greet us, the Tibetan way of showing respect. Penpa and the driver hand him our presents; he puts them to one side and introduces us to his other guests, two of his business associates, and his father. His young wife, Drongdha, nods towards us in greeting, and goes to the cupboard to get some cups for us. I compliment her on how stunning she looks in her long green robe, like a man's but shorter, showing her graceful hands. My crew has voted her the beauty of Gyantse; she does have a lovely face, long and symmetrical, with big dark almond-shaped eyes and glowing cheeks, set off today by her elaborate silver necklace heavy with amber and lapis lazuli. Rincheu beams at my remarks, while trying to rein in his son who is toddling around the table, excited and laughing. The boy is handsome, taking after his father, who towers over him, tall and upright, with a rather Western tanned face and gleaming white smile. He is festively dressed too, in a black Chinese leather jacket trimmed with mink, though I miss his usual dashing beige stetson.

Rincheu urges us to drink. I ask for a Coke and Penpa starts on the Budweiser. I am relieved that Richeu does not pressure me to take something alcoholic. Drongdha hands me my cup and I ask her whether she is happy with the house – we have been filming the decoration as it has progressed. 'It is ready now. Let me show you round,' she says. We leave the men in the sitting room and go into the master bedroom that leads off it. It stops me short. It is a vulgar version of a Chinese hotel room for the nouveaux riches. Everything is loud and shiny, but clashing. Two of the walls are dark, painted with garish flowers and birds. The huge pale wooden bed has a cream bedhead stretching two thirds of the way to the ceiling, and a gold and crystal chandelier hangs over it, matching it in extravagance. What could I say? Rincheu has given her the best he knew, whatever money could buy in Tibet.

Rincheu breaks off his conversation with Penpa – his business friends have left. 'What do you think?' he says eagerly.

I am a bit stuck, but come up with a diplomatic reply. 'It is very different from your house in the village.'

'Oh, that's so old fashioned. This is the latest,' he says.

I really liked his other house, in the village next to the Rikzins'. The village is small and all the other houses are made of mud bricks, painted white. His is stone built, and enormous, with thirteen rooms, more even than his large family needs. There were just his father, his stepmother, his two younger brothers and the wife he shared with them, and their children. Half the rooms were empty, though the ones they used were charmingly decorated in traditional style. The youngest brother is not at home these days, working in northern Tibet all year round, nor is Rincheu, now he has left them and set himself up in town with the beautiful Drongdha and their new child.

But I am feeling uncomfortable with the conversation. My remark was not so diplomatic after all, and I try to get off the subject of the other house. I ask them what their New Year has been like.

'You know what it's like,' Rincheu turns to Penpa. 'A lot of family, a lot of talk, a lot of eating and drinking.'

'But you don't drink,' I say.

'Maybe not, but as you see I offer *chang* and beer to my guests. It is the Tibetan way, just like we eat porridge made of *tsampa* and *chang*, and then drink *chang* the first thing on New Year's Day, to bring us good luck.'

I told him briefly about the ceremony the day before with the villagers.

'Every occasion is for drinking. Is there one when we don't drink?' Rincheu says, his eyes fixed on the string of cans on the table. Penpa is glugging down the Budweiser. 'We drink our money away, our time away, our opportunities away, our lives away. The amount we drink every year must be enough to build several Potalas. It's such a waste.'

His father, an old man, all wrinkles and with a head full of wiry white hair, is following the conversation with interest. He nods.

Rincheu's metaphor is telling: I have looked for but never found a figure for how much Tibetans spend on drink. But judging from the people around me, I think it is not a small sum. Penpa often asks me for 100 *yuan* for a night out; that is twenty-five bottles for an evening for three people, and he does it four out of seven evenings. I do not know how he manages without this 'subsidy'. At least he is honest: 'I am a drunkard and a beggar,' he declares. One of Penpa's drinking mates says his record is 250 cans of Lhasa beer with four friends, two nights in a row. Even for the Rikzin family, who can afford *chang*, Yangdron would turn 4 kilos of barley into *chang* every other day: that is more barley than they eat.

But it is more than money. Lives are at stake. Pasang killed a man in his prime; and he has lost ten years of his own life already in jail, because of drink. I have heard of any number of accidents and deaths due to drink. Penpa asked for leave twice to attend the funerals of friends who died that way. The blacksmith who fixed our stoves came in one day and said his brother had just died of alcohol poisoning. Our housekeeper had to go home because her uncle was about to receive his sentence for nearly crippling a woman in a drunken rage. Dr Lhamo's husband crashed his motorbike in a ditch a few weeks ago on his way back from a night call. 'He was so drunk I didn't even need to use an anaesthetic when I stitched him up,' Lhamo told us. Every weekend in the emergency room of the Gyantse hospital, young men and women are rushed in with knives still stuck in their bodies. I was told by doctors there that over 10 per cent of all the deaths in the hospital are alcohol related. But the saddest story to me was the other blacksmith who sold his own son for drink, and died from it.

I remember what Phuntsog said to me after the sky burial, when I asked him about the blacksmith's short life. 'He had drunk so much his liver was hard as stone. He should have been more responsible, a better man to himself and to his family. It was such a waste.' From the sky burial master, the man who sends the souls of the dead to their next life, in a society that believes karma is the fundamental principle of existence, that was an astonishing admission. Perhaps he has seen too many lives cut short, too many families torn apart, too many parents without their sons, too many children without fathers – all due to drink. The cost of the joy of life is too high. But I guess nothing will stop Tibetans from drinking, from enjoying themselves and their lives. They live for pleasure and die for it too.

Looking at Rincheu, his beautiful wife and laughing son, I cannot help thinking it is a kind of parable. This is a man who does not drink, and see what he has achieved. He trained as a stonemason when he was fourteen, and became a skilled carpenter and carver working on building sites. He saved every penny he earned, and was soon taking on men himself to build houses. No worker can fool him or get away with a mistake. His reputation grew. These days he is always busy – and he always looks as if he does not have a worry in the world.

Today his smile is broader than ever. I guess he has had a good year: he has expanded his company – he has more than a hundred workers now – taken on another successful businessman as a partner, and won his first big government contract for an irrigation project, for which he has bought a £20,000 bulldozer. He deserves his success. He is the hardest working Tibetan I know, up at the crack of dawn almost every day, going from one building site to another, sorting out problems, checking the quality of the workmanship, and giving the workers their tasks for the next day. And he does not drink. His youngest brother used to work for him, but everything Rincheu gave him he spent on drink, and was often drunk on site. Rincheu threw him out of his company.

Now I think of it, of all the Tibetans I have come to know during the year, the ones who have got where they want to be in life are non-drinkers. Tsultrim, the deputy head lama in the monastery is one, but that goes without saying. Tseten has not taken any vow of abstinence, but he rarely touches alcohol. Jianzang, the hotel manager, shares Rincheu's hatred of drink. 'I see through all these so-called pleasures. When I was a doctor, I saw so many people coming into hospital because of alcohol. Drink costs money and ruins your life,' he once said to me. Another is Penpa's oldest brother, whom I have never met but heard a lot about. He is furious with Penpa for wasting all his

Yangdron and Dondan planting barley.

Above left Tsultrim,
deputy head of
Palkhor Monastery.

Left Dondrup,
Tsephun's master.

Above Palkhor
Monastery.

Right Tsephum,
in front of the
giant *tankga* of
the future Budha.

Above Dance of the Black hat. *Below* Death Dance.

Above Masked Dance.

Below Death Dance.

Left Monks of Palkhor Monastery.

Below left The Budha in the
Prayer Hall at Palkhor Monastery.

Right Photos of the
10th and 11th Panchen
Llamas hanging in the
Palkhor Monastery.

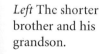

Left The shorter
brother and his
grandson.

Right The
taller brother.

Above Mola in her room.

Below Jianzang, the hotel keeper.

talent and money on drink. He himself became head of City Planning in Lhasa, responsible for the city's transformation, for better or worse. But these men are rare beings in this society.

'You can see for yourself what drink is doing to our people,' Rincheu sighs. 'I wish I had been tougher with my son. I love him so much. However rich you are, you can't eat more than three meals a day. I don't need all the money. It is all for him and the other children. I just hope he's learned his lesson.'

Just then a couple with a young girl come through the door. Rincheu stands up to greet them, and Penpa signals to me that we should make a move. Perhaps all the talk about drink and the damage it does has made him uncomfortable. And I sympathise: it is not something to tackle when everyone is supposed to be enjoying themselves. Rincheu follows us downstairs to say goodbye, and Penpa asks him how his son is getting on. I had wanted to follow Rincheu on a prison visit but he had asked us to wait a while. He has been trying to get Pasang's sentence reduced, arguing he is a model prisoner. Of course, good behaviour alone is not enough; money would be needed too. Last time Penpa asked him about it, Rincheu said the prison authorities were considering his request. A film team showing up at this crucial time might disturb things. As soon as he got confirmation, he told us, we could accompany him on his next prison visit.

'We've got some good news,' Rincheu says, looking really glad. 'Pasang might have his sentence reduced by half. That means he will be home before the autumn. I'm so pleased.'

That is very good news. Another ten years behind bars would completely ruin his son's life. I shake Rincheu's hands to congratulate him. The release, if it happens, will also make a dramatic end for our film.

As we wave goodbye and walk towards the street, I cannot help feeling quite elated. I am happy for Rincheu; they seem such a contented family apart from this tragedy. 'It will be interesting to see what happens. I guess they will cope,' Penpa mutters to himself behind me. Something in his tone, slow and meaningful, makes me turn round and ask what he means.

'You know you told me a while ago that Rincheu used to share a wife with his two younger brothers in the village? You were wrong,' he says.

I look at Penpa, not sure what he is getting at.

'Rincheu shares his stepmother with his father; she is Pasang's mother. Drongdha is Pasang's wife. Rincheu has taken Drongdha while his son is behind bars.'

I stop. Rincheu shares one woman with his father, and then another with his own son? What else do I not know?

'Rincheu told me himself a few days ago,' Penpa says pointedly. 'I know it's a very complicated relationship even by our standards. And he still has a grudge against the Rikzin family: Dondan did not stop the fight, and the family never put in a word on Pasang's behalf.'

Now we are standing in the street outside Rincheu's house. It looks deserted, all the shops are closed; all the families are at home. I am trying to figure everything out. Could the Rikzin family have done anything? I should check with them. Should the little boy call Pasang uncle, when Pasang is his father's son? Or should he call him father, as he is married to his mother? It sounds like a riddle. Perhaps Penpa is trying to tell me something: just because Rincheu works hard and does not drink, it does not mean he is a good man. Obviously Penpa thinks I am a poor judge of character. I have so many questions to ask him. But he turns away, and begins to walk off, saying, 'I think I'm going to the tea house. Don't worry, I'll be ready when we start in the morning. Seven o'clock?'

NINE

Three Million Prayers

IT IS LATE APRIL, but winter is reluctant to loosen its grip. The ground is still hard, and the first shoots are struggling to push up in the fields. Three snowfalls in quick succession seem to be warning them not to take anything for granted. But spring is coming, however haltingly. The well-kept fields are soaking up the sun; a cuckoo is darting about, pecking here and there – a sure sign of spring, the villagers say. The tips of the poplar trees are turning the faintest green, and the wind that has been blowing dust in our faces since October is dropping. At last the soft blue of iris lilies sprinkles the roadsides, and here and there tiny pink primulas appear. It is all a welcome relief to me. But for the villagers, spring signals work: the long idleness of winter is over, and planting is starting in earnest.

Down the valley, as far as the eye can see, families are ploughing and planting in every field. They have been getting ready for some time, selecting their seeds, buying the fertilizer, sharpening their tools, and watering the fields. Now they have to get the seeds in quickly before the sun sucks the moisture away. Apart from the harvest, this is the only time I have seen so many farmers working. The Rikzin family is out there like everyone else. Their two bulls are draped with coloured scarves, and they are pulling the wooden plough; Dondan is gently guiding them with a switch made from some twigs. Yangdron walks behind them with two bags, from which she takes a handful of fertiliser and one of seed, spreading a bit of each in the furrow. Loga is standing in the middle of the field, staring, and then remembering that he is supposed to be helping. In the next field, a little girl in a big straw sun hat keeps her grandmother company, refilling her bags from sacks of seed and fertiliser, and spreading them for her when the grandmother takes a rest. Loga can just about be counted on to refill Yangdron's bags, but he cannot seem to manage the actual planting that the girl is doing, and she is just a toddler.

With so much to do, the Rikzin family would love to have more help from Loga. But they know not to expect it, and by now, so do I. I have seen him almost daily for nine months. I try to bring him an apple, chewing gum, or a Coke every time I come; he takes them greedily and flashes a big grin. But I have no idea whether he really knows who I am. For some reason, the only member of our team he knows by name is Loten, our researcher and assistant cameraman, though he only visits occasionally. I have asked the family how Loga got this way. Yangdron has told me the most about him, but she's not sure what ails Loga, exactly, or how it started. Our filming is nearing the end, and I want to find out more. How does Tibetan medicine regard such an illness? As a shaman and healer, Tseten ought to be able to tell me.

I find Tseten back at the house, seeing patients. When I get there he is blowing saliva at the face of a baby boy held tightly by his mother. There is fear in the boy's eyes, and tears on his face. When Tseten stops spitting and starts reciting a mantra, the boy begins crying again, bawling as if he'd been holding back a flood of tears. His mother is embarrassed and strokes his head to calm him down. Then Tseten hands the mother the 'medicine' for her son; it looks like brown soil, wrapped in a piece of the *Tibetan Daily*. He says she should give it to the boy in water once a day, and that he will be better in three days.

I wonder whether the boy might just be teething.

The next patient asks Tseten to diagnose her son, though the son isn't with her, because his legs have suddenly swollen up. Tseten asks for her birth date and her son's. After going through the astrology book, he says, 'The main cause of the swelling is the veins in his legs. The dragon god has got into them.'

'Where does the dragon god live?' the woman asks, gingerly.

'You have a big pile of wood in front of your house, and I think the dragon god is on top of the pile. Your family hasn't shown proper respect to the dragon god, and you have dirtied its abode.'

Tseten prescribes some sutras to be read and offerings of *tso* and incense to be placed on the wood. If they want a quick recovery, he says, he suggests they go to hospital for antibiotic injections after the rituals.

'The hospital in which direction?'

Tseten consults his astrology book again. 'In the easterly direction. The one in Gyantse.'

'Do you take a commission for each patient you recommend to the hospital?' I say, jokingly, after the woman leaves. I have heard that in Lhasa, shamans are paid by the hospitals or clinics they send their patients to; sometimes they even specify which doctor patients should see and get a cut from him too. The hospitals play along and direct patients back to the shamans for more rituals for their recovery. It is corruption with a Tibetan twist.

'Find me patients like that,' Tseten says. 'Most villagers cannot even afford the simplest treatment. Perhaps you are thinking of the lucky ones working for the government.' He goes on to describe what he regards as the saddest moment in his practice: praying for the soul of a young bride whose family was too poor to send her to hospital. 'She did not have to die.'

Just as I'm about to ask Tseten more questions, an old man walks in. He's bow-legged, with white hair and rheumy eyes, and he looks worried. Seeing me, he hesitates, but Tseten signals for him to sit down. The man tells us that he fed his bull chopped dried white radish yesterday, as he does every day, but that this morning the animal's stomach was so swollen he could not get him through the door. He called the vet, who gave the bull an injection, but there'd been no improvement. It's planting time, and the man needs the bull to plough his field. He wonders if Tseten could determine whether his family was under some sort of curse.

I have never before seen Tseten asked to treat an animal. 'Was anyone in your family born in the year of the pig?' Tseten asks.

The old man nods, and Tseten flips through his astrology book, and then asks the ages of each of the nine members of the man's family. Do human horoscopes have anything to do with the white radish stuck in a bull's throat?

'I have found the cause,' Tseten announces, after a few minutes. 'The trouble comes from the local deity at the edge of your village. Do you worship it?'

'Yes, I do, but I only bow to it from a distance and have rarely been near it.'

'Do you do it regularly?'

'No, only when we are in some kind of trouble.'

'You should do it regularly. There are many evil spirits around. The book also shows another very powerful spirit from the southerly direction. The two spirits have joined forces.'

'Yes, a relative lives in that direction and he held a ritual in his house yesterday. I went to help them.'

'Some of you, possibly you, have your inauspicious time in

158

May. So your inauspicious time, and the spirits have combined to make trouble for the bull.'

Tseten prescribes three days of worshipping the local deity at sunset, with an offering of incense, and then advises placing a photocopied image of the local deity on a south-facing wall, burning juniper branches at the foot of the hill outside the village, and having several different sutras read by monks in the monastery.

'We had a prayer said before the planting started,' the old man murmurs, perhaps worrying about the cost.

'That was for something else. You need sutras specifically for this purpose.'

Tseten hands him a little sachet of white power, telling him to put it in a jar and burn it, and to walk this around the bull. 'Keep your eye on the bull for the next three days. After that, he will be fine.'

The old man takes the sachet and stands up; he gives Tseten a deep bow and walks backwards towards the door.

'Suppose the bull dies in the next three days?' I ask, cheekily.

'It won't die.'

Can we have a bet?

'Any sum you want.' Tseten says confidently.

'A case of soft drinks for each day.'

'That's a deal.'

'But if the bull dies, won't they blame you?'

'No. They will come again and ask me what they may do with the dead animal. What they should do with the meat, and can they use the skin. They will have a prayer said for it.'

I have noticed that in all three cases, the diagnosis that Tseten gave has to do with the influence of spirits. Tibetan medicine lists 404 diseases, 101 of them fall into this category, and are literally called 'imaginary diseases'. They are things like nervous breakdowns and mental illness, shellshock. The spirits that cause these diseases are said to live both inside and outside the body. There are thousands of these spirits – female spirits linked with desire, males with aggression; there are water spirits, earth spirits, spirits in rocks and stones and forests – they are everywhere. To cure the ailments they cause, either the evil spirits must be exorcised, or the benign spirits must be cajoled back into the body. There are different mantras and different protector deities that are used to help with each spirit. A shaman like Tseten is charged with determining which spirit is troubling the patient, and with finding the appropriate prayer. Medicine will only be effective after this prayer has been said. Such a diagnosis may sound arbitrary, but the precise details of the practice are all laid out in a book called *Gyushi*, the *Four Tantras of Tibetan Medicine*. This is the canonical source, and is supposedly derived from the teachings of the Medicinal Buddha himself.

I wonder if Loga's problems fall into this category too? What prayers did the family say for him? Did they not work? What did the doctors say? Now that the patients are gone, I have a chance to ask Tseten about him.

Tseten tells me what he learned from Mila. Loga got a lot of attention as the first born of the Rikzin family. He was a sweet, healthy, and strong baby. Everyone loved him and wanted to hold him. When he was ten months old, he was looked after by a female relative for a week. 'Something happened to him during that week,' Tseten says. 'When he came back, he was completely changed. He refused to eat and threw *tsampa* everywhere. He could not sit or lie still and cried day and night like a frightened animal. And then he had a rash all over his body.'

Mila took him to Gyantse. The traditional Tibetan doctor confirmed Mila's suspicions: he said an evil spirit had entered Loga's blood. The doctor ordered rituals to purify him. The rituals had to be performed in secret – this was 1961 when the anti-Buddhist campaign was in full swing. But Loga got worse.

He was taken to the hospital in Gyantse, where a doctor said there was poison in his blood, though he could not determine the cause. He prescribed a lot of pills. Mila said they helped, because Loga's condition did not deteriorate: he could talk and walk. He could feed himself, he was not incontinent, and he was not mad.

The purification rituals, though, had clearly not worked. Mila determined that the trouble could not have been due to an evil spirit entering Loga's blood – it must have been something more fundamental. He performed a different ritual and more divination. The result was stark. 'Loga's illness had nothing to do with this life, or with anything that happened to him after he was born,' Tseten says. 'It had to do with something in his previous life.'

What on earth could Loga have done in a previous life?

'Our divination determined that Loga had been a powerful landlord with hundreds of serfs. He was a greedy and violent man and treated them badly. He may have had blood on his hands. The illness was retribution for his bad karma. The *Four Tantras* call it karmic disease. Just as it lists 101 different imaginary diseases, it lists 101 types of karmic diseases, too.'

What other diseases are karmic? Can anything be done about them?

'There are many of them: fatal illnesses or things children are born with, like a missing limb. You cannot cure them. All you can do is to perform prayers, rituals, pilgrimages, good deeds, everything that will help to atone for past sins and ensure a better rebirth.'

The family must be doing that for Loga then?

'Yes, we have been doing all those things,' Tseten says. 'And there is a particular passage from a sutra that we have to recite three million times. We are in the middle of that.'

It seems quite a labour to me, and possibly all for nothing.

Everything Tseten has said just makes me want to look for a scientific explanation. Fifty years ago, Loga's doctor was unable to find a cause, but the blood test did show an abnormality. Since then, the family hasn't tried to explore further. They are set on their path of attempting redemption. And I imagine that a sophisticated investigation would probably be beyond the capacity of the local hospital.

It may be beyond our local doctor, Lhamo, too. I decide to see what she thinks of Loga's trouble, and also to see what is going on in her clinic, which serves the twelve villages in the valley and beyond. The clinic is a ten-minute drive from Tseten's house, next to the Karmad *xiang* headquarters building. We enter by way of a courtyard that has two rows of poplar trees and two vegetable plots. The trees have nails in them from which the patients hang their intravenous drips. There are half a dozen patients attached to these drips today. The patients are sitting on the ground, with needles in one hand and a cup of *chang* in the other. Everyone has a 2-litre plastic container of *chang* next to them for a refill. Surely liquor will reduce the effect of the medicine – or even create complications? I ask Lhamo about it, and she says that she tells them not to but nobody listens. 'The drips make them thirsty, and *chang* is just water to them,' she sighs.

The vegetable plots are supposed to help Lhamo to supplement her meagre income – she makes only 300 *yuan* (£20) a month – but they are fallow. Lhamo is too busy to tend to them. She does not have much time for her little boy either; he is playing in amongst the patients, hugging them, taking a biscuit from one and a pat on the head from another. Every time I see him doing it, I shudder. He is bound to get sick one day. I said so to Lhamo; but the clinic is her son's playground – she has nowhere else to put him.

Beyond the courtyard is a one-storey building, which has the operating room and the consultation room at one end, and the doctor's tiny home at the other. The consultation room has just a table, a chair, a bench, and a line of cupboards holding the drugs. On the walls there are Red Cross posters giving information about hygiene, child care, and TB. Outside the operating room, two old ladies are having a fierce argument. It turns out that the daughter-in-law of one of them is inside. She is pregnant and in a lot of pain; she has been suffering for eighteen hours, but still the baby has not come. The other woman's son is having a fit at home and cannot breathe – she wants the doctor to come at once. Meanwhile there are three people waiting in the consultation room.

Lhamo decides to send her doctor husband Tashi on the house call, and pulls out a rather dusty leather case from under the table and helps him put the right medicines inside. She absolutely has to stay behind to deliver the baby; it will probably come some time tonight. The woman has already had one still-born baby, and Lhamo wants to make sure this one will be all right. The odds are against her. The infant mortality rate is high in Tibet – even according to the Tibetan government figure: out of every hundred live births, as many as thirty babies will not make it to their first birthday in some areas.[49] We have been hoping to film a birth. Usually the family does not want us there – they think we will bring them bad luck. So far we have twice been allowed to film, and in both cases the babies were stillborn. We still hope to film a happier scene – with a crying baby and a smiling mother at the end of it. This could be the moment. I tell the cameraman to stand by.

The first of Lhamo's patients is a little girl who has been brought in by her grandfather; her cheek is swollen as big as a fist. Next are a young man who can not lift his arms, and a pregnant woman who is very pale. Lhamo puts five 'dry needles', the Tibetan name for acupuncture, in the young man's shoulder, prescribes a drip for the pregnant woman, and gives the girl an antibiotic. The grandfather finds he does not have the 3 *yuan*, 20 pence, for the medicine; Lhamo tells him not to worry, but she makes a note in her notebook. He bows and shakes her hands gratefully. She gets up and follows them out. Then she goes in to check on the pregnant woman in the operating room, before walking around the courtyard looking at the patients on their drips. All that done, she pours us some butter tea and sits with relief on the bed in her room.

Now we have a minute to talk, although Lhamo looks so tired I do not feel like bothering her with questions. And she is obviously anxious about the pregnant woman. So I just sit and watch her for a while. Lhamo is small, quiet, and serene; she looks like the nuns in the big nunnery down the valley. She is just as compassionate and kind. I am very fond of her, and often struck by the sympathy and patience with which she treats each and every person who comes to see her, but also by the sadness on her emaciated face that never seems to leave her. I am not sure I would call on her though if I was sick. She and her husband Tashi received only two years of medical training from the Chinese Red Cross in Shigatse and they are now running the clinic with another doctor. This is not unusual – most of the *xiang* clinics are run by doctors like them. And intravenous drips are their main resource: they prescribe them for most patients, whether they have a cold, fever, stomach or gall-bladder complaint, toothache, or indigestion. I wonder whether it is good for them; they can develop immunities if they have too many antibiotics, and I have also heard that the high rate of hepatitis B infection in Tibet has something to do with them because the needles are not always sterile.

Suddenly Lhamo's boy dashes in from outside screaming, and pulls her out of her moment of rest. He has had a fall, and she picks him up and cuddles him, calming him down. I find him a piece of chewing gum; it distracts him enough to make him smile. He grabs it and runs back outside. Lhamo smiles too, gratefully. She seems to have perked up a little and I ask her whether Tseten's patients come to her as well. I was thinking of the woman that morning whose son had a swollen leg. 'Yes, she came and I gave her an antibiotic for him,' Lhamo says.

What does she think is wrong with the boy?

'I haven't seen him, but it sounds like it might be thrombosis.'

I tell her what Tseten said about the dragon god. 'He may be right,' she says. 'In traditional Tibetan medicine many illnesses are caused by the spirits. If they are, only shamans like Tseten can help.'

Why do they come to her then? I had not expected her to defend Tseten's practices. She thinks for a minute. 'Well, we have illnesses that we say are due to karma or to the influence of spirits. Doctors cannot treat them. But then there are diseases in our medicine that are due to circumstances, like changes in the weather, or infection, or diet, or the way people behave – drinking, or getting into accidents. Patients will come to me for those problems, but they might go to Tseten as well.'

Does his healing work?

'It only works if you believe in it. If you think about it, when the patients have done everything they can, they are calm and that's actually good for their recovery.'

I guess that makes sense. So often you hear of cancer patients with the same diagnosis, but some live much longer than others. People say it is the will to live that keeps them going. Their attitude can make a difference. But will Dr Lhamo try traditional healing herself?

'Yes, I have seen a shaman for my own illness. He lives in another valley, near my mother,' she says.

I know Dr Lhamo has been suffering acute stomach pain for some time. We saw her when she last came to Gyantse to visit the hospital. The doctor said it was an ulcer, probably caused by the long hours she worked and by not eating properly. She was given some pills and told to take it easy. Obviously the pain had not gone away.

I ask her if she has had an endoscopy.

She shakes her head, saying the hospital in Gyantse is not equipped to do one. And she can't go to Shigatse, just half an hour's bus ride away, because she cannot afford the treatment. As a doctor she is entitled to free health care – but only in Gyantse.

Probably she will end up visiting Shigatse even if it means going into debt. But first she will try a shaman's blessing; it will cost next to nothing, and her illness might just lie in the spirit realm.

'Perhaps I did something bad in my previous life. Perhaps I acquired it in this life. I deal with so many patients every day; I may have got it from them, or the influence of their spirits. I am not sure,' she says.

Of all the Tibetans I have met in my year here, Lhamo is the most caring. When she delivers a baby, she does everything a doctor should, but she also treats the mother like a sister, buttoning her jacket, tucking a scarf round her neck, telling her husband to look after her, rearranging the cloth the baby is wrapped in. She is the same with everyone: warm, affectionate, fussy even, like family. And they respond with reverence. Whatever they can afford to give – a block of butter, some potatoes, sheep's tripe – they press into her hands. I can't imagine she has committed any evil deeds that have led to her illness, and I tell her so.

'I don't think I am a bad person,' she says with a blush. 'I was born into a Tibetan farmer's family. But medicine does not seem to be helping me, so I want to try the traditional way.'

Lhamo goes on to tell me about her plan for a pilgrimage to a cave twenty-five miles away. 'It is in the shape of a belly. The old people say if you touch it with your belly, it will help to heal your stomach problem. It might help my illness, or maybe it will help to make sure that my next life has less pain.' I am about to ask her more, but the woman whose daughter-in-law is in labour rushes in to say she thinks the baby is coming.

Lhamo goes into the operating room, and the cameraman goes with her. They come out after half an hour. She is completely crestfallen, and is holding a bag full of blood with the foetus inside it. Another stillbirth.

The cameraman looks at me, shaking his head. 'I stopped the camera.'

It has been a very long day. The woman who has lost her baby looks drained, but seems unemotional, even resigned. At least this time the pregnant woman has survived. The rate at which mothers die in childbirth is high in Tibet, around 400-500 deaths for every 100,000 live births,[50] much higher than for China as a whole, where the figure is thought to be about 45 per 100,000.[51] She puts on her trousers and gets ready to go home. Lhamo takes her arm, leads her to the cart her mother-in-law has got ready, and says goodbye, telling her to take a few days' rest (even after giving birth a traditional Tibetan woman will typically go straight back to work). Lhamo relieves four patients in the courtyard of their drips, picks up her little boy, goes into her room and collapses on the bed. I follow her. She is quiet for a while, and then says, chokingly: 'Another one. I don't know how long I can take this. I have lost count of the dead babies in the valley in the past eighteen months. Whenever there's a knock on our door at night, I fear the worst.'

I ask Lhamo why the maternal and infant mortality rate in rural Tibet is so high, considerably higher than in the rest of China. According to reports by non-governmental health organisations I have read, the one thing that would most to reduce infant mortality rate is having a trained health worker present at every birth, either at home or at the clinic. What does Lhamo think?

'Most of the mothers won't even come to the clinic,' Lhamo says angrily. 'You know we Tibetans believe in ghosts and spirits. The women worry about people being jealous and putting the evil eye on them, so they don't talk about their pregnancy, let alone come in for regular check-ups. They also think the clinic is full of evil spirits because babies die here. So they give birth at home. Then because they believe giving birth is unclean, they will do it in a store room or a stable so as not to pollute the rest of the house. You can imagine how easy it is to get infected. Even if they have their delivery here, it can be too late. I need to tell them how to look after themselves, how to prepare. So often they rush here at the last moment when there is a complication at home, and the baby is stillborn; then they blame the clinic.'

I can see how frustrating it must be for Lhamo trying to per-suade women who are encumbered with all these superstitions. The clinic may be primitive and Lhamo's training limited, but still it is safer than delivery in the village. Butri, the Head of the Women's Association in the valley, has even threatened them with fines if they do not comply. To her frustration too, many women prefer to pay the fine and have what they think is a safe delivery in their stable. I have been struggling all along to accept the locals' beliefs and respect them, be it offerings to Yul Lha to avert hail, or praying for the souls of the dead, or hiding rather than taking pleasure in their sons going to university. If rituals and beliefs make people feel better, all well and good. But these are different. Mothers and babies are dying, unnecessarily.

But Lhamo has her superstitions too. I hesitate to point this out to her; but it does seem just a matter of degree. Lhamo, a doctor, thinks her illness may be due to spirits or to her bad karma. Can she expect the village women to be rational? I have read a very interesting article by a group of Western anthropologists working with health NGOs in Tibet, looking for ways to help bring infant mortality down.[52] They find part of the problem is that the rural health workers have these beliefs too. The anthropologists try to design 'culturally sensitive' approaches, making use of women's beliefs rather than 'eradicating' them. For example, the village women believe blood from the birth is unclean, so they tell them the clinic will dispose of the blood faster. But such efforts have not been very successful. Others say that giving health workers such as Lhamo better training and improving conditions in the clinics is the way forward.[53] But progress by whatever means is painfully slow. In the battle between old beliefs and modern medicine, tradition is far too strong.

Tashi comes back late, dirty and as distressed as Lhamo had been. 'I don't think the man can be saved. All I could do was make him as comfortable as I could. I think the family will have a funeral soon,' he says, taking a cup of tea from his wife.

Lhamo asks him to take care of the remaining patients in the courtyard. They talk between themselves for a little while, then Lhamo asks me: 'Can I go back with you to Gyantse? I think I will go to the hospital for a check-up tomorrow, and I have to buy more medicines for the clinic.'

We leave the clinic. As we pass through Tseten's village I remember that I wanted to ask Lhamo about Loga. She says she knew him from the clinic; the last time she saw him, Dondan brought him in after he had scalded himself. She says she does not know the cause of his condition, and she has seen very few people with it. But she mentions that Loga's cousin, who also lived in the valley, has it too. 'People say it must be their karma.'

There she goes again, I say to myself.

The next morning when we get up, I give Lhamo and her son a big breakfast: steamed buns filled with beef, fried doughnuts, eggs and milk and *tsampa* and butter tea. The boy has never seen so much food at breakfast, and does not know what to eat first. He keeps stuffing things into his mouth, at the same time trying to tell his mother how delicious everything is. She worries that he might burst, but she's smiling, and says it has been a long time since they've eaten so well.

We walk to the hospital from our house. It's a big modern building, only ten years' old. On a marble block the sign reads 'Gyantse People's Hospital' in large gold characters. It's like a palace compared with Lhamo's clinic: beige tiles on the floor, windows everywhere with sun streaming in through them, white walls with a green painted border. The hospital was built with help from Shanghai, and it serves all 70,000 people in Gyantse County.

But while it looks impressive, I doubt if I would want to be treated here if I were seriously ill. Two months ago Loten was admitted, complaining of vomiting and diarrhoea. A doctor examined him and said it was appendicitis, and insisted that he needed an operation urgently. I thought we should seek a second opinion in Shigatse. It turned out that Loten had an upset stomach, brought on by binge drinking and overeating. The doctor in Gyantse was either incompetent, or he wanted to make money. I have seen this reported all over China: you go in with a bruise and they order an MRI scan; you have a fever, and they say you need a blood transfusion. There was a notorious case last year, when a man ran up a bill for more than half a million *yuan*, £36,000, for two weeks in hospital with a heart complaint. The blood they put on the bill added up to twenty-five bathtubs-full a day. They never discovered what was wrong with him, and he died. In our rapid move to the market, hospitals too have become money-making machines, and doctors are now called the 'new prostitutes'. The Chinese health system no longer looks after people from cradle to grave, as it once promised, but it should not be sending so many to early graves after emptying their pockets.

I hope Lhamo will have a good experience today. I leave her in the outpatients department while I go to the clinic for nervous diseases to see if I can find out anything about Loga. I don't have much luck. A young Tibetan doctor on duty tells me he could not say anything without seeing the patient. He asks if I can bring Loga in. He says if I can tell him the name of the disease, he might be able to tell me whether it was treatable here. But of course I don't know this; I decide to do a little research online.

Lhamo's exam goes swiftly too. The doctor can't say why she isn't responding to the pills for her stomach ulcer. Her blood test last time was normal. He recommends that she continue with the medicine and take some leave. We leave the hospital together. She's disappointed. She told the doctor that her pain was getting worse, but he had nothing else to suggest. I try to put her mind at rest. I tell her that I had an endoscopy three years ago which found an ulcer. Mine was painful too, but it went away when I took a break from work and lessened the stress I was under. Lhamo smiles sadly, and tells me she wants to go to the monastery. I offer to accompany her, but she says she will be quite a while. She is going to offer butter lamps to all the Buddhas and deities in the monastery, and walk around it a hundred times – she normally does this thirty times, but she thinks she would like to do more today. It is like going on a pilgrimage. It is supposed to cleanse one's sins from a past life and help towards a better rebirth.

Watching her walk away holding the hand of her little son, I feel sad. Next time I go to Shigatse, I will take her along for an endoscopy, so that she can be reassured. I also think she could do with some rest and better food. On what she and her husband make, she has to feed her son, her mother, and her parents-in-law too. They eat *tsampa* for breakfast, *tsampa* for lunch, and noodles or rice for supper. Very occasionally I see some veg-etables in their bowls, even an egg, probably contributed by a patient. When she has morsels of meat, she gives them to her son. She is as thin as a stick.

At least with Lhamo, I may know what the problem is. Loga's case is much more complicated. After drawing a blank at the hospital, I head to the internet bar next door to try to do a little research. I don't know what I'm looking for. I put in 'mental retardation', and find this: 'The three major known innate causes are Downs syndrome, fetal alcohol syndrome and fragile X syndrome.' But when I read further, none of these causes sounds likely. I take a long shot and email my husband, asking him to consult our child psychiatrist friend, or a teacher special-ising in children with learning difficulties.

While I wait for an answer about Loga, I decide to do a small experiment. My idea was triggered by what I saw at Lhamo's clinic: that grandfather who could not afford to pay the 3 *yuan* for his granddaughter's treatment. Lhamo told me they were not unique. 'If it's a small sum like that, I will take it out of my salary,' Lhamo said. 'But if it's a lot, I may have to turn them away. I hate that.' Her voice grew faint. 'But what can I do? You see the clinic. We have no money, nor do the patients. It is so sad.'

I call Lhamo and ask if she would like to hold a clinic in Tseten's village. I tell her it will be free for patients, and she takes a moment to reply. 'It will cost you a lot of money,' she says.

'That's why I want to try it in one village first – to see how much it costs. And we will pay.' That gets her excited and she agrees.

Then I ring Dondan and Tseten to make sure we can use their house. They think the clinic is a good idea. 'Are you certain?' I ask Tseten. 'It won't take your business away?'

'Don't worry,' he says. 'People will always come to me.'

A few days later, in the warm May sunshine, we set up in the upper courtyard, putting down carpets where Lhamo sits with her medicines in a big travelling bag. Dondan puts nails in the outside doors to hold the IV drips. I am a bit anxious. It is planting time and most villagers are out in the field. We did not make any formal announcement – I did not want to appear to be upstaging the government health system – so we just told half a dozen villagers. But they start to dribble in, most of them bringing their own butter tea or their *chang* in thermoses.

More and more people arrive, quite a few with their babies and small children. Soon the courtyard is crowded. Men are drinking and laughing, passing their *chang* around. Lhamo rummages in her bag, while the women around her crane to see what she has inside it. Tseten was right. Many of them go into the prayer room to consult him while they are in the queue for Lhamo. Loga is very happy, running in and out of the house. He drinks with the visitors, and asks their names over and over again. He always likes a party. And I keep thinking, what is really wrong with him?

A grandmother slips a little girl's shirt off so Lhamo can see the rash on her back. Two mothers lower their boys' trousers for them to be injected with penicillin. They cry bitterly and are comforted with sweets. Tibetans have a particularly bad start in life; one study a few years back found 51 per cent of rural children below the age of seven suffered from stunted growth due to malnutrition, compared with 17 per cent in China as a whole.[54] And the common illnesses Tibetans die of are those found all over the poorer parts of the Third World: TB, gastric disorders, infectious and parasitic diseases.

Lhamo stops frequently to ask me about cost. Can she prescribe a particular medicine, and for five days' worth rather than three? Normally, she says, when she prescribes antibiotics, patients only want a couple of days worth, worried about the cost. She tells them they should finish the full five-day course, otherwise the body will develop resistance. But they cannot afford it. Each time I tell her to go ahead, and she bows. She treats her last patient four hours after we start. Altogether nearly forty people come to see her that day, and at the end of it, I tot up the bill. It comes to 470 *yuan*, just over £30, mostly for antibiotics, drips, injections, cough medicine, pain killers, and bandages. Lhamo is pleased. 'If we had asked them to pay, probably only eight or nine of them would have wanted the treatment.' But she apologises again and again for spending so much of our money.

I agree with Lhamo, we should not be spending our own money. It's like throwing a cup of water on a forest fire. In theory, the villagers have subsidised health care. They pay 8 *yuan* a year under what is known as the Cooperative Medical System, and can get reimbursed for 70 per cent of any treatments they pay for. But they have to fill in a form, in Chinese, and bring it to the *xiang* HQ. Most of them cannot read or write in Tibetan, let alone Chinese, and the bureaucracy scares them. For a small sum, it's not worth the effort. They can get back 70 per cent of a large bill too, say for hospital treatment in Gyantse. But they have to come up with the full amount in cash first, which they simply do not have. No wonder the villagers go trustingly to Tseten.

Tseten has told me that he is on the last leg of his qualification as a practitioner of traditional medicine. Of the four Tibetan Tantras of Medicine, he has passed exams on three, with one to go. Then he will be able to treat patients not only for their spirit-inflicted illnesses but for those of this world too, another 101 diseases. These are mainly due to diet or climate, or habits and lifestyle, which cause imbalances in the elements of the body. He will not earn more: doctors of Tibetan medicine traditionally do not charge. But they command high status in the community. With medical care as it is, Tseten knows he will stay in demand.

Subsidised care, such as it is, is special to Tibet; in the rest of rural China, it does not exist. Villagers are scared of getting sick. Chinese newspapers report people throwing themselves off buildings after they hear they have a serious illness – they do not want to get treated and bankrupt their families. What a change from the old days when all over China everyone was treated for free, by paramedics or in hospital. But since the 1990s the whole health system has been 'reformed' to relieve the state of the burden of caring for its people. There was no debate, no public consultation, no way to complain. A billion people have to fend for themselves, and if they cannot pay, tough luck. Or karma.

I wonder whether modern medicine, if it had been there, could have saved Loga. I still do not know what he suffers from. At last, after two weeks of waiting, I get a reply from the child psychiatrist my husband consulted; he thinks Loga might be afflicted with something called phenylketonuria. The disease fits Mila's tale of 'poisoned' blood, and Loga's sudden change from normal to abnormal at ten months, after staying with the relative. I researched the disease further on the internet. 'PKU', as it is known, was discovered by a Norwegian doctor in 1934. An afflicted baby will look perfectly normal for the first few months; then he or she will begin to have symptoms like vomiting, irritability and sometimes pale hair, irregular teeth, and muscle problems. By 1954, a treatment was discovered – it consists mainly of a special low-protein diet. The diet must begin early, preferably in the first three months, and has to continue for life. After a year without treatment, brain damage is irreversible. All this seemed to match Loga's case. The disease is hereditary, which would fit with the cousin having it too.

The faulty gene that gives rise to PKU was identified in 1992. What is missing is an enzyme in the blood that allows the body to convert an amino acid essential for growth and development. It is a fairly rare disease, affecting one in 10,000 births. In many parts of the world babies are routinely tested for it at birth; this is still not done at all in Tibet or in fact in most of China. Even if Loga had been correctly diagnosed, it would have been next to impossible nearly fifty years ago to put him on the right diet. Mila and the doctors were almost certainly wrong to think that the pills Loga was given made any difference.

In the Google sea another website caught my eye. It was a news announcement from 2005. 'New gene therapy techniques cure mice with PKU.' The scientist who identified the faulty gene made the breakthrough. This is science at work: taking time, observing, looking for cause, effect, remedy, and, ultimately, a complete cure, all probably within a century. As a doctor working in the field has written: 'If one were to construct a fantasy about a human genetic disease for which all is known and a cure available, phenylketonuria (PKU) is likely to come to mind…It is an astounding story, the standard to which all genetic disease is held.'[55] How far it all is from Tseten's world of spirits and mantras.

I drive to the village the next day. I catch Tseten about to leave, locking the gate. A young man in a leather jacket is standing by his motorbike, holding Tseten's drum. 'Someone in his family is sick. He's come to fetch me. Everyone else is out in the field. What can I do for you?' Tseten asks, as he climbs on the back seat of the bike.

'I've got something to tell you.' I explain what I've found out about Loga. This won't change anything for Loga, but it might at least save the family from the remainder of their three million prayers.

Tseten listens patiently, and then says: 'What the experts say may be right, but it does not explain why I didn't get it, or Dondan. Why was it only Loga? There must be something in his karma.'

The bike roars off, spraying me with dirt, and Tseten's robe billows out behind him. He may accept what science can do, but he still has complete faith in his world too.

TEN

Crime Is Its Own Punishment

SOMEONE IS KNOCKING GENTLY on the iron gate of our courtyard. At first I did not hear it amidst the chattering of the birds outside my window. I have been lying in bed enjoying their singing. The winter has been so long, so silent, and now the birds have suddenly appeared in force, filling the branches of our willow tree and the young poplars. They seem to be as cheerful as I am that spring is finally here. The knocking persists. Who could it be? It's only seven o'clock, too early for the housekeeper. I run out to open the gate. To my great surprise, it's Mila.

It has been quite a while since I've seen him. He'd been staying with his daughter in Shigatse for the winter; the family was worried that their village house was not warm enough and that he might catch pneumonia. He did not even join them for the Tibetan New Year in February. But he should have been back some time ago. Everyone is busy preparing for the spring planting, and they really could do with his help.

There is no rain at this time of year. Irrigation has to be diverted down a canal from the Nyangchu River before planting can begin. Dondan has been working day and night with other villagers to clean and repair the canal. Each household has a member sleeping there. They have to pay for the electricity that runs the pumps. It costs a lot of money, and they cannot afford to let anything go wrong. Last year the water burst through a breach in the canal and a huge amount was wasted. Yangdron has had to bring out Dondan's meals, and get the family's plots ready too, while looking after everything else at home. Tseten has performed the ritual for the village, asking for forgiveness for disturbing the soil and killing insects while they are planting. Mila would have been a help, not least for keeping an eye on Loga. I have missed him too.

Mila's hands are cold when I shake them. I rush to put cow-pats in the stove and get the fire going. It is still chilly in the early morning. I put a steamer on the stove with some buns in it and go to wake Penpa so he can make butter tea. Buns dipped in the tea will be Mila's breakfast.

'You must be busy, filming the villagers getting ready for planting, and the monastery preparing for the Buddha's birth-day,' he says.

He's right. We have been shuttling between the fields and the Palkhor Monastery. The Buddha's birthday celebrations, called Sagadaba, will start on 15th May, and last for a whole month. It is one of the most important events for the people of Gyantse. The monks will perform an elaborate fire ritual, praying for those who have departed. Then there will be the great mask dance for which the monks have to practise weeks in advance. At the same time, they will make three big *mandalas* in front of the statue of the Buddha in the main hall. The climax is the display of an image of the Future Buddha on the side of a hill, a giant *tangka*, 30 by 40 metres, and people from all over the county will congregate at the monastery on the day. The deputy lama, Tsultrim, one of our film's characters, is in charge of the celebrations. It is a big responsibility for him: given how precarious and sensitive things are in Tibet, so much can go wrong.

I feel the tension in the air as we follow him day after day making his meticulous preparations.

'I'm busy too,' Mila tells me. 'Today, I have to catch a bus to Kangmar. I am doing a special service for a big family there. It will last ten days.'

I ask him if it's a wedding or a funeral.

'Neither. As you know it is the custom here for every family to invite a monk or a shaman to say prayers. It is to protect them against illness and misfortune. You can do it any time of the year, but doing it this month, during Sagadaba, doubles the merit and the protection. I've got prayers lined up for the whole month, almost every day.'

This explains his absence. I watch him eating his breakfast, slightly stooped over, and wiping steam from the tea off his spectacles. He looks frail, and I wonder why he has taken on so much. 'I have to do it; my father and my grandfather did it for them. We have to keep it going,' is all he said. He did not mention it but I also sensed money was a factor: with Jigme and Gyatso in college, the family is barely coping. If his other two grandchildren were to go to college too, the family would be overwhelmed.

But what I really want to ask Mila has little to do with this world of rituals. On my journey to retrace the footsteps of the Chinese monk Xuanzang from China to India and back, my greatest insights came not from any scriptures or preaching but from the people I met whose lives embodied their faiths. I recall one old man in particular, Duan, who lived in Xian. In many ways his history was not unlike Mila's. He was thrown out of his monastery in 1963 and forced to marry, but he never gave up his beliefs, even though he had to meditate and pray silently and in the dark for almost thirty years. Monasteries could be destroyed, but inside himself he had a shrine that was inviolate. When I commented on his suffering, he just said: 'So many people were tortured to death, but I'm alive. So I can't really say I have suffered.'

I always thought that I would discover even more by coming to Tibet, the wellspring of another great Buddhist tradition. The spirituality of this mystic land and its people is so well attested by travellers and explorers whose fervour shines out in their numerous accounts and photographs. George Bogle, the first Englishman to enter Tibet in 1795, was envious of the Tibetans' faith: 'I wish you enjoy this happiness which the advanced nations have already lost. When they are in the endless pursuit of their greed and ambitions, you live in peace and joy under the protection of the wildness.'[56] I too was impressed on my earlier visits by the omnipresence of faith in Tibet. But I had never had the opportunity to stay long enough to educate myself more thoroughly.

I thought making *A Year in Tibet* would give me the chance I was waiting for. Right at the start I decided to make the monastery a pillar of the film. I soon picked out the tough, serious, and workaholic deputy lama, Tsultrim. He recommended Tsephun, the sixteen-year-old novice monk, who is still learning the basics of Buddhist scripture and practice. Tsephun, in turn, is guided by his hot-tempered, but kind, master, Dondrup – one of the oldest monks in the monastery and a survivor from the old Tibet.

Filming in the monastery could not have been more exciting, but not for the reasons I expected. In fact it has made me feel a deep sadness. First the tension of the Panchen Lama's visit in late September. Then in December, a priceless statue of the Buddha was stolen from the monastery, along with five ancient *tangkas*. The Gyantse government and police sent in a joint team to investigate, and more treasures went missing on their watch. Three monks were arrested – one even attempted suicide – but the crimes have remained unsolved. At great expense, sixteen

CCTV cameras were installed throughout the monastery, and all the valuable statues were placed behind floor-to-ceiling bars. The day after these security measures were completed, another *tangka* was stolen from the one chapel that was not monitored.

Clearly it was an inside job. But perhaps some of the monks were trying to make a point. The team was not just investigating; they were using the incident as an occasion for questioning the monks, hoping to weed out those they thought were trouble-makers. The senior monks made an effort to keep things smooth – the government has the final say on the number of monks in a monastery. But the relationship has become irksome. The monastery has not been allowed to recruit in recent years and if monks are thrown out now, their numbers will decline even further. There seemed to be a silent battle of wills. The monks demanded evidence before anyone was thrown out. And so far, there is no conclusive evidence. The case is still unsolved. Tsultrim has been losing sleep for months. Now he looks totally ragged. I have stopped calling him daily in case there is more bad news.

Tsultrim has plenty of other troubles. Tsephun, the novice monk, is a star: natural, innocent, curious, and always with a spark in his eyes. But his heart does not seem to be in the monastery. He dropped out before he finished primary school, and his family sent him here, hoping it would make something of him. Tsephun has a habit of running off to the tea shop, and likes to watch kung-fu films and play video games. Then a month ago, a girl's mirror and comb were found in his cell, and the master feared the worst: a girl turning up with a baby, claiming Tsephun was the father. The master called Tsephun's father to the monastery, showing him the evidence, and saying he could no longer control Tsephun; it would be best for him to go home.

The only time I feel at peace in the monastery is when the

monks are chanting their morning prayers. For me, Buddhism is lived. It is how we refine our thoughts, our words, and our deeds. Rituals are there to help us along the way. As the deep, soothing voices fill the prayer hall, I can at least feel something of the elusive transcendence I am seeking. And then, all too soon, I am brought back to reality: I watch Tsultrim's eyes darting back and forth, checking who of the monks is missing – there is a fine of 3 *yuan*. Then I watch Tsultrim stand, walk down the rows of monks, and slap the ones who are dozing. The young monks have probably been out late playing pool or travelling to perform rituals for money. They are not spending much time on their sacred texts either. In the annual test in February, there was a sutra set to be memorised; only two monks passed the exam on it, despite the fact that those who failed were fined 200 *yuan* – the fine was supposed to be an incentive to study harder.

All this is going on in one of Tibet's greatest monasteries. The Palkhor Monastery used to attract the most distinguished lamas for debates, a tradition which started with the 1st Panchen Lama. Of all the sects of Tibetan Buddhism, Geluba – the Yellow Hat – is the most recently formed, with the Dalai Lama, and later the Panchen Lama, as its spiritual leaders. Founded in the fifteenth century, at first it had only a modest following. The 1st Panchen Lama came up with an ingenious way to make a name for his sect. He chose a monastery where all the sects could congregate and hold a debate – the Palkhor Monastery. His knowledge and oratory skills were so powerful that he won over the entire assembly. Ever after, to commemorate his achievement, monks from all of the big monasteries in Tibet came to Gyantse every year to debate. The tradition survived right up to Mila's time.

This is why I hope Mila will tell me more about his monastic life. There is something special about him. He is warm, compassionate, erudite. He has told me before that he joined the

Palkhor Monastery when he was twelve, and not, as so often in Tibet, because his family was poor, but because they wanted him to pursue a higher calling. That dream dissolved in 1959 after the Tibetan uprising.

The monks from the Palkhor Monastery were among those leading the uprising in Gyantse, attacking Party offices and military posts. They even formed a death squad of 150 monks. But Mila was not sucked into the political mayhem. He said he was more interested in sutras than politics. That did not save him. A government work team took up quarters in the monastery after the uprising, and one of the officials told him: 'You can be a good Buddhist anywhere.' Of the 1,520 monks in the Palkhor Monastery, barely a hundred – mostly the old and infirm, orphans, or those whose families could not take them back – were allowed to remain. The rest were either sent to prison, or told to go home.

'How did it feel to be sent home?' I ask Mila.

'What could I do? I was not the only one. The monks from the three big monasteries in Lhasa were also sent home. My sister was thrown out of her nunnery too. It was fate.'

By getting married, Mila had at least showed that he was 'progressive'. Did he manage to keep up his practice at home? How did his training at the monastery help him? I was thinking of Duan, the ex-monk in Xian. He meditated for nine hours every night, hardly sleeping at all.

'I was so busy, I hardly had time to think of the Buddha,' he says, with a wry smile. He goes on to explain that, after the uprising, the Chinese government concluded it was high time to dismantle Tibet's old governmental system, which they had left more or less intact up until then. They called it the Democratic Reform. The monasteries were just one of what they termed the 'three pinnacles of evil'; the other two were the old government, and the aristocrats and landlords. The Party maintained that all three had oppressed the Tibetan people for centuries; they were also the leaders and instigators of the uprising. Now they must pay for their crimes against the Tibetan people and the Motherland. At the grass-roots level, the Party enlisted Tibetans like Mila who could read and write. They would join in work teams and take the message to the people.

'After I went back to the village in 1959, it was one campaign after another: like a wheel, it never stopped turning,' Mila says. 'First we did political education, telling people they no longer had to respect their old masters; they were liberated new men and women. Then we had the "Three Strikes and Two Reductions", against the uprising, against the old government, and against the feudal system of slavery. The "reductions" were about rent and interest. Now the people would get the bulk of their harvest, not hand it over to the landlords. And all the time there was a constant struggle against "superstition", as they called it, and religion.' The people had to be persuaded that it was not karma at the root of their misery, but exploitation, and their willingness to submit to it. Doctors, not shamans, would cure the sick; and it was not evil spirits that entered the body, but bacteria. There was no hereafter, so the dead could just be dumped for the vultures without the expense of sky burial ceremonies.

I came across some government records which give a good idea of the intensity of this political work in a district just fifteen miles from Mila's village. In one campaign, the district government organised 87 special issues of wall posters, 1,583 articles, 543 struggle meetings, 671 keynote speakers, 101 training events for 2,681 activists, 45 propaganda teams to help the villagers, and 48 newspaper reading groups.[57] It was much the same where Mila was, and he was expected to take part in all of these things. 'It was day and night,' he said. 'Even after a day's work, we still had to do political study for two or three hours.'

Keeping busy did not keep Mila out of trouble. In 1963, in Tibet as in everywhere else in China, another political campaign began – this one even more intense, and more far-reaching. It was known as the Socialist Education Campaign. It called on the masses to struggle against enemies of the people, to love socialism, and to love the Motherland. In Tibet, 'enemies of the people' meant anyone remotely connected with the old hierarchy or anyone who showed sympathy with the Dalai Lama. Everyone was under pressure to dig deep and look within themselves for any wrongdoings. And one day at a meeting, the Party official in charge turned to Mila and asked: 'Do you have anything to confess? Are you hiding something? Because we know about you. Now is your chance. Tell the truth and we will be lenient.'

'I tried to think what they were getting at, but nothing occurred to me,' Mila tells me now. 'It must have been about my time in the monastery, but I had never done anything wrong or harmed anyone.' But they had something on him. He had collected rent for the monastery from its properties nearby. 'It wasn't money for me. Every penny went to the monastery. Someone had to collect it.'

But that was not how the Party saw it. It was exploitation and he had not admitted to it. What else might he be concealing? Now the whole meeting rounded on him. It was the start of a long ordeal.

After this, Mila became a target at the daily struggle meetings. He was marched from village to village in a moving column of the guilty – lamas, nuns, aristocrats, landlords, estate managers, and rich farmers. They were made to wear their old costumes, in Mila's case his monk's robe. He was also made to carry a big papier-mâché key, symbolising the rent collector's coffer. He was accused of being a parasite, of cheating people of the money they gave in donations, of falsely claiming to intercede with the

186

gods, and of killing people because he pretended to be able to cure them as a shaman. As the villagers shouted at him, listing his crimes, they also attacked him with sticks, whips, stones, hoes, needles – whatever they could find. Often Mila had to be carried home. Every morning when he woke and heard the gong summoning him to yet another meeting, he shuddered, wondering whether he would be alive at the end of the day.

He was told he would be pardoned if he confessed. But anything he wrote down became fodder for the next struggle meeting. He had to work hard to think of new things to confess, always careful to keep them fairly mundane. A trader from his village, tired of saying he'd cheated people, had written down the name of a group he'd once heard of in Lhasa. Because it was a rebel group, the Party officials seized on it, and sent the trader to prison. Mila's stories reminded me of a confession I'd once read, by the head of the Sakya Monastery, one of the oldest and greatest monasteries in Tibet: 'I have confessed whatever I am guilty of. Now I understand it is the custom of your Party to say I have done things I have not done. So now I apologise to the people for everything done or left undone. I am guilty of everything on earth.'[58]

Shamans are supposed to have extraordinary powers. I've read that some people ask shamans to perform special rituals against their enemies. Did Mila ever contemplate placing a curse on his torturers? 'What?' he asks, looking up from his cup of butter tea. 'The cardinal principle of Buddhism is never to harm anyone, not even your enemy. Never! I don't know where you got that from.'

I ask him if he ever despaired and considered taking his own life in those terrible times.

'No,' he says, firmly. 'Life is too precious. As a Buddhist, you don't kill anything, let alone take your own life. Everything has a reason. Sometimes I thought perhaps it was all happening because of something I had done in a previous life.'

I still find the idea of karma hard to swallow, though I suppose it helps Mila not to blame anyone or bear grudges. I begin to feel I understand Mila a little bit better. I want to ask him more, but he has to catch the bus to Kangmar. I walk him to the market to buy him something for his trip. He insists that he already has a thermos of tea and some *tsampa*, and does not need anything else. The day has turned warm; the trees, bare two weeks ago, are now tipped with yellowish green leaves, though I can still see snow lingering on the mountains in the distance. There seems to be more oxygen in the air; even my steps feel lighter. As I wave goodbye, Mila tells me he will be back at the end of Sagadaba, so I can catch up with him then.

For days after this visit, I think about what Mila went through. No matter how much I think I know about the Mao era, every time I come across a personal experience, I feel amazed all over again. The suffering is infinite, it seems. In Tibet, the oppression took place on such a massive scale, I find I can hardly comprehend it. But I do not have many moments for contemplation. Filming the preparations for Sagadaba is all-consuming. We spend quite a bit of time following the monks practising their dances. Their styles and abilities vary quite a bit. Some dance as if they have air in their bodies, lifting and stretching – they are solemn, graceful – almost majestic. Others can't even follow the basic steps – left foot, right foot, then a 360-degree turn. They trip and fall over, inviting loud booing and laughter from the other monks. Tsultrim is rather portly, but he dances every step with them, as if to show them that if he can dance with his bulky body, so can they. They take regular breaks from rehearsing to play poker, or for refreshments and a special lunch of stewed beef meant to inspire greater effort.

Finally, the big day arrives. People begin to gather outside the prayer hall, families or even whole villages together. They put down carpets or pieces of cardboard on the ground and claim the best spots. Women lay out snacks and sweets, thermoses of tea and big plastic bottles of *chang*. Inevitably, some in the crowd have already started drinking. Meanwhile the monks are donning their costumes in the chapel behind the monastery kitchen. Some wear brilliant red brocade robes, patterned with dragons and clouds; others wear deep blue ones with white cranes flying on the back, and bright yellow chrysanthemums blooming on their chests. They wear large gold or black hats, masks, and ropes of beads over their shoulders.

Two old men help the dancers get ready. One is tall, with silver hair and a rather sweet demeanour – his round spectacles tied behind his head with elastic; the other is shorter and darker, with a gaunt, heavily lined face and pinched cheeks. They tie pleated skirts around the dancers' waists and put sashes over them, help them into silk tunics, and decorate their big black conical hats with ribbons and tassels. The young monks are joking or making faces at each other, but these two older men are completely focussed on their work. As soon as they finish dressing one of the monks, they take a step back to survey their work. Then they break into huge smiles.

It occurs to me that the men might be former monks from the monastery. I check with Tsultrim who tells me that the two men are brothers, and that both were monks in the monastery before being forced to leave in 1959. They have been coming here for more than twenty years, first to teach the monks the dances, and now to help with the costumes. The grandson of the shorter brother is now a monk in the monastery.

Once all the monks are fitted with costumes, I ask the shorter of the two men whether he knows Mila.

'Of course I know him. We were in this monastery at the same time and went home at the same time. I suffered for more than ten years because of him.'

'What did Mila do to you?' I ask, completely taken aback.

'He reported me.'

'How can you be sure it was Mila?' I don't want to sound as if I doubt the old man's story, but I simply can't believe what I'm hearing.

'I know it's shocking,' he says. And then he adds: 'If you don't believe me, ask my older brother.' He points to the taller man with the spectacles, still making some last-minute adjustments to the costumes.

I suppose I shouldn't be so astonished – such stories are a common characteristic of Mao's China. Unlike Stalin, Mao had no need for a vast secret police. He put everyone to work spying on those around them – in the village, in the street, in the workplace, in the monastery, even inside their own homes. People reported on others for any number of reasons – to gain favour with the Party, for power, or simply to save their own skins. In the days of the continuous political campaigns that culminated in the Cultural Revolution, everyone lived with suspicion. People stopped trusting their husbands or wives, even their own children. The shadow of such betrayal is still with us, particularly in Tibet. With so many Tibetans and monks following the Dalai Lama, it is easy these days to find something to report. But, still, I have trouble attributing this kind of behaviour to Mila. When I'm finally able to ask the taller brother about Mila, he nods his head. 'My brother suffered a lot,' he tells me. 'For more than ten years, he was the target at endless struggle meetings. He was the only one singled out in our village, so he had to bear all the attacks on his own. And no matter how often he protested his innocence, nobody would listen to him. They all believed Mila.'

The monks are ready to leave for the performance now. The brothers stand back and watch them. I ask the shorter brother what his feelings are about Mila.

'Mila and I still meet, quite often,' he tells me. 'There aren't enough monks in the monastery, and sometimes villagers invite us both for a big ceremony, and I'm asked to be his assistant. I don't mind. We talk as if nothing happened between us.'

Does he not hate Mila?

'No I do not. What is the use of hatred? It makes us bitter and accumulates bad karma. It is my fate. All I want now is for my grandson to continue where I could not and I hope I will be reborn as a monk in my next life.' He points to the tallest of the masked dancers. 'That's him,' he says proudly.

A drum roll announces the beginning of the dances. Both brothers stand back to watch the dancers file out of the chapel.

Now, transformed into demons, animals and ghosts, the monks are ready to take to the stage. I follow a stag, a horse and a buffalo onto the open ground in front of the main hall, where thousands of people are waiting. To the sound of bells, drums, long horns and cymbals, the monks dance gracefully and energetically in a circle. Their masks are frightening – grinning or scowling. The children in the crowd scream when the monks come near. The taller brother, standing near me, tells me there is nothing to worry about: these are the guardian deities. Their appearance is meant to frighten evildoers and protect the faithful.

Then comes the Dance of the Lord of Death. Two monks appear, wearing large grinning skulls, close-fitting white costumes, and shoes like deep-sea divers'. They have a skeletal look. As they dash about vigorously, the taller brother tells me that he used to play one of these parts. He says the men are trying to teach us the Buddhist concept of impermanence – that death is not the end of life, but the beginning of another stage of existence. There is nothing to fear. I think he may be right: perhaps once you can look death in the face, particularly under a brilliant blue sky, it is not so scary.

My favourite is the Black Hat Dance. Twenty monks make their entrance, wearing towering black hats and shooting angry looks at the crowd. Their aprons are painted with monsters' faces, with long fangs and bulging eyes. This dance is based on the assassination of a king called Lang Darma, who ruled Tibet from 836-842. He is the monster on the dancers' aprons. During his reign, monasteries were shut down, monks were thrown out, forced to marry, or ordered to hunt wild beasts, and those who refused were killed. Translations of Buddhist texts were halted, and the Indian masters who came to Tibet to propagate the faith were threatened with death. One day, a monk named Lhalong Pedor hid a bow and arrow in the sleeves of his cloak, and rode on a black horse to Lhasa to dance before the King. In the middle of the dance, he drew out his bow and shot an arrow through Lang Darma's chest. Then he jumped on his horse and took it across a river. The water washed away the black charcoal he had painted his white horse with, and he reversed his black cloak to show its white lining. He escaped unrecognised. Soon after Lang Darma's death, Tibet fell into turmoil and civil war. Even though scholars are revising their opinions on Lang Darma (some claim he was not anti-Buddhist at all), legends persist. Now the Black Hat Dance is one of the most important dances, performed in almost all the monasteries and by all Buddhist sects. It is symbolic of the protection of the dharma. It is also believed to have the power of invoking all the guardian deities of the monastery.

To me the dance calls to mind the hatred, violence and destruction of the Cultural Revolution. As I watch the whirling dancers quickening their pace, the monster eyes on their flying aprons seem to blur into the contorted faces of the Red Guards, who once unleashed their frenzied rage against Buddhism here in this very monastery. In the summer of 1966, a dozen major Red Guard factions took over Gyantse and the monastery.

They had fanciful names: the 'Grand Alliance to Safeguard Chairman Mao's Thought', 'Forever Alliance HQ', 'Struggle Against Your Own Selfish Thoughts', 'Revisionism', 'Liberated Serfs', 'Revolution Forever', and 'Follow Chairman Mao's Grand Strategy'. They battled ferociously to outdo each other as the true soldiers for Mao's cause. One day the few monks remaining in the monastery were reciting their morning prayers in the main hall, just behind where I have been watching the dancers perform. A group of Red Guards marched through them shouting slogans, and then screamed: 'Shut up, all of you.'

'From that day on, we were indeed silenced,' one of the older monks told me. 'We never gathered in prayer again.'

Inside the hall, the Red Guards tried to pull down the giant statue of the Buddha – they couldn't move it, so instead they broke off its arms and head. The Buddhas in the side chapels were smashed, and statues were pulled down, just as the Red Guards had done at the Tashilunpo Monastery in Shigatse. Sutras and scriptures dating back to the fifteenth century were collected and burned near the monastery entrance: the fire raged for three days and three nights, the red flames lighting up the sky. Mountains of ashes were taken to the fields as fertiliser.

Once the statues and sutras were disposed of, villagers from each district of Gyantse were invited to tear down one of the monastery's sixteen halls. A few were spared and converted into government warehouses for grain. The beautiful white pagoda to the left of the main hall, for which the monastery is famous, survived. I heard that someone had cleverly argued with the Red Guards, reasoning it was a proof of exploitation of the people by the monastery. But all the doors were taken off, and the murals on the walls were smeared with mud or red paint. Another hall behind the pagoda, but further up the hill, is also still standing. Perhaps it was just too much effort for anyone to climb up there to knock it down.

After the dances, I follow the monks to the kitchen where tea is served. There, hanging on the wall and draped with a white *khata*, is a framed print depicting the monastery in the old days. Its sixteen halls are dotted across the hill, surrounding the beautiful white pagoda. The sight of it never fails to amaze me: this great repository of minds and hearts, of centuries of devotion, wisdom and love – destroyed in a matter of weeks. Four decades after the Cultural Revolution, the monks have not succeeded in restoring any one of the halls. The ruins have been left standing, a reminder of what the place once was, and of what happened here.

As soon as Sagadaba is over, I go to Shigatse to see Mila. I feel really uncomfortable. Should I mention my encounter with the two brothers? Should I ask him why he did it? I'm still undecided when we meet outside the Tashilunpo Monastery. Mila is turning prayer-wheels. I wait until he's finished, and then we walk together to his daughter's home, about a hundred yards away. Along the way, I ask him whether, after he was denounced, he thought he would ever practise again. 'Never!' he says. 'I thought it was what the books of prophecy had warned us about: the end of the dharma.'

He was referring to one of the many volumes of prophecy in Tibet, written in the ninth century, and widely believed by the Tibetans to have predicted the arrival of Communism: 'The subjects will rule the kingdom, the king will be made a commoner. A sacrilegious act will be considered a deed of heroism.' Another passage reads like a direct prophecy of the Cultural Revolution: it mentions a time 'when Tibet's monasteries become empty, and when the great lamas roam like street dogs'.[59]

Once we are sitting down inside his daughter's prayer room, I ask Mila about his services in Kangmar. He says that there's a large demand for them and that he's going back in a few days' time. This might be the last time I see Mila. I hesitate, but I find I cannot hold back. I tell him about the brothers I met during Sagadaba, and ask if he knows them. Mila lowers his head, counting the rosary in his hand. He replies that he knew them during his monastery days, and changes the subject. He asks how I enjoyed the Sagadaba.

I tell him about what we have filmed – the dancers in their dazzling costumes, the three stunning *mandalas* made of coloured sand that took forty monks five days to create. I say that even the lazy monks, the ones who usually had so much time on their hands, seemed to be transformed by the work – and that the results were achingly beautiful.

At the end of the festivities, the *mandalas*, symbols of a perfect universe, were destroyed with one stroke of a broom, in order to demonstrate the impermanence of things. And then, just before sunrise the next day, the giant *tangka* was unfolded on the hillside for the world to see. It took my breath away. We were lucky enough to be able to film it up close, but at the same time I felt sad. I knew that, fearing unrest, the government had issued instructions that no one in government service and no students could take part in the Sagadaba celebrations. Only local villagers came, so what should have been a crowd of 30,000 was instead a crowd of a few thousand.

Mila listens to what I have to say about the festivities. Do they remind him of his time there, I wonder? Like the two brothers, he was invited back by the monastery twenty years ago when all the traditions had been forgotten. He helped the monks to restart the dances and the celebrations. But he stopped doing it soon afterwards. Why? I ask. Mila does not say anything. His eyes are half-closed and he is telling his rosary. He is in another world.

I'm deliberating about whether to tell Mila that I have invited the taller brother to our house for tea. Unlike his younger brother or Mila, he was actually imprisoned for over a decade, 'Just for shouting some slogans during the uprising,' he said. 'It was a mad time. Lots of people went mad and did unspeakable things. Anyone who was not mad had to suffer.' He was a keen talker, quiet, but very expressive, giving me lots of graphic details of his time in prison, bearing out everything the Panchen Lama wrote in the *70,000-Character Petition*. I could see why he had got into trouble in the first place. Now old and fragile, he was no threat to anyone.

When it was time for the tall brother to take leave, he turned to me and said, almost as an afterthought, 'I told you that Mila reported on my brother. You ought to know my younger brother did the same thing to Mila. They were both young, very clever, and competitive. I know it doesn't sound very Buddhist, but their rivalry, and then the political pressure, got the better of them.' Then he left, refusing to let us drive him to the bus station. I stood there speechless, watching his bent figure padding slowly down the dusty lane.

It was another astonishing revelation. I did not know why he decided to reveal the secret, or why he left it until then to tell me. Perhaps after all these years of learning to be cautious, years in which no one wanted to talk about these questions, it was a relief for him to be able to speak. Perhaps he did not want to leave me with the impression that Mila alone was guilty. Perhaps he was returning to being himself. His profoundest hopes for a monastic life had been destroyed but he remained very much a Buddhist, determined to be truthful. He stayed celibate too – a very difficult choice in a Tibetan village, where it takes a family to make a decent living. Without a robe, without a monastery, he was still a monk inside.

I look across at Mila, sitting under a *tangka* of a benign deity. He is almost in a trance, as if his prayers and meditation might

196

be taking him beyond the pain and disillusion of the past. I remember an old man in the village telling me once that in the old days in Gyantse if someone broke the law and ran away, the authorities would not pursue him. People believed that crime was its own punishment; the guilty person's karma would be his penalty. Mila has faced trials and choices more difficult than most of us will ever know. Like so many others, he is living with what he has done. I decide I will not ask him any more questions. I will leave him in peace, if peace it is.

ELEVEN

Keeping the Faith

WHEN I FIRST ARRIVED in Gyantse in July 2006 I found a town full of excitement. I was on my own, making preparations for the film, and I had shown up just in time for the town's biggest annual event, the Horse Race Festival. Cars, motor rickshaws and tractors were converging on the racetrack at the edge of town, behind the No. 1 High School. They were loaded to breaking point with boxes, tent poles, tables and chairs, carpets, and tanks of water. Government organisations, from schools and hospitals to the police and the court, would be arriving in force, together with teams from the county's eighteen *xiang*, and traders from hundreds of miles around.

Beyond the commotion, green seas of sprouting barley, broken here and there by bright yellow mustard fields, stretched all the way to the mountains. Thickly leaved trees and wild-flowers grew beneath them. The snows on the horizon had vanished under the brilliant sun, and the Nyangchu River was in spate, making it live up to its name: 'the place for everything delicious'. I could breathe easily, and the weather was at its best – the ideal time for the people of Gyantse to enjoy themselves.

After touring the festival site, I walked back to the Jianzang

Hotel. I was staying there while I looked for a house to rent and characters for the film. I found Jianzang, the hotel's owner, sitting in the lobby with a cup of tea and his English vocabulary notebook, speaking the words aloud. His wife and two maids were folding piles of sheets from the morning's wash and putting them on the reception desk. Across from Jianzang an old lady wearing glasses and black traditional dress sat watching them quietly. Hardly before I had joined Jianzang on the sofa, he asked me, 'What is the English word for *bahe*? I want to tell our guests what they are going to see at the festival.'

'Tug-of-war,' I replied.

'That's funny; it's supposed to be fun, not war,' he said.

He was not sure what the Tibetan word was for tug-of-war, so I tried out on him some other words and phrases I had picked up that day. This was the pattern we adopted from the start: I taught him English and he taught me Tibetan. But he always had other ideas, too. Could I help him design an English language brochure for his hotel? Or could I write the opening speech for the eighth anniversary of the opening of his hotel in 2008? 'What is the hurry?' I asked him. 'That's after the Beijing Olympics.'

'You'll be gone by then,' he told me. 'I might as well make use of you now.'

I decided to ask Jianzang to be one of our film characters after my first day in his hotel. He is short and compact, a bundle of energy, and always eager to learn, his small eyes on the move, ever dreaming up new schemes. He was the first man in Gyantse to quit a government job, as a doctor in the hospital, and set up on his own. With the profits from his clinic, he built a hotel in 2000, the year construction began for the railway from Beijing to Lhasa. He spotted the tourism trend before anybody else in Gyantse. His character comes through in his hotel. It is clean and orderly, the staff are conscientious and attentive and all in uniform. With an entry in the *Lonely Planet* guide as the 'best budget hotel' in town, he is not short of customers – that was how I found him – so there would be a lot to film.

As I was parroting the Tibetan words he'd taught me, a Land Rover drove into the courtyard. Jianzang got up. 'I hope they are booked, otherwise I'll have to turn them away,' he said with a smile on his face.

The old lady sitting on the sofa across the lobby came over to me. 'I'll help you,' she said. She looked at my notebook. I had written all the Tibetan words in the English alphabet. 'Why don't you write it in Tibetan?' she asked. I said I just wanted to learn to speak the language, I thought learning to write would take too long. 'You're a clever girl. You can do both. You have to learn things properly. I'm going to show you the Tibetan spelling.' And she took my pen and my book, and began to write Tibetan letters for me. Her hand was very firm, her writing utterly precise, like musical notes on a stave. I looked up in surprise at her ancient lined face, her long white hair plaited in a coil on top of her head, her tiny magnifying spectacles, too small for her broad features, held on with a woollen thread over her ears. A Tibetan woman of her age who can read and write is rare. Who was she?

Jianzang came back in, saying to me in English: 'No booking, sorry, no room,' and then in Chinese: 'Did I get that right?' But then he stopped himself, and pointed at my new instructor: 'You should have my mother in your film. She has lots of stories. She is really clever. She taught me Tibetan – in fact, she insisted that I learn it; she used to slap me on the face when I couldn't remember my lessons. I promise you, you won't find a better teacher.'

And that was my introduction to Mola. I would soon discover she was Mila's sister – though at that point I had not yet met Mila. She was in town because her second son, Jianguo, had given her a ride. He was competing in the tug-of-war, as part of the team from Karmad *xiang*. She wanted to see Jianzang and her youngest son, Kalsong, who also lived in Gyantse.

I was intrigued why Jianzang had had to learn Tibetan at home. Did they not teach him in school?

'You should know. Chinese is the language at school. The little Tibetan we learned was very rudimentary, not good enough for my mother,' Jianzang recalled. 'But as the oldest child I had to help in the house and look after my siblings. I was too tired and hungry to learn. My mother just insisted.' From the way Mola was teaching me, a stranger, I could imagine.

As it turned out, Mola's insistence changed Jianzang's life. When he was sixteen, the Gyantse County government was recruiting barefoot doctors to be given basic training in Tibetan medicine. An exam was required, and Tibetan was the only subject – the canonical work, *The Four Tantras of Medicine*, was only available in Tibetan at the time Jianzang got the highest score, and his new life began from that moment: from village boy to doctor to successful businessman.

Did she know that Tibetan would do Jianzang so much good?

'I'm not an oracle,' Mola said. 'So, no, I could not foresee the results. But I felt strongly that, as a Tibetan, my son should know our language. It is basic.'

Mola persuaded me to learn Tibetan properly, written and spoken. She had a point; I had forgotten almost everything about it that I learned at Oxford. In any case, I enjoyed it: just making the sounds gave me pleasure. The alphabet made it easy – less trouble than Chinese; I told her I would do my best. The problem was that I was more interested in talking to her than studying right then, especially as she said she would be leaving in a couple of days. She struck me as a fascinating character. I really wanted to find out as much as I could about her.

Mola began her story by telling me that she had started learning sutras at the age of five, and by the time she was fifteen she had memorised all of the major ones. 'My brother and I studied with our father as teenagers,' she told me. 'He would tell us which prayer to recite and we would follow him. Afterwards, he would correct us if we made a mistake. We would also be given something delicious to eat. It was a good way to learn.' Content with her life, she never thought of marriage or entering a nunnery. 'It's not *where* you learn and practise, it's *how* you learn and practise, with your heart and mind,' she said. But soon people began to hear about her, and a call came from the local nunnery – the nuns wanted her to lead it. 'I couldn't refuse because, out of eleven nuns, ten could not read or write. How could they help others? I had to teach them.' But three years later, in 1959, after the Tibetan uprising, the government sent her home. 'If you just want to practise Buddhism, you can do it at home. Nobody will bother you then,' a Party official told her.

And then a marriage broker, none other than the local Party Secretary, approached her with a proposition. She should marry, he told her. It was not good for a woman to be single. People would gossip. He had just the right person for her: an activist in another village up the valley. She said that she did not want to marry, but he wouldn't take no for an answer. She had to agree: disobeying the Party was a serious crime. The Party Secretary was the witness at their wedding. Before he was transferred he even came up with the names for their first two sons: Jianzang, which means 'building Tibet', and Jianguo, which means 'building the country'. Mola had two more sons and one daughter. 'I was overwhelmed. There was never enough to eat. The children were always hungry and crying for food. My new life took me over and I did not have time to think about the old one.'

I found Mola truly remarkable. I had hardly been in Tibet a week and here was such a telling story – strong, moving, and full of history. If I could find half a dozen characters like her and

Jianzang, my job would be almost done. I could have talked with her for hours more but I thought I might tire her out. She was seventy-six. I asked her if she would come with me to the festival in the morning, but she said she had seen it many times before and just wanted to stay put and talk to her sons.

A big parade launched the Horse Race Festival the following day. The first column of the parade was the school children in their blue and white uniforms. It took me straight back to the National Day celebrations of my school years: weeks of preparation, and then walking in formation until the big moment when we saluted the Party leaders with our plastic flowers. The children were followed by monks wearing crimson robes, and teams of villagers and competitors from all the various *xiang* of the county. Everyone marched or danced to the upbeat rhythm of a patriotic Chinese song, 'Fifty-Six Nations Are One Family', which blared out non-stop from loudspeakers, piercing the ears and drowning out all other noise.

The villagers wore traditional dress, each *xiang* having its own colour for their blouses and shirts. They were bright, cheery, and beautifully coordinated, like their steps to the music. Following the villagers were some residents of Gyantse: men wearing the costumes of the old Tibetan officials, long gowns and enormous red hats with drooping tassels, and riders on horseback dressed as ancient warriors. It took almost two hours for everyone to file past the podium, where the local officials clapped and beamed at the marchers. The Party was getting its message across: our people are united and happy.

After the organised display of unity came the real, wild excitement. First off were the mounted riders demonstrating their horsemanship: with archery, then by picking *khatas* off the ground at speed, or by slicing rows of sticks with swords without missing a single one. These riders were part of a performing troupe from Lhasa – in Gyantse the skills have died out; all the local riders could do was take part in the more humdrum race around the track. The yak race between the eighteen *xiang* was slower, but more fun. I never imagined the ponderous yak could run so fast.

The tug-of-war drew a huge crowd. Someone pointed out Jianguo, who was taking part in the event. He stood like a yak himself. He is strongly built, and as tall as Mola, nothing like his older brother Jianzang. For the tug-of-war, a heavy rope is wound around the two contestants' necks and shoulders and through their legs. A flag dropped, and Jianzang and his fellow competitor began, swathed in dust, urged on by the shouts of the onlookers. Jianguo looked immovable, his head bent, his hands holding tightly on to the rope below his crotch. They both took the strain with all their strength. Then, without warning, Jianguo gave the rope a powerful yank, and the other man fell. The crowded erupted with applause. Jianguo seemed embarrassed by his win, and just smiled humbly, wiping the sweat from his face.

Having watched Jianguo's victory, I decided to thread my way out of the crowd. Tents and stalls jostled for space, every inch was taken. Laughter and singing came out of the tents, where families and friends were chatting away, drinking and playing mah jong and games of dice. Behind the trees, men and women were even making love; by now I had seen this unabashed behaviour often enough in Tibet not to be shocked. More surprising to me was the extraordinary variety of goods for sale in the stalls, from the huge piles of white wool from northern Tibet to Taiwanese sausages. Traders in their hundreds were selling everything you could think of. I succumbed: at the height of summer, I bought a length of heavy black woollen cloth, one of my more curious purchases. I left the fair, taking care not to trip on the plastic bags, torn-up newspapers, instant chopsticks and take-away boxes scattered everywhere on the ground.

When I got back to the hotel in the late afternoon, there were several Land Rovers in the courtyard: another full house tonight. With a big smile on his face, Jianzang was signing in the new guests. I went up to the tea room on the roof. With a view of the fort, over a mug of tea, it is a wonderful place to put your feet up. That afternoon Mola and her youngest son Kalsong were there, Kalsong speaking animatedly, Mola listening intently, her eyes fixed on his.

I had met Kalsong already. Jianzang had taken me to his house, behind the hotel, to see whether it might be suitable for the crew and myself. It was brand new: the walls had not even been plastered. Kalsong showed us around without saying much – Jianzang told me he would use the rent to pay for the loan on the house. I really wanted to help him, but in the end we did not take it – if we were going to be here for a whole year, the crew would need much more space.

I learned a little about Kalsong at this time. As was the custom in Tibet, a family with more than one son would send one to the monastery. Kalsong, the youngest, was the son the family chose. 'He was always keen on the dharma and always asked our mother questions about it. Instead of going to secondary school, he joined the monastery,' Jianzang said. Kalsong soon became a star monk, clever, diligent, and full of laughter.

But his monastic life was cut short in 1995 during the controversy that raged over the new – the 11th – Panchen Lama. Traditionally it was the Dalai Lama who chose the newly reincarnated Panchen Lama, and vice versa. He announced his choice, a boy named Gedhun Choekyi Nyima; the Chinese government chose their own candidate, and the Dalai Lama's choice disappeared from view. There was outcry and widespread protest both inside and outside Tibet. Kalsong led the protest in the Palkhor Monastery and was promptly arrested, bringing down the abbot too, who was sacked for failing to rein in his unruly monks. After three years in prison, Kalsong was released. He did not give up his calling altogether. He has been in great demand to perform rituals for local people, sometimes on his own, sometimes with other excommunicated monks. He did marry though – his wife, the sweet and delightful Droma, works as the receptionist in Jianzang's hotel.

Seeing Kalsong and Mola converse, I was struck by the concern on her face. He is the youngest son, and she clearly has a soft spot for him. She knew well what Kalsong had suffered, and what he was still suffering. She too had had her religious calling abruptly cut short. 'When I go to the monastery to pray, I keep thinking he should still be there,' she told me. 'That would have been the life for him. It is such a pity.'

Did she regret sending Kalsong to the monastery?

'You know, after I was sent home in 1959 and after the three big monasteries in Lhasa were nearly destroyed, I thought that was the end,' Mola said. 'My nunnery was razed to the ground during the Cultural Revolution. Without monasteries, without lamas, where was hope? Then, in 1984, the government allowed some monasteries to be restored, and people began to take up the religious life again. I couldn't believe it. When people from the village asked me to pray for them, at first I could not. But slowly I was persuaded. And finally we decided that Kalsong was to join the monastery. Who knew it was not to last?'

Did she resent Kalsong's fate?

'He knew what the law was and he broke it. He had to accept the consequences,' she said firmly.

This was the Mola I had admired from our first meeting: intelligent, capable, and forthright. But now I knew her history as well, not just the defeat of her own hopes, but seeing her son's dream broken too. Perhaps she had been too optimistic that he would escape her fate. She wanted Kalsong to finish what she could not, but it was not to be. I had felt tears in my eyes as I listened to her. But I managed to hold them back. She was so strong, how could I get emotional in front of her?

The day after Jianguo took part in the competition, Mola left for her village on the back of her son's tractor. I bought her bags of sugar, powdered milk and tea on Jianzang's advice. When I pressed them into her hands, she held me tight and said that I must come and see her. I told her that she didn't have to worry, she'd have a hard time getting rid of me.

I did not pursue Mola as a major character for the film, though. She said that she was pretty much housebound, because she had cataracts in both eyes. She was still invited for rituals and prayers but she only performed them for the people in her village – and I knew this would limit the scope of our filming. But I kept in touch as much as I could. I constantly asked Jianzang about her and about when she might be coming again. 'Oh, she's fine,' he would say. 'Nothing much new, she just stays at home.' Then he would move on to some piece of gossip. 'I saw Penpa, your researcher, at seven o'clock this morning. He was leaving a tea house. It looked like he had not been back to the house all night. I hope you know what he's up to …'

Soon we were all consumed by a case Jianzang was fighting, representing his Chinese builder, Mr Su, in an appeal. A factory owner was suing Mr Su after his prefabricated cement plant had collapsed in a flood; he claimed it was due to the builder's construction work blocking a waterway. The court ordered Mr Su to compensate him 60,000 *yuan*, but Mr Su decided to appeal and asked Jianzang to help him. Jianzang had won a similar case four years ago representing himself against his neighbour, who had engaged one of the most famous lawyers in Tibet. It caused quite a stir and earned him a reputation as a self-made brief. We filmed him sitting with his legs crossed in the hotel's roof-top tea room, holding a legal tome on construction in the People's Republic of China. He had a new notebook filled with pieces of paper and the evidence he had already collected, and was going through the clauses in the book one by one. He was so meticulous, so thorough. And he wasn't even doing it for money. 'I have no guests in the winter. I thought I should use the opportunity to refresh my legal knowledge. Also, crooks shouldn't get away with things that are their own fault,' he said.

Then he found something. He cried out, 'Listen to this clause, Teacher Sun! Number 84. It says "all factories must obtain certification from the government that the buildings have passed construction quality control". I asked his lawyer for the documents, and he did not have them. So his factory is badly constructed. He cannot blame Mr Su for its collapse. That is what I will argue.' He clapped his hands and laughed. 'I've nailed him.'

Shortly after Jianzang won the appeal, our film crew prepared to follow him and his wife on a trip to Nepal. He was going to find a Nepalese cook. Although the *Lonely Planet* guidebook had spoken well of his hotel, it did not think much of his food. 'Mediocre. That is their verdict,' Jianzang grumbled. He showed me the entry as we discussed his forthcoming trip. 'I will prove them wrong. You won't find the bad reference in the next edition of the guidebook. My Nepalese cook will win over the foreign guests,' he said.

'How about his Chinese guests?' I asked.

'Oh, I don't like Chinese tourists. They are the worst. They bargain with you hard on the price, and then complain about everything. They treat me as if I were their servant. I much prefer foreign tourists.'

I said I hoped I was not one of those Chinese guests.

'Oh, of course not,' he protested. 'You've travelled the world. Most of my Chinese guests seem never to have left home before. They insist on the comfort of a five-star hotel, here in Gyantse, but they only want to pay 100 *yuan*, what's that, £7. It's a joke.'

I wanted to point out to him that his Chinese guests might not be so green – anybody who comes to Tibet must be quite adventurous; and it would not be the first place they had visited. But Jianzang was quite capable of flaring up when crossed. I did not want to rile him just when we were about to leave for Nepal with him. Instead I asked him about Mola. 'Oh, I'm planning to bring her back here to have her cataracts done. But it's too cold now. We'll do it in the spring, perhaps.' Well, at least he was a good son.

'Could I go and see her?' I asked.

'Yes,' he said, 'go now. My mother would love to see you. She often talks about you.'

Did I need to warn her?

'She is an old lady, and she is in the village, you don't need an appointment.'

I went with Penpa, taking tea, sugar and powdered milk again. But she was not there. She had been out the last time I'd tried to see her too. Then later I found out Jianzang had brought her to Gyantse and did not tell me. Was he annoyed that I had not made her a character in the film and concentrated on Mila instead? Jianzang had told me himself that when his father died ten years earlier, Mila had not helped them enough, and the two families had not seen much of each other since then. Perhaps I was caught in a family feud.

But Mola remained on my mind. After Sagadaba I made another effort to reach her in the village. I did not ask Jianzang. We just went to her house. I knocked at the gate. A woman opened it. Again Mola was out, but the woman said that if we could wait, she would go and get her. So she really was not so housebound after all. I had a sinking feeling that dropping her from the film was a big mistake, one I would always regret.

We sat in the family's big sitting room. It seemed newly decorated, with pillars and beams painted bright red and covered with elaborate flowers and animals. A row of cupboards against the wall had the same ornate decorations. It must all have taken months to paint and at quite a cost. Perhaps this was why the room was otherwise sparsely furnished. The few mattresses on the floor looked like rejects from Jianzang's hotel.

When I first visited Tibet, I found the bold colours of the decorations, the loud jewellery the woman wore – corals and ambers and lapis lazuli – overwhelming. It was hard to take, with my minimalist tastes. But I now think there are good reasons for the extravagance – in the winter especially, when there is so little sign of life in the vast void, just the starkness of nature, the boldness can be endearing. Coming in from the cold outdoors into a room full of colours that shock the senses can be reassuring.

While my thoughts were wandering, Mola came home. She smiled broadly when she saw me, and held my hands tightly. She apologised for keeping me waiting – she'd been in the middle of a ritual for her neighbour, and she had to find an appropriate moment to stop. Now I felt guilty for interrupting her service, and said I would come back another time.

'Not to worry. My grandson Langkha is doing the service. I was just making sure there were no mistakes. It's a prayer for the wellbeing of the family, nothing too complicated. He can handle it on his own.' Mola seemed confident.

I was surprised that after the painful experience with her son, she still wanted her grandson to continue on the spiritual path.

'The villagers need a shaman,' Mola said. 'But I decided to teach him myself. I have been doing it since he left primary school. Now he is twenty-one. He is very clever. I only have to teach him a sutra once and he remembers it.'

I did some quick maths in my head: she must have made the decision to teach Langkha around the time Kalsong was thrown into prison. Clearly she had thought hard about it.

Mola stood up and pointed at a flower on the pillar near the table, which I had been admiring. 'You know Langkha painted all these himself? Even things he has never done before, you show it to him, and he can do it. He looked at a few houses and found a pattern book, and just copied the flowers and animals on to the wood with a pencil and filled the colours in. It took him months, but it saved us a lot of money. Most families get painters and craftsmen to do theirs.'

Langkha was gifted, and I could see how proud of him Mola was. But what fascinated me was the fact that she had taken it upon herself to train him. In Tibetan Buddhism, the guru and his disciple are described as father and son. It is the most important relationship for the disciple. The guru has not only to transmit the letter and the spirit of the teaching, but to 'awaken the sparks out of which blaze forth the fire of mystical experience'.[60] As the great Italian Tibetologist, Giuseppe Tucci, says: 'An instruction based simply on the written word, without the participation of a lama, is not only ineffective; it can even lead one away from the right path and be destructive.'[61]

'The monastery is *the* place to learn. That is why I sent Kalsong there, to get a proper education. But after what happened to him, I thought it would be safer to teach Langkha myself. It is not the best way, but it is the safest,' Mola told me.

She explained that she had taught him the main sutras, and the basic skills. Then she'd sent him out to learn from different masters. He went often to a monastery near Shigatse, where the incarnation lama was particularly good with commentaries on the sutras. Langkha also listened in on the monks' debates – the traditional way of learning, during which a monk is cross-examined by his fellows on points of doctrine. He had learned the elaborate rituals from Mila, and he had been Tseten's assistant for a while. Another ex-lama had taught him astrology. He had just come back from southern Tibet where he studied the

Tibetan Book of the Dead for four months with a renowned shaman, and other rituals for sky burial. 'I won't be here for ever, and I want to prepare him to send me off,' Mola said with a laugh.

'How long will his training last?' I asked.

'How big is knowledge?' Mola looked at me. 'Langkha still has a long way to go.' She had yet to find him a meditation master who could initiate him into the mystic world. After that he would have to meditate on his own for four months of every year. He will also have to go on pilgrimages and prostrate millions of times to accumulate merit. 'Perhaps by his late thirties and forties, he will become a good shaman,' Mola said, counting the years on her fingers. 'But before then, I will find a good wife for him.'

I was keen to ask Mola for more details about this learning process, in particular what Mila had taught the boy and could teach him still. I was sure their feud, such as it was, would not stand in the way of anything Mola thought Langkha needed. But I would have to come back another day. The sunlight was receding from the room, and we had drunk a dozen cups of tea. Perhaps Mola wanted to go back and see how Langkha was doing. I said I would love to take her photograph before I leave. 'Let's do it in my room,' she said, happy to oblige.

Her room was small and cosy, but something of a religious sanctuary: every wall filled to the ceiling with paintings of protective deities, Buddhas and Bodhisattvas, photographs of famous lamas, and *tangkas* draped with white *khatas*. Flowers and figures made of solidified butter and painted in bright colours occupied the centre of the altar table; below them a row of brass bowls filled with sacred water and three burning butter lamps. On the table next to the low bed and on the bed itself were piles of sutras, wrapped in yellow silk. Mola sat down on the bed, took off her glasses and put them on the table. Then she looked straight into the camera, a strong, confident woman, smiling, but with depths of melancholy in her eyes.

Mola insisted on seeing us off at the edge of the village. The path was winding and uneven, and an open drain ran alongside it. I was worried for her because of her poor eyesight. But she would not let me help her. Instead, she led me by the hand, pulling me along. Suddenly I heard the rhythmical sound of a drum and cymbals. I could not tell where it was coming from; it was echoing over the village. Then I heard a chant, faint but discernible, floating in the air. 'That is Langkha doing the ritual,' she said with a smile on her face, pointing to a big white house to the left of the path, with its doors closed.

'Do you want to go in and see him?' she asked.

Although I was tempted, I decided not to. Even with an apprentice shaman in the house, the family would not have welcomed strangers at such a time. My sudden appearance might have distracted Langkha too. I thanked Mola and we continued on our way.

'A family in the next valley has requested a service for tomorrow,' Mola said quietly, still pulling me along. 'I told them I could not come and asked if I could send my grandson. They were very happy. So he is off doing the ritual on his own tomorrow. He needs a lot of practice. That is when he'll find out what he still needs to know, and that's how he'll learn.'

She was imparting all of her knowledge to Langkha, and giving him her clients too. She had set her four sons on their paths in life: a farmer, a doctor turned businessman, a soldier turned deputy-governor of a county, a monk or ex-monk. Through her grandson she had one last chance to pass along the values she held so dear.

Holding Mola's hand and following her closely, I began to understand something that had puzzled me in the early days of our filming, when I watched Tseten performing all his rituals and the villagers coming to him for treatment. How had these traditions endured? Monasteries could be destroyed, Buddhist statues could be melted down, lamas could be unfrocked, prayer flags could be taken away. But in the heart of the people, in remote villages and grasslands, in Mola's family, the traditions survive. Mola was indomitable, an inspiration. I was witnessing one woman's mission to carry on the faith.

At the centre of the village there was a stupa and rows of prayer-wheels. I went around the stupa with Mola and pushed the prayer-wheels alongside her. I silently said my prayer. It was that Tibet would endure, and remain its own spiritual self.

EPILOGUE

Four days after Sagadaba we threw a farewell party in our house for all our characters, their families, the officials we had worked with, and all the people who had helped us over the past year. We had to find another cook though: Mr Li had given up on his restaurant business. 'It isn't worth it. I only have one life. I'm going home to be with my son,' were his parting words. We borrowed smart trays and burners from a restaurant, and put everything out on a row of tables in the courtyard, pork, beef, mutton, yak meat, duck, chicken: fried, preserved, and stewed, six hot and six cold dishes. More tables and chairs were set out among the trees and boxes of beer were piled up next to them – Penpa insisted we buy 800 cans and bottles – I agreed, as long as we could return anything we did not drink.

I put on a long Tibetan dress I had had made from the cloth I bought at the Horse Race Festival, with a blue silk sash round my waist and a blue shirt. I had never been confident enough to wear it before; I somehow felt it was just a pose. But that day I wanted to make the effort. These were the people who had made our year, who had allowed us to follow them as they lived their lives in front of our cameras, the people who opened to us their unique world of belief and ritual, and their struggle to come to terms with change; the people who had accepted us, helped us, and trusted us. I was going to do it right, if I could.

The crew laughed at me. They were going to stay in their jeans and T-shirts. Why all the effort?

Nearly sixty people turned up, including quite a few I did not know – Penpa's drinking pals perhaps. Jianzang, the hotel manager, and Rincheu, the builder, were both too busy to come and sent their apologies. I hoped they would always be so busy, and successful. If only more Tibetans were doing as well. Jianzang and Rincheu have shown it can be done. I missed Phuntsog too, the sky burial master, who we did not invite for fear of alienating the other guests. If he was so polluting, why was he allowed to send the dead to the next world? I asked my Tibetan friends. They could not answer me. All I could do was to send some gifts for him and his family.

When the guests saw me their eyes lit up. 'Wow, you're a Tibetan woman now!' Butri said, the first to arrive, with Tseten, Dondan, Lhamo, and all the people from the villages, in a minibus we sent for them. I was really pleased. 'But let me help you.' Butri came over, undid my sash, and tied it above my waist. 'It makes you much taller. And please stand straight. You should be proud, not look like an old lady like me.' That was quite something coming from her. Old lady? Not dressed as she was, in a bright pink blouse, and a very loud *bamdian*, with mustard yellow, sapphire blue and baby pink stripes. Butri had surprised me the most of all our characters, progressing from a staunch Party official and anxious mother, to an unashamed lover, and now a style guru. She had just been forcibly retired by the Party – after forty years of hard work – with no pension and no medical care. She felt betrayed. But you would not have known it to see her that evening with her old man. I did not think he would look after her, but she would cope. She was a survivor.

Tseten sat down in the far corner of the courtyard, surround-ed by a group of women I had never met. He introduced them as his clients in Gyantse. 'So you are going to set up house in Gyantse? Does Yangdron know?' I teased him. Yangdron had had to stay at home to look after Loga and the cows, and Dondan was with the other people from the villages, enjoying their beer quietly under a willow tree. 'You're being cheeky, Teacher Sun,' Tseten said with a smile. 'Now you look like a Tibetan, and you love Gyantse. I could set up house with you.' I laughed. It was good that we could joke like this with each other. We had come a long way from the decorum of a year ago. I offered him the customary three glasses – orange juice for him though, not *chang*.

Lhakpa and his family had probably never seen so much food and drink before, and made frequent trips to the buffet table. Before long he got tipsy. True to form, he came up to me and said, 'Are you ignoring me too, like Penpa? He wouldn't sit down and have a drink with me. We aren't good enough for him.' I really felt for Lhakpa. He had tried so hard to earn money, and respect. After the Tibetan New Year, he went to northern Tibet to do odd jobs. After only three weeks, he called us to come and rescue him. We found him in the street outside the bus station, covered with dust, his hair down to his eyes, his face criss-crossed with cuts, wearing just a thin jacket in the freezing cold. He burst into tears when he saw me. The contractor had been beating him and harassing his girlfriend Dadron.

Now Lhakpa had brightened up. 'You know what, Teacher Sun? I'm going to be a father,' he grinned. So Dadron was pregnant. And they were not married. I should have expected it. But how would they manage, I wondered? I could not see him becoming better off, given all the migrants he had to compete with. But I hoped his children would get educated and thrive, and not have to struggle like he did. I offered him three cups of *chang*, one on behalf of myself, one from Penpa, and one from the rest of the crew. He drank them gratefully, and immediately poured three cups for me. I had avoided *chang*, except for the odd sip, all the time I had been here, even when Dr Lhamo pricked me with a needle for not drinking it at New Year. But I could not refuse Lhakpa. For the first time I drank a whole cup. It tasted fresh and slightly fruity, a bit like pressed apple juice without the sweetness. It was a shame I was allergic to alcohol.

I was relieved to retreat to the tables where the monks from the monastery gathered. No beer or *chang*, no toasting, no lewd jokes, just soft drinks and gentle talk about their plans for the break now Sagadaba was over. Tsultrim and a couple of other monks were going on pilgrimage. They all needed it, especially Tsultrim, who looked preoccupied and tense. The theft from the monastery remained unsolved. And even if the thief was caught, there could be further burglaries and, more worryingly, political trouble. I had thought a monastery was where monks devoted themselves to higher goals. From my experience this year, it was anything but that. In fact I was surprised Tsultrim had any time for his scriptures, when his entire life seemed consumed by worldly worries. But perhaps guarding the monastery against political disturbance and indiscipline within was the transcendence he needed. That is after all the essence of Tibetan Buddhism, which follows the Mahayana tradition – personal salvation comes after the salvation of others. I prayed for him to succeed.

The mischievous Tsephun was demure, for now at least, under the watchful eyes of Tsultrim. I wished Tsultrim was his master, as he was strict but commanded his respect. He was too young to appreciate the severity of his actual master Dondrup, whose constant scolding and beating only made him more rebellious. He did not understand that Dondrup was trying to transfer his broken hopes and dreams onto him, having spent the prime of his life in prison. Despite Dondrup's threat to make the monastery expel him, I did not think it would. The government restricted the number of monks; the monastery would not sack any monk unless he broke his vows – and Tsephun had only been a little naughty. But I kept asking myself whether by following him, we actually tempted him with a glimpse of the outside world, which for now he seemed to love more than the monastic life. It would not surprise me if he turned his back on it one day.

Tsultrim and the monks left soon after the meal was over. They were going back for their evening prayers. With a simple handshake and a deep bow, I said goodbye to them. I told them I would send them the film when we finished it. It was remarkable that they did not ask about the film at all. Nothing could have demonstrated their trust more clearly – I am used to filming elsewhere in China, where people are cautious, and usually want to know how they will be shown and when the film is coming out. Here things are more sensitive, but Tibetans are as expansive as the landscape they live in. Once you are their friend, they give you everything.

I did what I could to justify their trust. I made trailers of our filming and made sure all our characters had a copy. I regularly invited them over to watch what we had shot of them – they were always delighted to see themselves on screen; they could not believe they were in a movie. I would like the final film to mean more than that. It would be a record of an extraordinary year, of an extraordinary people, at an extraordinary time in their history. Tibetans are struggling to keep their way of life and their beliefs, while they try to adapt to rapid change. If I could convey this vividly and sensitively in the film, through their stories, I would be happy; I hoped they would be too.

Tseten, Dondan, Butri, everyone from the villages, left soon after, except for Dr Lhamo. Always the considerate one, she stayed behind to help. Tseten came up to me as he was about to go. 'You have been so busy with all your guests, and we haven't had much chance to talk properly. But we wanted to give you something.'

He handed me a small parcel wrapped in a scarf. I opened it and found two dozen eggs, laid by their own chickens, not much bigger than quails' eggs. I knew that these were quite delicious, but Cook Li had rarely bought them because they cost twice as much as mass-produced eggs. The Rikzin family do not eat the eggs themselves – they are far too precious a source of cash for them. I was touched. I said I would only take three, and cook them to eat on my journey. They would remind me of him and his family all the way home.

'I will pray for you,' was all he answered.

For the rest, the party had just begun, with serious drinking accompanied by singing, solos, duets, and in chorus. They moved from the courtyard into the house, and by midnight, more than a dozen were completely drunk. Penpa had started drinking mid-morning, and was fairly plastered by three o'clock, when people were just arriving. He was supposed to be the joint host with me, but that was not to be: we would go around and offer every guest their three cups and get three in return, which he would drink. He was also supposed to give a speech to thank everyone on behalf of the crew. There was no speech. Instead he got into a fight with a local Party official, after they had started slanging each other about nothing very much. 'I don't give a damn. You're going to stay in this hole, and I'm going back to Lhasa,' he shouted; two men had to hold him back. Once again Penpa was out of control. It made me sad to think he might never get where his talents might take him. At least he was oblivious in his stupor.

By the time Zhao Dong, the cameraman, had bundled Penpa into bed and the last drunken guest had staggered out, it was 1.30 in the morning. The house stank like a bar, with beer spilled all over the floor and bottles and cans everywhere. The crew grumbled a lot at having to clear it all up. They had not been keen on the party in the first place, and it was supposed to finish three hours earlier so they would have time to pack for their trip. They were going on a tour of southern Tibet, the only area we had not covered in our year. It was a reward for all their work and for seeing the project through to a successful end. It had been hard going, and they had only had one break during the whole time. Our production managers quit one after another, none of them lasting more than three months. The remaining crew members were relieved it was all over, and they could not wait to get away.

I told them to go and pack; Lhamo and I would finish clearing up. 'Why not let's finish this together and then you pack too, and come with us?' one of them asked. 'Haven't you had enough of this place? Don't you want to see something new before you leave? It's not too late, there's room in the minibus.'

We had talked about this before; I did not want to go, and I had not changed my mind. But I had been thinking that Lhamo could do with a break, it would be good for her: the results of her endoscopy had been clear, so it looked as though stress and lack of nutrition were her trouble. Perhaps the trip would start her on the path of recovery. When I put the idea to her, she beamed. But what about her work? 'Don't worry. I'll call my husband and tell him I'm going, he'll take care of it,' she replied. I suggested she go and prepare her bedding in my room. The housekeeper would clean everything in the morning.

I love travelling in Tibet, but not this time. I had no desire to visit another lake, another mountain, another monastery. I had what I wanted here in Gyantse, the mountains, the river, the monastery, the fort, the old town – my everyday, never humdrum, always beautiful scene. I could not tire of it. And its people, those I had come to know but was never sure I fully understood – given more time, I would spend it here, to build on the friendships and trust we had gained with so much effort, to learn more about how they really feel, to enjoy their company, to experience more of those revealing moments – like when I offered a plate of apples to Tseten, and he took the smallest, the most bruised one, leaving the better ones for others. Like so many Tibetans, he did not just profess Buddhism, he lived it.

While Lhamo was getting ready for bed, I went outside. There was a huge moon casting a frost-like sheen on the trees in the courtyard. The white fort in the background shimmered in its light, tantalising and elusive, the symbol of Gyantse that had kept me company all year. Before leaving tomorrow, I would climb up to it and just sit there, enjoying the panorama of the monastery, the town, and the landscape beyond. I would breathe it all in, imprint it in my mind.

What would be my lasting memory of my year in Tibet? Most of all: of having got close to a place and a people unlike any other on earth. Is it Shangri-la? It is certainly not a paradise. There is too much poverty, too much illness, too much tension and control. But it is extraordinary, it is spectacular, and it is unique. I felt privileged to have lived here for a whole year and been accepted by the people we had followed. What would become of them, and of Tibet, in five years? In ten? As I gazed at the fort, I realised I was not thinking about going home, but of coming back.

NOTES

1 Record of the Rule of the Tibetan Kings, quoted in Hu, 2006, p. 12.
2 Wang, 1998, p. 39.
3 Tibet author on *http://bbs.nju.edu.cn*
4 Wang, 1998, p. 41.
5 Shen and Liu, 1953, p. 147.
6 Wang, 1998, p. 294.
7 Bell, 1928, p. 44.
8 Xu, 1999
9 Party School of Tibet, 1986, p. 238.
10 Milarepa, 1970
11 Cai Rang, 1999, p. 216.
12 Fischer, 2005
13 Waddell, 1906, quoted in Allen 2004, p. 57.
14 Allen, 2004., p. 60.
15 Goldstein, 1993, p. 821.
16 Ibid., p. 822.
17 Govinda, 1984, p. 117.
18 Dalai Lama, 1997, p. 9.
19 Sixth Dalai Lama, 2007
20 Bass, 1998, p. 148.
21 Ibid., p. 237.
22 Ibid., p. 21.
23 McKay, 1997, pp. 115–16.

24 Allen, 2004, p. 78.
25 Ibid., pp. 80–92.
26 Ibid., p. 81.
27 Ibid., p. 82.
28 Panchen Lama, 1997, p. 51.
29 Ibid., p.85.
30 Ibid., p. 29.
31 Ibid., p. 112.
32 Sun, 2003, p. 60.
33 French, 1995, p. 224.
34 Cited in ibid., p. 223.
35 Allen, 2004, p. 55.
36 Ibid., p. 61.
37 Ibid., p. 222.
38 French, 1995, p. 230.
39 Wang, 1998, pp. 418–19.
40 Ben Jiao, 2001, quoted in Fjeld, 2006.
41 Kawaguchi, 1904, p. 474.
42 Ibid.
43 Gyatso and Havnevik, 2005, p. 9.
44 Fjeld, 2006, p. 227.
45 Ibid., p. 10.
46 Anon., 1999.
47 Phuntsog, 2005, p. 87.
48 Kawaguchi, p. 253.
49 Adams et al, 2005, p. 823.

50 Tibet Information Network, 2002, p. 69, quoting a speech by the Chinese Health Minister. The figure is for 2001.
51 WHO, 2007.
52 Adams et al, 2005.
53 Ibid.
54 Tibet Information Network, 2002, p. 61, quoting the *New England Journal of Medicine*.
55 Levy, 1999, p. 1811.
56 Markham, 1879, p. 77.
57 Xu, 1999, p. 174.
58 Norbu, 1998, p. 164.
59 Ibid., p. 99.
60 Tucci, 1980, p. 45.
61 Ibid., pp. 44–45.

BIBLIOGRAPHY

Adams, Vincanne, Suellen Miller, Jennifer Chertow, Sienna Craig, Arlene Samen, and Michael Varner, 'Having A "Safe Delivery": Conflicting Views from Tibet', in Health Care for Women International, *Health in Tibet*, Taylor and Francis, Abingdon, 2005.

Allen, Charles, *Duel in the Snows*: *the True Story of the Younghusband Mission to Lhasa*, John Murray, London, 2004.

Anon., *Maiden Nangsa*, Tibetan People's Publishing House, Lhasa, 1999.

Aris, Michael, *Hidden Treasures and Secret Lives*: *a Study of Premalingpa* (1450-1521) *and the Sixth Dalai Lama* (1683-1706), London, 1989.

Barnett, Robert, *Lhasa: Streets with Memories*, Columbia University Press, New York, 2006.

Bass, Catriona, *Education in Tibet: Policy and Practice since 1950*, Zed Books, New York, 1998.

Batchelor, Stephen, *The Jewel in the Lotus*: *a Guide to the Buddhist Traditions of Tibet*, London, 1987.

Bell, Charles, *The People of Tibet*, Oxford University Press, Oxford, 1928.

—*The Religion of Tibet*, Oxford University Press, Oxford, 1931.

Ben Jiao, *Socio-Economic and Cultural Factors Underlying the Contemporary Revival of Fraternal Polyandry*, Unpublished PhD thesis, Case Western Reserve University, 2001, cited in Fjeld, 2006.

Cai Jingfeng, *General History of Tibetan Medicine*, Qinghai People's Publishing House, Xining, 2002.

Cai Rang, *Tibetan Buddhism: Custom and Belief*, Chinese Nationality Press, Beijing, 1999.

Candler, Edmund, *The Unveiling of Lhasa*, Edward Arnold, London, 1905.

Dalai Lama, *My Land and My People*, The Dalai Lama of Tibet, Warner Books, 1997.

Das, Sarat Chandra, *Journey to Lhasa and Central Tibet*, ed. W. W. Rockhill, John Murray, London, 1902.

David-Neel, Alexandra, *My Journey to Lhasa*, Virago, London, 1983.

Dhondup, K. (ed.) (I), Songs of the Sixth Dalai Lama (translated by K. Dhondup), Dharamsala, 1981.

Dummer, Tom, *Tibetan Medicine*, Paljor Publications, New Delhi, 1994.

Fischer, Andrew M., *State Growth and Social Exclusion in Tibet*, NIAS Press, Copenhagen, 2005.

—*A Theory of Polarisation, Exclusion and Conflict within Disempowered Development: the Case of Tibet in China*, Unpublished PhD thesis, London School of Economics, 2007.

Fjeld, Heidi, *The Rise of the Polyandrous House: Marriage, Kinship and Social Mobility in Rural Tsang, Tibet*, Unpublished PhD thesis, University of Oslo, October 2006.

French, Patrick, *Younghusband: the Last Great Imperial Adventurer*, Flamingo, London, 1995.

—*Tibet, Tibet: a Personal History of a Lost Land*, HarperCollins, London, 2003.

Goldstein, Melvyn C., *A History of Modern Tibet, 1913-1951: the Demise of the Lamaist State*, University of California Press/Munshiram Manoharlal Publishers, New Delhi, 1993.

— 'When brothers share a wife', *Natural History* 96(3): 39-49, 1987.

Goldstein, Melvyn C., and Kaplan, Matthew T. (eds.), *Buddhism in Contemporary Tibet: Religious Revival and Cultural Identity*, University of California Press, Berkeley, 1998.

Govinda, Anagarika, *The Way of the White Clouds*, Rider, London, 1984.

Grunfeld, A. Tom, *The Making of Modern Tibet*, New York, 1996.

Gyatso, Janet and Hanna Havnevik, *Women in Tibet: Past and*

Present, Hurst & Company, London, 2005.

Health Care for Women International, *Health in Tibet*, Taylor and Francis, Abingdon, 2005.

Hilton, Isabel, *The Search for the Panchen Lama*, Penguin Books, London, 1999.

Hofer, Theresia, *Tibetan Medicine in Ngamring*, Diplomatarbeit zur Erlangung des Magistragrades der Philosophie an der Fakultät für Sozialwissenschaften der Universität Wien, 2005.

Hu Ji, *Retrace the Ancient Road to Tibet*, Shangxi Shifan University Press, Xian, 2006.

Huang Mingxin, *Tibetan Astrology and Calendar Making*, Qinghai People's Publishing House, Xining, 2002.

Karmay, Samten Gyaltsen, *The Arrow and the Spindle: Studies in History, Myths, Rituals and Beliefs in Tibet*, Mandala Book Point, Kathmandu, 1998.

Kawaguchi, Ekai, *Three Years in Tibet*, Theosophical Publishing Society, Madras, 1909.

Levy, Harvey, 'Phenylketonuria: Old disease, new approach to treatment', *Proceedings of the National Academy of Sciences USA* 96(5), 1999.

Lopez, Donald S., *Prisoners of Shangri-la: Tibetan Buddhism and the West*, Chicago, 1998.

Luorong, Zhangdui, *Research into the Issues of Poverty in Tibet and Poverty Relief Efforts*, China Tibetology Press, Beijing, 2002.

Markham, Sir Clements R. (ed.), *Narratives of the Mission of George Bogle to Tibet, and of the Journey of Thomas Manning to Lhasa*, 2nd ed., Trubner and Co., London, 1879.

McKay, Alex, *Tibet and the British Raj: the Frontier Cadre, 1904-1947*, Curzon Press, Richmond, 1997.

Milarepa, tr. Garma C. C. Chang, *The Hundred Thousand Songs of Milarepa*, abridged and ed., Harper and Row, New York, 1970.

Nebesky-Wojkowitz, René de, *Oracles and Demons of Tibet: The Cult and Iconography of Tibetan Protective Deities*, London: Mouton & Co., 1956.

Norbu, Dawa, *Tibet: the Road Ahead*, Rider, London, 1998.

Panchen Lama, *A Poisoned Arrow: the Secret Report of the 10th Panchen*

Lama [1962], Tibet Information Network, London, 1997.

Party School of Tibet, 1986, *Compilation of Major Events in Tibet, 1949-1985*, Lhasa, 1986.

Phuntsog, Tashi, *Secular Tibet*, Writers' Publishing House, Beijing, 2005.

Sambhava, Padma, tr. Robert Thurman, *The Tibetan Book of the Dead*, Aquarian, London, 1994.

Samuel, Geoffrey, *Civilized Shamans: Buddhism in Tibetan Societies*, Smithsonian Institution Press, Washington, 1993.

Sautman, Barry and June Teufel Dreyer, *Contemporary Tibet: Politics, Development, and Society in a Disputed Region*, M. E. Sharpe Inc., Armonk NY, 2005.

Schell, Orville, *Virtual Tibet: Searching for Shangri-La from the Himalayas to Hollywood*, New York, 2000.

Shakya, Tsering, *The Dragon in the Land of Snows: a History of Modern Tibet since 1947*, Pimlico, London, 1999.

Shen Tsunglien and Liu Shenchi, *Tibet and the Tibetans*, Stanford University Press, Stanford, 1953.

Sixth Dalai Lama, tr. Geoffrey R. Waters, *White Crane: Love Songs of the Sixth Dalai Lama*, White Pine Press, New York, 2007.

Sogyal Rinpoche, *The Tibetan Book of Living and Dying*, 10th ed., Rider, London, 2002.

Sun Shuyun, *Ten Thousand Miles Without a Cloud*, HarperCollins, London, 2003.

Taring, Rinchen Dolma, *Daughter of Tibet*, John Murray, London, 1970.

Taylor, Michael, *Le Tibet de Marco Polo*, Office du Livre, Fribourg, 1985.

Teltscher, Kate, *The High Road to China*, Bloomsbury, London, 2006.

Thomas, Nicholas and Caroline Humphrey (eds.), *Shamanism, History, and the State*, University of Michigan Press, Ann Arbor, 1994.

Tibet Information Network, *Delivery and Deficiency: Health and Health Care in Tibet*, London, 2002.

Tsering, Phuntsog (ed.), *The Annals of the All-Revealing Mirror*, Lhasa 1987.

Tucci, Giuseppe, tr. Geoffrey Samuel, *The Religions of Tibet*, Allied Publishers, New Delhi, 1980.

—tr. Mario Carelli, *To Lhasa and Beyond, Diary of the Expedition to Tibet in the Year MCMXLVIII. With an Appendix on Tibetan Medicine and Hygiene, by R. Moise,* Istituto Poligrafico dello Stato, Rome, 1956.

Waddell, Laurence Austine, *Lhasa and its Mysteries, With a Record of the Expedition of 1903-1904*, Books For Libraries Press, Freeport NY, 1906 (reprint 1972).

Wang Lixiong, *Sky Burial*, Mirror Books, New York, 1998.

WHO, *Maternal Mortality in 2005*, World Health Organisation, Geneva, 2007.

Wu Fengpei (ed.), *Compilation of Travels in Sichuan and Tibet*, Sichuan Nationality Press, Chengdu, 1985.

Xiong Wenbin, *Medieval Tibetan Buddhist Art: Research in the Murals of Pel Kor Monastery*, China Tibetology Research Centre Press, Beijing 1996.

Xu Ping, *Life in the Himalaya*, Yunnan People's Publishing House, Kunming, 1999.

Xu Ping and Lu Fang, *Famous Historical and Cultural Town: Gyantse*, China Tibetology Research Centre Press, Beijing, 2004.

ACKNOWLEDGEMENTS

I want to thank all the characters in our film, all the crew, all the production team, many Tibetan and Chinese friends and colleagues. Richard Klein deserves special mention for his staunch belief in the project.

I have been blessed with a wonderful agent, Kate Jones at ICM. Kate's tragic death early in 2008 hit me hard. She will be mourned and profoundly missed by everyone who knew her.

Much appreciation must go to Sienna Craig, Andrew Fischer, Heidi Fjeld, Resi Hofer, Caroline Humphries and Shakya Tsering, who drew my attention to a wide range of research. They helped me to confirm the truth or otherwise of what people told me locally and set it in a broader context.

Peter Firstbrook and Sue Haycock have been great to work with. Carin Besser made outstanding contributions to the book; thanks too to John Lahr for recommending her, and for all his other excellent advice. I am also greatly obliged in various ways to Gordon Barrass, Mick Csaky, Philip Graham, Daphne Hyman, Jiang Zuwu, Brian and Anne Lapping, Kristen Lippincott, Isobel Losada, Dr Zhang Qin, and Zhao Dong. And Tian Yibin, who contributed some stunning photographs.

I owe a special debt of gratitude to Fang Xichen for his wisdom, friendship and unstinting generosity of spirit.

As always Susan Watt at HarperCollins has given me the invaluable benefit of her wisdom and insight. I could not ask for a better editor.

My year in Tibet has been particularly hard on my husband: he has with his usual good grace put up with my longest ever absence.

His unfailing support has meant more to me than I can easily say.

GLOSSARY

Amban: representative of the imperial Chinese court in Tibet
bamdian: traditional Tibetan apron
bardo: the stage between death and rebirth
chang: barley wine
chiema: a basket filled with edibles, used as an offering
dharma: Buddhist teaching or doctrine
dorje: a small ceremonial sceptre, made of metal, symbolising a
    thunderbolt
karma: fate, the influence of past incarnations
khata: a ritual white scarf with a fringed edge
mandala: a representation of the cosmos, depicting deities
    and other symbols
momo: Tibetan meat dumplings
pulu: woollen cloth
tangka: religious painting
torma: shapes made of barley flour, used in rituals
tsampa: barley flour
tshatsha: small clay sculpture made in a mould
tso: brown dough containing barley flour, sugar, butter, and raisins,
    shaped into cones and used as an offering
xiang: an administrative unit of rural area in China, normally a
    district of a county

INDEX

Ambans 3, 37
Aris, Michael 3

bamdian (traditional Tibetan apron) 88, 216
Beijing University 1, 54
Bell, Charles 19
Bön 10
Book of Changes, The 98–9
British Empire 4, 90–2
Buddha 2, 10, 11, 42, 43, 72, 79, 84, 121, 144, 179–80, 188–92, 194, 195, 209, 215, 218
Buddhism 14, 16; *bardo* (the stage between death and rebirth) 28, 31, 32–3, 42; Chinese attitude towards 13, 22–3, 30, 38, 43–4; concept of impermanence 191; Dalai Lama 5, 8, 19, 44–5, 50–2, 72, 83, 89, 123, 146, 183, 186, 190, 205; dances 191, 192; death and reincarnation, view of 25–39, 42–3, 45–52; diet 77; essence of Tibetan 218; giving, concept of 24; introduction into Tibet 2, 10, 31; lamas 1, 5, 13, 15–19, 28, 44, 47, 126, 210–11; living 183, 222; Mahayana tradition 218;

meditation 31, 35, 212; monasteries *see* Tibet: MONASTERIES; monks and nuns *see* Tibet: MONKS AND NUNS; no harm, concept of 187; Panchen Lama 5, 81, 72–4, 81–5, 90, 136, 181, 183, 196, 205–6; Sagadaba (Buddha's birthday celebrations) 179–80, 188–92, 194, 195, 209, 215, 218; sects 146, 183; shamans *see* Tibet: SHAMAN; survival of 213–14; view of women 124–5; wastefulness 43–4; *see also* Tibet: RELIGIOUS LIFE
Butri, Pasang 73, 74, 113, 127–31, 216, 219

Chandler, Edmund 76, 91
Chang (Tibetan beer) 34, 40, 74, 106, 116, 128, 137–54, 162, 173, 189, 217–18, 220
Chiang Kaishek 3
China: astrology, tradition of 98–100, 157, 158–9, 211; Buddhism, historical attitude towards 13, 22–3, 30, 38, 43–4; closure of monasteries and

temples within (1949) 90;
Cultural Revolution 9, 21–3, 29,
30, 89, 90, 99, 112, 190, 192–3,
194, 206; Tibet, historical
relationship with 1–3, 6, 37, 88,
92–3 *see also* Tibet: CHINA,
RELATIONSHIP WITH;
National Day 203; population
explosion 38; women, view of
within 121
Chisongdezan, King 69
Chumik Shenko, massacre at 91
Collected Works (Mao) 23
Communist Party, Chinese:
Buddhism, attitude towards 13,
22–3, 30, 38; burial, policy on
39; Cultural Revolution 9,
21–3, 29, 30, 89–90, 99, 112,
185–6, 190, 192–3, 194, 206;
Democratic Reform (dismantles
Tibetan governmental system)
184–5; Red Guards 22, 30, 84,
192, 193; Tibetan activists 73, 74,
127–31, 216; Tibetan monasteries
and monks, attacks upon 13,
22–3, 45, 84–5, 184–97; Tibetan
uprising against (1959) 13, 84,
89, 184, 189, 202
Confucius 3, 121, 124
Cook Li 76–8, 88, 89, 90, 216
Curzon, Lord 76

Dadron 81, 217
Dalai Lama 5, 8, 19, 44–5, 50–2, 72,
83, 89, 123, 146, 183, 186, 190, 205
Dagchen 125, 126
Daily Mail 76, 91
Darma, Lang 192
Detsen, King Trisong 10

Dolkar 101–3, 104–5, 106–8, 109, 114
Dondrup 72, 181, 218
Dorje 25, 26–7
Droma 96–8, 99, 100, 102–3
Drongdha 148, 149, 150, 154
Duan 180
Dzong 91, 92

Gampo, Songtsen 2
Gansu 89, 125
Gnyan Chen Tanggola 10
Goldstein, Melvyn 45
groma 141
Gyaltsen, Choekyi 83
Gyantse County 25, 27, 101, 102, 103,
179; Agriculture and Animal
Husbandry Department 20;
alcohol use within 147; British
army in 19, 91; Chinese
migration into 85–6, 89, 90;
climate 20, 22, 75–6, 143;
Communist Party in 128, 129;
construction projects 73–4;
districts (*xiang*) of 11; Horse
Race Festival 198–9, 203–4, 215;
hospital 151, 160–1, 160, 161, 166;
landscape 23, 75, 221; location
4; monasteries 13, 181 *see also*
Tibet: MONASTERIES; police
181, 197; population 4; Red
Guards take control of (1966)
192–3; restaurants in 85–6; sky
burial masters 27; white fort 34,
221, 222; Winter Fair 135–7
Gyatso (bridegroom) 106, 107, 109
Gyatso, Tsangyang 50–1
*Gyushi, the Four Tantras of Tibetan
Medicine* 160, 161, 174, 201

236

cost of health care 164, 166, 170–1, 172, 173–5; cost of living 94; education, cost of 14–15, 59–60, 180; effect of religion upon 43–4, 83; fees for shamanic rituals 18, 157–8

EDUCATION 5, 6

effect on Tibetans of lessons taught in Chinese 62–5, 201; English School 44, 45; government employment of graduates 60; National Exams 54–7, 60, 63–4, 69; schools, primary and secondary 28–9, 61–8, 198, 201; Tibetan Inland Schools 66, 67; university or college, choosing a 57–9, 60–1; university, cost of 14–15, 59–60, 180; university, departure for 53–4, 68–70

HEALTH CARE AND MEDICINE 5, 6, 75–6, 156–77

acupuncture ('dry needles') 163–4; altitude, effect of 72, 76, 96; antibiotics, use of 64, 162, 164, 165, 173–4; birth control 129; clinics 162–3, 165–6; Cooperative Medical System 174; cost of 164, 166, 170–1, 172, 173–5; free clinic 172–4; doctors 162–3, 165–7; hepatitis B 174; hospitals 166, 170–2; incompetence within 170; infant mortality rate 129, 163, 167–8, 169; karmic disease 161–2, 165, 166, 175; malnutrition 173; maternal mortality rate 167–8; medical training 164, 168, 169; modern Chinese

health system and 170–1; rural health workers, superstitions of 162–3, 165–7, 169; subsidised health care 174, 175; traditional Tibetan medicine 156–62, 165, 168–9, 172–3, 174–5, 201

HISTORY OF 1–3, 4, 10, 44–5, 90–2

LANGUAGE 5, 6, 14, 62–5, 201

MARRIAGE 5, 74, 79, 95–110, 114

bride uninformed of marriage and partner until wedding day 100–10; dowry 104–5; law 129; polyandry (multiple marriage) 1–2, 5, 110, 111–21, 129–32; shaman chooses partners for 95–110, 114

MONASTERIES 10, 128, 179

attacked by Communist Party 13, 22–3, 45, 84–5, 180–1; Communist Party and Chinese government, modern relationship with 182, 218–19; Communist Party closes 84, 89, 202; Communist Party's historical attitude towards 9, 22–3, 30, 45, 84–5, 180–1; Cultural Revolution's effect upon 9, 22–3, 30, 180–1, 190, 192–3, 194, 206; exams 183; filming in 181–3; lack of discipline within 5, 44, 146–7, 183, 218–19; percentage of Tibetan population within 44; pilgrimages to 43, 80, 171; power within Tibetan society 45; rebel against reform 45; thefts from 5, 181–2, 218; Tibetan economy, effect upon